CALLED to **BE**
CALLED to **DO**

Finding Your Purpose and Destiny
in Your Unique Gifting

PETER WOLLENSACK

Called to BE, Called to DO

Published by
Harvest Equippers
Surco, Lima 33
Peru
www.harvestequippers.com

ISBN: 978-1-936443-01-7

All Scripture quotations, unless otherwise indicated, are taken from the King James Version of the Bible. Abbreviations for other Bible versions cited are:

AMP ~ Amplified Bible / ESV ~ English Standard Version / GWT ~ God's Word Translation / ISV ~ International Standard Version / JPS ~ Jewish Publication Society Bible / LITV ~ Literal Translation of the Holy Bible / MKJV ~ Modern King James Version / MNT ~ James Murdock New Testament / MSG ~ The Message Bible / NASB ~ New American Standard Bible / NET ~ New English Translation / NKJV ~ New King James Version / NLT ~ New Living Translation / PNT ~ J B Phillips New Testament / RV ~ Revised Version / WNT ~ Weymouth New Testament (1912)

Cover and book design by www.ChristianBookDesign.com
Cover photo: BigStockPhoto 459242

The accounts in this book are factual; however in some cases the identifying details and names have been changed to protect confidentiality.

For bulk order purchases or other inquiries please contact:

ministeriosdinamicos@gmail.com

Endorsements for
CALLED TO BE, CALLED TO DO

As a new Christian, I read a passage of Scripture that profoundly affected my life—Ephesians 4:12: "… for the edifying of the Body of Christ." I knew immediately what I was CALLED TO DO, but didn't know how. Peter Wollensack's easy to read book and the simple to apply Biblical precepts in it will save you (and could have saved me) much frustration in seeking the means TO DO what we are all "CALLED TO BE." Let me commend Pastor Peter for writing this insightful book, and recommend it to you for reading.

~ Rev. Ben Kinchlow,
Author and long-time co-host of The 700 Club
Virginia Beach, Virginia

Do you know what your endowment gift is? This book is practical, insightful and helpful for those who want to know where they fit in the Lord's body, what their gift might be and how to grow in that gift.

~ LaMar Boschman,
Bible teacher and author
Grapevine, Texas

Somewhere between God's uniquely intentional formation of each one of us and the ultimate fulfillment of those precise purposes for our existence, there must be a process of self-discovery. We are only able to fully cooperate with God's plans for our lives when we have seen, understood, and then fully embraced our divinely instilled uniqueness. Pastor Peter has written an indispensible manual for those who are trying to see themselves from God's perspective. Be forewarned, *Called to Be, Called to Do* is a life-changer … precisely the one you've been waiting for!

~ Rev. Todd Foster,
Senior pastor , Church on the Rock,
New Haven, Connecticut

Be prepared to find yourself challenged to identify your endowment gifts and mature spiritually as you approach this very readable book from the pen of Pastor Peter Wollensack. *Called to Be, Called to Do* is a gift from our Heavenly Father and is appropriate for group or individual study. This book is destined to make a difference in the lives of pastors and congregations, mature believers and new Christians, alike.

~ *Rev. William and Rev. Yvonne Hunter*
Loshunter Ministries
Sun City, Arizona

By discovering your unique spiritual *DNA* (gifts and callings), and functioning in them, you effectively release Christ Jesus into the world around you and thus fulfill your God-given purpose and destiny. Allow this wonderful book to help you accomplish this tremendous feat.

~ *Dr. Mark Virkler, president and founder*
Christian Leadership University
Cheektowaga, New York

God has a special plan and purpose for each one of us. Unfortunately, many Christians are completely unaware of the wonderful and unique part they are meant to play in that plan. As a result, they live without vision, direction, focus, and passion. Other Christians believe and agree that they have a destiny, but they have no idea what it is or how to reach it. Pastor Peter's book provides the key to finding destiny—understanding the unique gifting that God has put into us and how the gifts play out in real life. I am very happy to recommend *Called to Be, Called to Do* to every Christian who wants to move forward in reaching their destiny and mature into all that they are called to be in Christ.

- *Rev. Brick Cliff, president and founder*
World Impact Now (WIN) Ministries
San Benito, Texas

The apostle Paul prayed that believers would have a revelation of the hope of their calling. Unfortunately most Christians have great difficulty discerning their calling. *Called to Be, Called to Do* is a comprehensive and well documented study by a seasoned missionary to Peru that will help believers identify their callings using their spiritual and natural gifts as a roadmap. Pastor Peter combines years of experience with personal revelation to bring forth the truths in this important book.

~ Dr. Berin Gilfillan, president and founder
International School of Ministry (ISOM)
Redlands, California

ABOUT THE COVER

God wants each one of us to grow to our potential.

The spiral form of the interior of a nautilus shell symbolizes the type of progressive growth our Creator desires for each one of His children. A nautilus begins life with just a few tiny chambers and then adds new, larger chambers in a spiral pattern over the years as it develops toward maturity. The step-by-step growth process is beautifully recorded by the nautilus' strikingly iridescent inner shell.

Just as the gleaming chambers of the nautilus reflect a natural progression toward maturity we as Christians are to mirror the glory of the Lord as we grow in Him. His precious Holy Spirit moves us from "glory to glory" as we reflect His radiance (2 Corinthians 3:18).

The growth potential of the nautilus is contained within the first chambers that appear—even before it was born. So too, a divine pattern for our own spiritual and physical development has been placed on the inside of each one of us. We do not grow to our full potential overnight but, rather, move from one stage to the next as we move toward our destiny. As we discover and yield to Yahweh's plan and purposes for our life we experience increased capacity and fulfillment.

The starry blue border of the cosmos represents our Creator's involvement in the entire process. The vast potential within us is as great as the expanse of the heavens above.

DEDICATED TO …

Those whose heart's cry is to find true meaning and purpose in their life.

Those who are busy "doing" but have found that they are neither effective nor satisfied.

Those who are longing to hear the cherished words, "Well done, good and faithful servant. Enter into the joy of the Lord."

Those who wholeheartedly believe the Master's words: "Ask, and it will be given to you; seek, and you will find; knock, and it will be opened to you." (Matthew 7:7 NASB)

ACKNOWLEDGEMENTS

I would like to express my love and appreciation to my wife, Blanca, who has been a constant source of encouragement, inspiration, and sound advice during the course of writing this book. Thank you for being helpful in so many ways and for being patient and understanding as I "burned the midnight oil."

I am also grateful to Pastors Todd and Leslie Foster, our spiritual covering, as well as to my family and friends at Church on the Rock in New Haven, Connecticut, and elsewhere who have so faithfully supported us on the mission field. By sharing with us the vision and the burden of training literally thousands of church leaders, you have helped enable this book to be written, strengthening believers and the church in many parts of Latin America.

I also wish to give a special thanks to Regina and Gary Johnson of the Global Transformation Network for sharing Regina's unique insights into several key spiritual aspects of the gifts Yahweh has placed in each one of us.

Thanks also to Ysabel Alvarez whose creative talents are so amply displayed in the illustrations. Thanks as well to Angie Kiesling for her skillful editing as well as to Wendy Schnur, my sister, for her meticulous proofreading of the manuscript for this book.

CONTENTS

PREFACE

HOW THIS BOOK CAME TO BE

The Lord began stirring my heart a few years ago about the need to bring His people to a greater understanding of the wonderful gifts that He's placed inside each of us. Having studied the "motivational gifts" extensively almost a quarter century ago—along with many personal observations in the intervening time—I was well prepared to begin teaching pastors and leaders in Peru and elsewhere about the endowment God has placed within each of us.

The plain truth is that too many of God's children live far below their potential. In terms of abilities, some of us have been living like a homeless pauper who isn't aware that his father set up a trust fund on his behalf before he was born. He's lived on the streets as a beggar because he didn't know what he'd been given. Likewise, our loving Father has made a deposit from His great storehouse into our account, which is there for our use—and yet many of us have left the account virtually untouched.

Some have lived like Samson in the time of the judges of Israel—awesomely endowed, but foolishly wasting our potential. Since we haven't understood or appreciated what has been given to us, we've failed to tap into the resources our mighty God has deposited within us.

In a time of prayer not long ago the Lord instructed me to write a book about the motivational gifts. At the time of this prompting, He also gave me a title for the book: *Called to Be, Called to Do*. Its primary significance is that according to His priorities, our first calling is to discover what we are meant to be—that is, what Yahweh has made us to be—and from that insight we are then to go forth and fulfill our purpose and destiny.

The English-speaking world is fortunate to have several notable books that delve into the characteristics of the "motivational gifts."[1] These are what I refer to as the "third set" of gifts because the other two sets mentioned in the New Testament are much more widely recognized and the subject of a great deal of teaching. These better-known gifts are commonly called the "gifts of the Holy Spirit" and the "fivefold ministry gifts."

In ministering on the missionary fields in Peru and elsewhere, I have found that there is very little knowledge of this "third set" of gifts, with perhaps only one out of a hundred pastors or leaders having even heard of them. Called to Be, Called to Do not only opens up a greater depth of understanding of the connection between our innate gifting and our purpose in life, which is groundbreaking in itself, but it also provides a more in-depth study of what these gifts "look like"—in everyday life and as they have been portrayed in the Scriptures—than has been previously available.

Yahweh has revealed to me several basic truths included in this book. These are spiritual realities which for the most part have been hidden to the vast majority of believers or ignored by them. Furthermore, to arrive at a greater level of understanding of the gifts within us, we must dig deeper than the obvious. Certainly each gift has an observable set of personality traits and characteristics. But these gifts deposited inside each one of us are much more than that. They are "grace packages" that are essentially spiritual in nature, each with its own particular anointing and purpose.

THE PRACTICALITY OF THE MESSAGE

We are able to understand ourselves and others far better as we learn to appreciate the foundational nature of our giftedness. Misunderstandings and conflicts are easier to avoid, and interpersonal relationships improve. We are able to develop in the way God has intended, but only as we also learn to abide in His presence. Understanding these gifts even helps in decision-making and enables us to lead more wisely.

As I have discovered more and more how to apply the knowledge of these grace packages, I have increasingly been able to avoid various pitfalls over the years. To the degree that I have understood my own gifting—with its own strengths and weaknesses—as well as that of others, I have been more discerning in making choices. In fact, many of the mistakes and detours in my life could have been avoided if I had a better appreciation of my own particular gifts and calling and that of others at that time.

The wisdom gained by understanding these gifts is very practical in its application. For example, I have been invited on several occasions to partner with others in various endeavors but have declined in some cases because I knew the undertaking would never succeed. How was I able to discern this? It began with the insight that if a person demonstrates a significant lack of development of their innate gifting, which is observable through their actions and attitude, failure is almost a foregone conclusion, no matter how spiritual that person professes to be. In each instance, the eventual collapse of such proposed ventures later on proved that great wisdom is contained in understanding the operation of these gifts!

Insight into these various gifts is indispensible for the proper functioning of the local church as well. Yahweh has provided each of the gifts so that the many-membered body of Christ is equipped to reach its full potential. When a local congregation recognizes and appreciates the full variety of gifts with which it has been endowed, it will function together more harmoniously, be able to release a greater degree of corporate anointing, and be better equipped to fulfill its God-given purpose.

If we fail to recognize the many truths the Lord is restoring to His people in these end times, it is at our own peril. Abiding in the Lord is the basis of developing our God-given gifts and fulfilling our destiny. If we choose to live or do ministry in any other way, some of us may accomplish seemingly mighty exploits in the name of the Lord, but the reality is that we have done such things neither His way nor for His purposes, which is ultimately to bring Him glory. The better way is to recognize that we are first called to be and then called to do!

Developing our spirit man involves allowing Him to work through us. In fact, our primary "work" is to "rest"—rest in Him—and then do.

PART ONE: OUR MAKING

"Know that the LORD Himself is God; it is He who has made us, and not we ourselves; we are His people and the sheep of His pasture." Psalm 100:3 (NASB)

Chapter One

THE MYSTERY OF THE TREASURE WITHIN

We Are Wonderfully Made

TREASURE IN EARTHEN VESSELS

"But we have this treasure in earthen vessels, so that the surpassing greatness of the power will be of God and not from ourselves."
2 Corinthians 4:7 (NASB)

There is a divine purpose on the inside of you. The Lord your Maker has placed it there. It's much like a buried treasure—one hidden within your very own heart.

Only one person holds the key to this treasure within, and that is you, the one for whom God's purpose and plan was intended. You are His unique creation. You're one-of-a-kind, not part of some assembly-line production. His purpose for you can be fulfilled by no one else.

We catch a glimpse of this truth when we look at the astounding revelation God gave to the prophet Jeremiah, when He said, *"I knew you before you were formed in your mother's womb ... before you were born I made you a prophet."*[1]

Now, just pause for a moment and ponder this brief word given to Jeremiah, for it provides an amazing insight. The Lord said that even before Jeremiah was made—before he was formed in his mother's womb—God knew him. In other words, the Lord had Jeremiah in His heart and mind first—and then, some time after that, he was fashioned. Furthermore, God revealed that He had a purpose for Jeremiah at that time, long before he was born—to be a prophet.

Since our heavenly Father is *"no respecter of persons,"*[2] what was true for Jeremiah is equally true for each of us as well. He had each one of us in His heart and mind before we were formed. He had our purpose well thought out and planned. You see, your birth didn't catch the sovereign Lord of the universe by surprise. He didn't say, "Wait a minute, let me see here … I know I can find a purpose for this one somewhere. Let Me just look around …"

We need to open our eyes to how God does things. In the Psalms David wrote, *"You alone created my inner being. You knitted me together inside my mother. I will give thanks to you because I have been so amazingly and miraculously made … Every day of my life was recorded in your book before one of them had taken place."*[3]

It is God who created your inner being—your spirit and soul. This is the part of you that is the real you, for it is the eternal you. So the spirit and soul combination that's uniquely yours didn't just happen by chance. The essence of who you are was God's doing because He was the One who fashioned your innermost being.

Furthermore, David speaks of God's foreknowledge concerning his life; he said the Lord wrote down all the days of his life in His book before David had seen so much as his first day on earth. This truth goes far beyond our human ability to understand. While we may marvel at God's awesomeness and His reality we are left—even with the insights gleaned from the Scriptures—with a sense that we have just a mere inkling of God's ways.

AMAZINGLY MADE

It's clear that Yahweh planned and designed each one of us before we

were made—and did so according to a specific "blueprint" He created
for each of us.

A little more than a generation ago scientists discovered that a highly
complex molecular structure, called DNA, exists in every cell of the human
body. They found out this fundamental building block of life determines
every one of your physical characteristics down to the minutest details.
The shape of your nose, the length of your eyelashes, the size of your feet,
the texture of your hair—everything that comprises the physical "you" is
determined by the double-helix blueprint of your DNA.

What scientists discovered merely confirmed what the Holy Scriptures declared three thousand years ago, that our physical being has been
"miraculously" designed and made. God used the mechanism of DNA
to fashion every human being as a unique creation, unlike any other
person who has existed or ever will. This DNA blueprint was created at
the earliest moments of your conception. It's simply astounding!

Do you think the all-wise God, the author
of your unique DNA, would take any less
care in designing the inward you? Your body,
a temporary abode for your innermost being,
will pass from the scene in short order—a
few decades at most—and will return to dust.
Be assured that the God who is a Spirit[4] has
taken as much care in designing the inside
of you, your soul and spirit, as He has your
"outward man," which is perishing.

Your "inner man"[5] lives in a realm that is beyond the five senses. In the
natural we can only observe the outward manifestations of this "inner
man." What is most obvious is an individual's personality, which is
unique in every person.

Since we are all "one-of-a-kind," that means we each have a personality that is the sum of our mannerisms, temperament, character
traits, talents, and ways of thinking and doing. In fact, even "identical"
twins—who share the same physical DNA—have unique personalities
even though they may be raised in the same environment. The reason

for this is simple: Each one of us has been created differently on the inside according to a *spiritual* blueprint. What makes every person truly unique is the "spiritual DNA" our Maker used when He fashioned us. And while "identical" twins have the same predetermined genetic code comprised of their physical DNA, which causes them to look alike, their predetermined "spiritual DNA" is another matter. The inner qualities and personalities of even "identical" twins can be quite different, according to God's plans and purposes.

When King David wrote in the Psalms about his "inner being"[6] having been "knitted together" and "amazingly and miraculously made," he was referring to much more than his physical being. David had glimpsed into the spirit realm where he received a revelation of that which formed his innermost being. Whether we, in our twenty-first-century world, refer to this God-ordained fashioning of the inner being as our "spiritual DNA," or opt for other terminology, matters little. What is important is that we recognize that neither our physical being, "which is perishing," nor our inner man, which is eternal, was produced by chance, for "… it is He that has made us …" and He did so with a plan and a purpose in mind. Each one of us has a destiny that, at least in part, was designed into us by our Maker because it is intimately connected with the way He fashioned us.

As an analogy, consider the design of two vehicles, each with a very different purpose: a car and a boat. A car is meant to travel on land and the four tires on it are a good indication of that function. The engine and steering wheel point to the fact that it was designed to go. Not just go anyplace, but to travel on land. Likewise, the purpose of a boat can also be found in its design. Its water-tight hull makes it buoyant in water. The hull's shape is a good indication that the boat is useful for moving around on the surface of water. It is also clear that the propeller will move the boat in water but is of no use on land.

So, just by looking at the basic design and characteristics of a car or a boat, much can be deduced about their purposes. The maker of each vehicle intended it to meet very specific needs for transportation—one to travel on land the other on water.

As we consider how each of us was designed, it becomes clear that our Maker had a special purpose in mind when He created us. Everyone has his[7] own particular characteristics that were not placed there randomly. The divine pattern of our spiritual and physical DNA was arranged to fulfill a purpose Yahweh had in His heart and mind. Simply put, our purpose is found in the way we've been made, and our destiny is tied to our creation.

Just as the characteristics of your physical body have been predetermined by DNA, so God has amazingly designed your "inner man"—the eternal you—according to an elaborate and unique pattern—your "spiritual DNA"— before you were born!

Questions: Chapter One

1. There is a divine purpose on the inside of you that is much like a buried _____.

2. Scripture says before Jeremiah was formed in his mother's womb God _____ him.

3. The Lord had each one of us in His heart and _____ before we were formed.

4. When King David wrote of his "inner being" having been "knitted together" he was referring to much more than his physical being. David had glimpsed into the _____ realm.

5. According to King David in Psalm 139:16: "Every day of my life was recorded in your book _____ one of them had taken place."

6. The real "you," the eternal "you," is your _____ and your _____.

7. It's clear that God planned and _____ each one of us before we were made.

8. Everyone has his own particular _____ that were not placed there randomly.

9. Just like the purpose of a car or a boat can be seen by its design, so can a person discern his purpose in his _____.

10. Each one of us has been created differently on the inside according to a _____ "blueprint."

11. What makes every person truly unique is the "spiritual _____" that was used by our Maker when we were fashioned.

12. Our purpose is found in the way we've been made, and our destiny is tied to our _____.

13. Do you believe that God's purpose for you can be fulfilled by someone else?

    _____ yes _____ no _____ not sure (check one)

14. In the last century scientists discovered that DNA determines even the minutest details of a person's physical characteristics. In light of the fact that our body lives for only a few decades and then perishes, while our soul and spirit live for eternity, do you think it is reasonable to believe that God planned our spiritual characteristics by a template we could call our "spiritual DNA" as well?

    _____ yes _____ no _____ not sure (check one)

15. God recorded every day of David's life in His book before David was even born according to Psalm 139:16. Since God is "no respecter of persons" (what He does for one He'll do for another), what do you believe that says about you and your future?

    _____

    _____

    _____

Chapter Two

APPRECIATING OUR ENDOWMENT

Starting at the Right Place

"The LORD *called me before my birth; from within the womb He called me by name." Isaiah 49:1 (NLT)*

Have you ever felt that a potential exists within you, deep on the inside, that's far beyond what you've experienced or been able to bring forth up to this point in your life? If you have, you're definitely not alone! That's because God, out of His love, has woven into our spiritual DNA a destiny and purpose that is far beyond mediocrity and the humdrum existence for which most folks have settled.

When King David saw into how Yahweh fashioned his inner being and how his days on earth were recorded even before he'd been born, what he was really marveling at was the awesomeness of the creation of his spiritual DNA and divine destiny. While three thousand years have passed since David received that astounding revelation, it's one that is hard to improve upon. In fact, most of us still need to catch up to it!

FROM THE INSIDE OUT

Those who've been born again are adopted into God's family and have found their true identity in Jesus Christ. But too many of God's children, after coming into His kingdom, have the mistaken idea that somehow they will find their destiny and purpose somewhere "out there"—by searching outside of themselves. They may go to church conferences, read Christian books, launch out in their own ministry, or be involved in any number of other seemingly worthy activities, but what they are truly seeking to find is a clear sense of purpose and direction.

The truth of the matter is that God's children should have been searching in a place they most likely overlooked (and therefore neglected) because they were too busy and because it was just too unfamiliar to them. However, doing things His way would have led them to abide in His presence and then, with God's help, look inside his own heart to find their true nature and identity. It is there that the hidden things are revealed and the treasure trove of divine purpose is unlocked. The Lord's help in this must never be neglected, for it is only as His children learn to rest in "the secret place" that purpose,

> *Precious few of us come even close to realizing the potential that's within us for we've settled for busyness, mediocrity, and conformity rather than doing things God's way.*

destiny, and calling are discovered. As the child of God is nurtured in the sanctuary of the Father's love, he grows in wisdom and understanding. The discoveries he makes in this safe haven will propel him down the road to fulfilling his destiny.

The primary failure of a believer who searches on the outside for his purpose is that he hasn't put "first things first." Jesus, speaking in the context of believers seeking after "things," told us that we are to *"seek the kingdom of God and His righteousness"* first. When we've done that, He's promised that everything else would follow afterward.[1] Since our purpose has been woven into our very being, we must start by finding out how we've been framed. As we grow in understanding, from *there* we will discover our destiny.

Contrary to Jesus' admonition, Christians commonly believe that purpose can be found in "doing." This is what might be called the "Martha syndrome," being busy and looking for meaning and significance somewhere in the midst of the busyness. In contrast to Martha's approach was that of her sister Mary, who chose to sit at the Master's feet savoring His every word. And what was Jesus' observation concerning these two ways? After chiding Martha for her misplaced priorities and preoccupation with serving and doing, He commended Mary for choosing what is best. In Jesus' view, a reverential attitude toward God and His Word is far better than the busyness of service toward Yahweh—especially when it precludes intimate fellowship with Him.

Too often we "put the cart before the horse." We start moving in a certain direction, becoming occupied with what appears to be a good thing, before we seek His counsel. Then, after we've launched out—in essence "doing our own thing"—we find ourselves so busy there's little time to hear what is on the Lord's heart.

How much more fruitful it would be, for ourselves and for God's kingdom, if we spent time in "the secret place" getting His instructions first! Any other way of doing things really amounts to our conducting an "experiment" in which at some point along the way we find out whether what we're doing is really God's will.

> *Launching out on any endeavor before receiving counsel from the Lord is like "putting the cart before the horse"—not much will come of it and it just doesn't make good sense.*

And, as we all know, while some experiments end successfully, more often than not they end up in failure. But that shouldn't be the case with us!

In humility we're to seek and knock, and having received His counsel, then do. It's incredible how much is squandered when we don't do things His way. Over the years I've seen so much calamity as many of God's children spent time in wasted effort and consumed so many kingdom resources, doing things they weren't called to do in the first place. It is painful to watch. How much tragedy and heartache could be avoided if believers followed His admonition and refused to launch out before getting instructions from "headquarters." Seeking *first*, not after the fact, makes all the difference.

ENDOWED BY OUR CREATOR

The modern-day church has gotten out of balance by overemphasizing certain parts of the Spirit-led walk while virtually ignoring other aspects. A major reason for this is that too many of God's children have "itching ears" and refuse to endure sound doctrine. Entertainment and "show" are big on the mega-church agenda while solid teaching on what it means to "abide in Christ" hardly registers on the church's radar screen. The line between New Age positive-thinking and the teachings of many prominent Christian ministries is so blurred it's no wonder the world has difficulty seeing the difference!

We can see this type of problem in the area of teaching on spiritual gifts. Most believers who have gone through basic discipleship training know about the Lord's provision of various gifts to the church for its healthy growth and development. Generally speaking, the two sets of gifts are commonly called the "gifts of the Holy Spirit" and the "ministry gifts."

The first set of gifts, which is also known as the "spiritual gifts" or "manifestation gifts," is found in 1 Corinthians 12.[2] They are really the various operations of the Holy Spirit at a given time and place to minister to individual needs and advance the kingdom of God. The nine gifts in this group include:

◈ Word of Wisdom
◈ Word of Knowledge
◈ Discerning of Spirits
◈ Tongues

- ❖ Interpretation of Tongues
- ❖ Prophecy
- ❖ Miracles
- ❖ Gifts of Healing
- ❖ Gift of Faith

The second group, also known as the "fivefold ministry gifts" or the "equipping gifts," is mentioned in Paul's letter to the Ephesian church.[3] One of the main functions of these gifts is to train believers so that they can mature in their faith and find their proper place in the body of Christ. The equipping (ministry) gifts include:

- ❖ Apostles
- ❖ Prophets
- ❖ Evangelists
- ❖ Pastors
- ❖ Teachers

However, there is also a third set of gifts mentioned in Scripture that by and large has received less attention than either of these other two sets. As a consequence they are generally less understood, though by no means less important for the health and vitality of the church. This third group is most commonly known as the "motivational gifts," though a more apt term is the endowment gifts because they have been endowed to us by God before our birth.[4] These gifts are found in Romans 12:6-8:

> [6] *Then having gifts differing according to the grace that is given to us, if **prophecy**, according to the proportion of faith;*
> [7] *or **ministry**, in the ministry: or [he who] **teaches**, in the teaching;*
> [8] *or he who **exhorts**, in the encouragement: he that **shares**, in simplicity; or he that takes the **lead**, in diligence; or he who shows **mercy**, in cheerfulness.*[5]

There are seven gifts mentioned in these verses[6]:

❖ Prophecy[7]
❖ Ministry (service)
❖ Teaching
❖ Exhortation (encouraging)
❖ Giving (sharing)
❖ Ruling (leading, presiding, administering, organizing)
❖ Showing mercy (compassion)

While these seven gifts find their true fulfillment only as they glorify God, there is a basic difference between them and the other two sets of gifts, which is that every person on planet earth has at least one of these gifts placed within him. In other words, the only requirement to receive an endowment gift is to be born into the family of man. Whether a child is born into a family that worships the moon and the stars or whether his father is pastor of the local Christian church, every baby is born with at least one endowment gift. By contrast, the manifestation and equipping gifts are clearly reserved for those who have been born again into the family of God.

A key to understanding the endowment gifts is that they are imparted to the individual by God before he is born and woven into his spiritual DNA, enmeshed in his "inner being." Furthermore, as the individual abides in the True Vine, Jesus, being nurtured by His love nature, the endowment gifts thrive and bring forth the fruit for which they are intended.

Much more emphasis and teaching has been given to the manifestation and equipping gifts, perhaps with the mistaken idea that there is a hierarchical order of importance to the three sets of gifts, which there is not. To think so would be like saying that among an apple, a banana, and an orange, one is inherently more important than another. Of course, that isn't the case, for each fruit has its own distinctive qualities and is to be appreciated for its uniqueness.

However, in discovering one's purpose and calling in life, the importance of understanding one's endowment gift package cannot be over-emphasized. After all, which one of the three sets of gifts would be most basic to the believer in discovering his purpose and calling: 1) the gifts that are part of the person's "inner being" and woven into his spiritual DNA, his endowment gifts? 2) the gifts that operate from time to time as the Holy Spirit wills, the manifestation gifts? or 3) the gifts with which only a select few in the church are endowed, the equipping gifts?

It should be obvious that the starting place in understanding one's purpose is knowing how he's been fashioned. That insight comes with discovering his endowment gifts. Once a believer knows which endowment gifts he's been given, he has a good start in realizing his purpose and calling. The reason for this is that his inner constitution and personality have been designed with God's loving purpose for him in mind. So, just as a building project starts with the construction of its foundation, the place where we should begin in understanding our divine purpose and potential in life is with appreciating our endowment gifts. In fact, the seeds of our destiny have been sown there.

The best starting point in determining God's purpose and plan for your life is to evaluate the endowment gifts with which you've been graced. He placed particular gifts in your inner being for the special calling He has for you. Determine your endowment gifts and you are well on the road to being able to find your purpose and discover your destiny.

Questions: Chapter Two

1. Too many of God's children have the mistaken idea that somehow they will find their destiny and purpose somewhere "out there" by _____ outside of themselves.

2. Precious few Christians come even close to realizing the potential that's _____ us.

3. It is in the "_____ place" that purpose, destiny, and calling are discovered.

4. Most Christians believe that _____ can be found by "doing."

5. Launching out on any endeavor before receiving _____ from the Lord is like "putting the cart before the horse."

6. God, out of His love, has woven into our _____ DNA a destiny and purpose.

7. The "Martha syndrome" involves being busy and looking for meaning and _____ somewhere in the midst of the busyness.

8. If we don't spent time in the "secret place" getting His instructions first, what we are really doing is conducting an "_____" in which at some point along the way we find out whether what we're doing is really God's will.

9. The three main sets of gifts mentioned in the New Testament are the _____ gifts of 1 Corinthians 12:7-11, the equipping gifts of Ephesians 4:11-12, and the endowment gifts of Romans 12:6-8.

10. All three sets of gifts are _____ gifts.

11. The manifestation and equipping gifts are reserved for those who have been born again into the family of God. However, _____ person on planet earth has an endowment gift that God has given him.

12. The endowment gifts have traditionally been called the "_____ gifts." They are generally less understood, though they are by no means less important for the health and vitality of the church.

13. Which one of the three sets of gifts would be *most* basic to the believer in discovering his purpose and calling? The _____ gifts.

14. In _____ we're to seek and knock, and having received His counsel, *then* do.

15. The endowment gifts are so named because they have been _____ to us by God before our birth.

16. By determining your endowment gifts you also will be able to _____ your purpose and discover your destiny.

Chapter Three

ADDING GREATER DIMENSION

The Importance of Your Endowment Gift

"For we are God's masterpiece. He has created us anew in Christ Jesus, so we can do the good things He planned for us long ago." Ephesians 2:10 (NLT)

YOUR GRACE-GIFT

There's wonderful truth in the saying "The best things in life are free." If you have a moment's doubt about it, then let me ask: Which is more valuable to you, sitting next to the one you love at the end of a gorgeous, sunny day and watching a sunset together, or having a handsomely framed painting you bought in an art shop of that same beautiful sunset? While you may appreciate beautiful art and would have paid a high price to put that "sunset" on your wall, sharing the real-life experience of a sunset with someone you care about is worth immeasurably more.

God has done so much for each one of us, and provided for us in so many ways we aren't even aware of, but most of us haven't taken the time to reflect on His wonderful provision. Take for instance the way you were made, the intricate design God used to make you the unique individual He created you to be. Do you really think there's anything you could do to deserve even that *one* thing He's done for you—and He did it before you even breathed your first breath? Of course not! You couldn't be good enough, pray long enough, or work hard enough to deserve just that one gift, even though He gave it to you *freely*.

When the apostle Paul made mention of the seven endowment gifts in Romans 12:6-8, he wrote about them as "grace-gifts," or charisma in the Greek text.[1] The word *charisma* means that these gifts are free and unmerited—we did nothing to deserve them. But they definitely come with "strings attached!" Their purpose is to glorify the One who made us. And so you need to realize that your endowment gift is neither *of* nor *by* nor *for* you.

A GIFT THAT AFFECTS EVERYTHING

Most of us don't have a clue as to how much of "who we are" is determined by these endowment gifts. Consider the fact that a person's gift causes him to:

◈ look at every life situation and relationship from a particular frame of reference
◈ act according to certain patterns of behavior
◈ be motivated in ways according to his spiritual DNA

It's as if a person goes through his life wearing a pair of tinted sunglasses that have the color of his endowment gift. Whatever situation he's in, he views it through the tint of his endowment gift "glasses." That lens color affects the way he sees and reacts to *everything* around him.

For example, a person with the gift of teaching will look and react to situations that confront him through the tinted glasses of a teacher and many times will be looking for "teachable moments." In situations where others couldn't find such an opportunity if they looked all week long, the endowment gift teacher will find just what he's been looking for and will be able to expound upon it at length. On the other hand, given the same situation, a person with the gift of mercy will look and react completely  differently according to the tint of his "mercy-colored" glasses. This person will be drawn to identify closely with those who are affected and will want them to know that he "feels their pain" and will commiserate with them in their difficulties.

Since a person's endowment gift shapes his perception of life and everything he sees and does, having insight into one's gifting will help him understand the inner working of his own heart. He'll gain insight into his attitudes, behavior, and motivation. Why does he think and react the way he does? He'll be more realistic and operate in a greater degree of wisdom and be apt "... *not to think of himself more highly than he ought to think, but to think soberly ....*"[2] In a world filled with self-delusion, this person will stand out of the crowd as someone who is down-to-earth and displays unusual common sense.

As a person grows in his understanding of all the endowment gifts he'll also gain greater insight into the motivation and behavior of others. By identifying the gifts that friends and acquaintances operate in he'll become more skillful in his relationships with them. He'll better appreciate what makes them "tick." This type of insight will obviously improve family life as well, helping a person to understand why his spouse thinks and acts the way they do, appreciating the unique qualities of each of his children, and understanding the temperaments of his parents as well as the dynamics of his own upbringing. In short, he (or she) will become a better marriage partner,

> *Your endowment gift affects how you view everything in the world around you. It's as if you're looking through sunglasses tinted by the color of your endowment gift—and everything you see is that color.*

parent, boss, or employee through the insights gained by understanding his endowment gifts and those of others.

This same understanding is valuable in virtually every aspect of ministry as well since people are at the very heart of ministry. A pastor will be a more effective leader and a better counselor as he gains insight into the endowment gifts of those he's leading and counseling.

BRINGING GLORY TO GOD

The ultimate purpose of each of God's gifts—whether a manifestation, equipping, or endowment gift—is to bring glory to God. Every one of the gifts is vital for the health of the church as well. It's for these purposes that God has provided them, and it is within the body of Christ that the gifts find their ultimate fulfillment during the Age of Grace in which we live. Ultimately these gifts enable the church to fulfill its role in Yahweh's plan.

It's significant that even though every human being—whether their home is an impoverished village in the Andes or a posh suburb of New York—is born with an endowment gift, it's only when a person is "born again" that their gift can be used for its intended purpose, which is to bring glory to God. Until that time, a person's gift will be used primarily for their own self-interest or for something other than its intended function. A God-created void will exist in a person's life, however, since the endowment gift is not being used for the job for which it was designed. In fact, a gnawing sense of a lack of fulfillment results when the person's endowment gift is applied solely to things other than its intended purpose. Of course, unless the person is born again there will be no way for him to understand the reason why he is suffering a sense of incompleteness and frustration within.

Even though everyone is born with at least one endowment gift, it's only when that person is born again that their special gift can be used for its intended purpose—to bring glory to God!

HELPING THE BODY WORK IN HARMONY

The apostle Paul described the operation of the manifestation and endowment gifts in the church by using the analogy of the working parts in a body. In his letter to both the church in Rome as well as to the believers in Corinth, Paul pointed out that a body functions according to the supply of each of its parts or members.[3] When the contribution of one or more of these parts is missing, the entire body isn't able to function as it should. It's the same with the body of Christ. When a particular gift is missing—whether it's an endowment or manifestation gift—the body of the Messiah can't work as it is meant to function.

Each endowment gift placed in a believer's spiritual DNA is there so he'll be able to fulfill his purpose in Jesus Christ. Part of that purpose is in relation to other believers as he takes his place within the body of Christ. Yahweh's plan for every believer is that he fulfills a particular function in the body. When that member fails to do so and doesn't contribute his gift, the entire body suffers.

While some parts of a physical body are more evident, like the mouth or the hand, some of the less visible parts are just as vital, if not more so, such as the heart or liver. Likewise, with the endowment gifts in the church, some are more visible—such as the teacher or the exhorter—but the body of Christ would cease to exist if not for the mercy gift, which represents the very heart of ministry. In other words, none of the seven endowment gifts is more important than another. Each gift has its own particular function without which the body of Christ suffers.

Furthermore, it is the Father's intention that the different gifts in the body work in harmony and bring wholeness. There should be a "flow" of ministry orchestrated by the Holy Spirit, not only during Sunday morning services, but also throughout the week as each member brings the gift God has deposited within him to the service of the body. This is true "body ministry" by which balance, wholeness, and harmony are brought to Messiah's body—ministering one to another and to the larger community.

LEADING REQUIRES 'SKILLFUL HANDS'

"So he shepherded them according to the integrity of his heart; and led them by the skillfulness of his hands." Psalm 78:72 (JPS)

Obviously, for anyone to lead or shepherd others effectively he must first have a heart for his sheep. This principle applies to wherever such leadership occurs. The above passage from the Psalms, speaking of King David, suggests that two basic qualities made him a successful leader: "integrity of heart" and "skillfulness of hands."

Integrity and skillfulness are absolute requirements to lead others successfully, whether it's as a pastor, mom or dad, boss, Girl Scout leader, or football coach. The first quality, integrity, relates to "who a person is" and the second, skillfulness, relates to "what a person can do."

"People skills," understanding those around you and relating to them, are essential for anyone who serves in leadership—especially those who are called by Yahweh to serve as an equipping gift to the body of Christ. To work competently with the wide variety of personalities found in a church, such a leader must understand the "spiritual DNA" of the people for whom the Lord has made him accountable.

As an equipping gift, the pastor's primary responsibility is to train those under his care to do the "work of the ministry."[4] To do so skillfully he needs to walk in understanding and be able to assess the endowment gifts of his people accurately. What motivates them? Why do they respond the way they do? What is their calling? Where do they fit best in the body? When such issues are understood in light of the way God has made them—that is, by understanding their "spiritual DNA"—it will make all the difference in his effectiveness as a leader.

The Lord declared to the prophet Hosea, *"My people are destroyed for lack of knowledge."*[5] However, in His mercy, oftentimes we're not *totally* destroyed by our lack of knowledge—just maimed, damaged, or enfeebled. Without a doubt, a lack of understanding of the endowment gifts *will* impair any leader's effectiveness in equipping his people. Lacking such knowledge makes it more likely that he will succumb to the natural tendency to place God's people in ministry positions based on the immediacy of the need and the availability of those willing to fill the spot.

We've seen it countless times. An urgent need arises for a pastor to appoint someone to fill a vacancy within a ministry, let's say the intercessory ministry—a place where someone with the endowment gift of prophecy or mercy would be a good fit. But instead the pastor places someone with the gift of sharing there, because he knows that person has been eagerly waiting to help out in whatever capacity he can. In this case the person the pastor has chosen is ready and willing but is simply a mismatch for the needs of the group. As a result, the intercessory prayer ministry starts to languish because the long-term members of the group can see that their newly appointed leader isn't capable, and the leader soon becomes frustrated because he's not suited to lead the group. In such a situation, conflict inevitably arises and the church begins to suffer because of the ineffectiveness of the intercessory ministry.

To be a *skillful* leader means that you need to place the right person in the right place at the right time—and to do that requires knowledge of your people and understanding their endowment gifts. By not doing so, a leader will too often end up mismatching God's people in positions where they are unsuitable, which in turn results in frustration, disappointment, and hindering the ministry.

> *A skilled leader needs to be able to place the right person in the right place at the right time—and to do that proficiently requires an adequate knowledge of his people and understanding their endowment gifts.*

The predominant, but dysfunctional, method of "doing" ministry in far too many churches, particularly smaller ones, is one in which the pastor is overloaded with responsibility—from fixing the plumbing in the church building to ordering the Sunday school material to preaching two or three times a week—while all but a few of the members look on. Beloved, it's never been God's intention for His people to sit and watch as spectators while the pastor has to "do it all." Since the birth of the church on the day of Pentecost, we've been meant to be members "one of another." The local assembly of believers is not, nor has it ever been, a "one-man show."

A DIVERSITY OF GIFTS

No *one person* has the *full measure* of each endowment gift residing within, and all seven endowment gifts are needed in a local church for it to function in a healthy way. It's crucial that each of the seven gifts be represented adequately and given ample opportunity to minister within the body. The pastor must clearly understand his own strengths and weaknesses in terms of his endowment gifting and then surround himself with others who bring those gifts that are lacking so there is a greater measure of balance in the ministry.

The tendency of a *weak* leader is to work within his particular comfort zone by surrounding himself with others who have similar endowment gifts. This is a natural way for many to do things, but it flies in the face of the purpose for which God designed a *diversity* of gifts—for the body to be inter-dependent, with each member's gift contributing to the whole. Truly appreciating this one principle can make a tremendous difference in the success of any ministry. Identifying the endowment gifts less represented within a church and its leadership team, and seeking out and promoting members with the needed gifts, will bring balance in the church as well as in the pastor's leadership team.

To illustrate this point, the endowment gifts (as well as other gifts) given to the local church by God are something like when a dad gives his son a toolbox with an array of tools inside. There's a saw, a hammer, screwdrivers, chisels, a tape measure, and other tools as well. Each tool has its intended purpose, and clearly it is of no use unless it is taken out of the box. If some of the tools just sit there the work that needs to get done simply won't get done.

Some church leaders are like the child who limits himself by taking only a few of the tools—his favorite ones—out of the box. Perhaps he doesn't like to use some of the others, or maybe he never even considered using them. So when he needs to cut a board, for example, he reaches into the toolbox and only takes out his favorite tools—a hammer and a chisel—but doesn't even think to pick up the saw. While it's true that a board *can be* cut with a hammer and chisel, it takes a tremendous amount of time and effort to cut it that way. It is neither effective nor efficient. In fact, choosing anything other than the saw to cut the board is a choice to do things "the hard way." The question is, Why not just use the saw that's in the box? It's there to be used. How much easier it would be if only the son would avail himself of what his dad has given him! The tools in the box were given to be a blessing and to be used—not to collect dust and rust.

The local church will function as God intended only when it utilizes all of the gifts at its disposal. When whole sets of gifts, such as the endowment gifts, are neglected the church suffers greatly. On the other hand, the church will fulfill its mission, and its members will mature beyond what could be imagined, when a pastor has a passion to nurture every gift within the body. To not do so is to fall short as a leader. Therefore, it's essential

The church will fulfill its destiny and the growth of its members will be energized when a pastor enthusiastically embraces and nurtures each of the gifts the Lord has provided.

for anyone in a leadership position to become skillful in recognizing, understanding, and working with the endowment gifts of the people around him—and then put each gift to use so that the local assembly functions properly.

Yahweh has spread the endowment gifts throughout the entirety of humanity, not just in the body of Christ. He's placed at least one gift in every one of us so that we fulfill our personal mission and purpose individually as well as corporately as the body of the Messiah. His desire is that no one be left out and everyone be part of the team effort in building the kingdom of God. By developing our endowment gifting and through teamwork, we will each fulfill our destiny—*together.*

Questions: Chapter Three

1. The purpose of the endowment gifts, like all of the gifts, is to _____ the One who made us.

2. A person's gift causes him to:

   ❖ _____ at every life situation and relationship from a particular frame of reference

   ❖ act according to certain patterns of behavior

   ❖ be _____ in ways that are God-given.

3. Every one of the gifts is _____ for the health of the church as well.

4. It's only when a person is born again that their special endowment gift can be used for its _____ purpose—to bring glory to God!

5. In the Greek text the apostle Paul used the word charisma concerning the seven endowment gifts, meaning they are _____-gifts. In other words, these gifts are free and unmerited—we did nothing to deserve them.

6. Your endowment gift gives you a distinct perspective, almost like having tinted "glasses." Each gift has its own color. Your endowment gift "_____" affect the way you see and react to everything around you.

7. Having insight into one's gifting will help a person understand the inner working of his own _____.

8. By understanding the _____ of each of the endowment gifts you'll be able to gain greater insight into the motivation and behavior of others.

9. It is God's intention that the diversity of gifts in the body works in _____ and brings wholeness.

10. God's purpose and plan for every believer is that he _____ a particular function or purpose in the body.

11. None of the seven endowment gifts is more _____ than another—they are all needed.

12. As an equipping gift, the pastor's primary responsibility is to _____ those under his care to do the "work of the ministry."

13. To be a skillful leader means that you need to place the _____ person in the right place at the right time.

14. The tendency of a weak leader is to work within his particular _____ zone by surrounding himself with others who have similar endowment gifts.

15. The local church will function as God intended only when it utilizes all of the _____ it has at its disposal.

16. The tools our heavenly Father has given us are meant to be a _____ and to be used—not to collect dust and rust!

17. By developing our endowment gifting and through _____, we will each fulfill our destiny—together.

PART TWO: THE GIFTS

"Now about the spiritual gifts (the special endowments of supernatural energy), brethren, I do not want you to be misinformed." 1 Corinthians 12:1 (AMP)

Chapter Four

GOOD THINGS COME IN SEVENS

The Healthy Characteristics of
the Seven Endowment Gifts

"As each one has received a special gift, employ it in serving one another as good stewards of the manifold grace of God." 1 Peter 4:10 (NASB)

SEVEN 'GRACE PACKAGES'

Each of the seven gifts (*charismas*) referred to in Romans 12:6-8 is in reality a God-given "grace package" that is pre-determined by an individual's spiritual DNA. Some of these characteristics are observable from the early years of a person's life while others depend on the individual advancing in their spiritual journey and reaching a spiritual threshold before particular attributes become manifest.

The totality of a person's characteristics—temperament, ways of thinking, comportment, and spiritual abilities—is determined by a variety of factors, including a person's spiritual DNA, the environment[1] in which he's raised, and how far along he is in his own spiritual path. All of these combined are what make the individual who he is and how he looks at the world.

Several aspects of a person's "grace package"—such as any special ability, spiritual authority, or anointing associated with his gift—become more evident as he matures spiritually. These special endowments are just as much an integral part of a believer's spiritual DNA as his temperament and personality, though they remain latent until his gift has been developed along godly lines. Once an individual is truly born again and growing in his gifting, being led by the Holy Spirit, he eventually will reach a stage where the supernatural endowment of the gift becomes a significant force, enabling him to walk in the fullness of his endowment gift.

For the sake of simplicity and clarity, the description of each grace package in this chapter focuses on the positive characteristics of the gift—that is, "what it looks like" when developed in a healthy manner. However, it should be noted that the endowment gifts also have a "downside" as well—negative characteristics that result from a person's failure to mature properly or walk in the God-kind of love. In reality, the vast majority of people are only partially developed, so they exhibit both positive and negative characteristics. Therefore, a good gauge of a person's spiritual development is to compare the "upside" with the "downside" characteristics.

Self-centeredness, carnality, spiritual slothfulness, worldliness, soul wounds, and strongholds in the mind are the main enemies of developing the endowment gifts as God intended. A person who is bound by any of these shortcomings, though he may be able to "speak with the tongues of men and of angels,"[2] will never be able to develop his God-given abilities to maturity, and his gift package will remain largely unfulfilled.

Though everyone has one principal endowment gift—the one that is strongest and usually most obvious—some people have a secondary or even tertiary gift that is evident as well. Just like the DNA that determines the properties of a person's physical body, spiritual DNA is highly complex. But, for the sake of gaining a basic understanding of these seven grace packages, we'll look at each gift as separate and distinct. This insight will also help us grow in understanding the purpose, plan, and destiny that God has for each one of us individually and corporately as the body of Christ.

1. PROPHECY

"However, when He, the Spirit of Truth, has come, He will guide you into all truth...." John 16:13 (NKJV)

One of the keys to understanding the endowment gift of prophecy is that a person with this gift has in the core of his being an extraordinary capacity not only to discern spiritual truth but also to sort it out in a clear and succinct way and to verbalize it. The prophecy-gifted person is endowed with the innate ability to "size up" individuals and circumstances quickly and to get a "feel" for things right away. Not only does he have the intuitive ability to see into the heart of a matter spiritually, he also has the facility to categorize it, normally in terms of a simple dichotomy, such as "right or wrong," "good or bad," or "true or false." He may not be right all the time, but it is certain that you will hardly ever see this person sitting on the fence, unable to make up his mind.

In other words, a healthy prophet has the ability to see things that others may not be aware of, express himself in clear and powerful terms, and draw vivid "word pictures" to describe what he sees and feels. This ability to articulate can be by the written or the spoken word. In both public and private meetings, a prophet often has the uncanny ability to "cut to the chase" as he slices through a clutter of peripheral issues and details to get to the heart of the matter at hand. Spiritually speaking, the prophet is able to see "the forest through the trees," put aside nuance, and then verbalize the essential truth of a matter.

I have found that the perceptiveness of most prophets will often cause them to notice what others normally overlook or take for granted. For example, it is common for a prophet to be sensitive and quick to detect injustice such as when a person or group is treated unfairly. While others may say, "That's just the way it is," when a spiritually mature prophet sees an individual or class of people held to a different standard or treated in a way that puts them down, he doesn't hesitate to come against such a situation. He is wired in such a way that he has a particular disgust for all types of wrongdoing, and this predisposition compels him to speak out or act against unjust treatment. Because of this, in such situations a prophet will come across to others as bold and outspoken. On less controversial occasions, however, a prophet who is developed in his gifting is just as likely to appear to others to be highly perceptive as well as articulate and persuasive.

One of the keys to understanding the motivation of a prophet is recognizing that he is by nature more vertically than horizontally oriented. That is, his natural inclination, when he is mature in his gifting, is to place greater emphasis on his relationship with God than with those around him. Because of this, a prophet will oftentimes grip truth more tightly than he will hold onto relationships. The result is that normally a prophet will develop few close relationships, but he is content with that.

While prophets may come across as frank and forthright to others, I have found that many will be very hard on themselves as well. Also, unless he is a carnal prophet, he will have developed an unusually high personal standard of honesty and integrity—one that is beyond reproach. This propensity can also cause him to suffer, as some with the prophetic gift have greater difficulty forgiving themselves than other believers.

Prophets enjoy being part of something new and doing things that are innovative. Maintaining the status quo goes against the spiritual inclination of most prophets, who if they are Christian usually desire to be on the cutting-edge of what Yahweh is doing. Because of the future-oriented frame of mind of this gift, a prophet working in the secular world often is well suited to fields that involve research or invention.

Also, I have found that prophets working in administrative positions seem to be able to find ways to improve, change, or enlarge upon what it is they're doing.

As a rule, a prophet can be brought into a situation that is near chaos and it doesn't bother him nearly as much as it would others. This is because his spiritual DNA makes him want to bring order to a given situation. While most prophets tend to be problem-solvers, once they are done they normally want to move on. They won't spend much time in celebration either. Since they are not "maintainers," they are best suited to start and develop an endeavor and then hand it over to someone else.

To sum up a few key points, people who are prophecy-gifted:

1. have an innate ability to quickly and accurately identify spiritual truths
2. are intuitive and insightful
3. can discern others' motives and character
4. have a keen sense of right and wrong
5. tend to see everything as either black or white; no gray or indefinite areas
6. sharply confront injustice and wrongs
7. are direct, candid, and persuasive
8. proclaim the truth—are gifted in verbal expression and need to express themselves, finding it difficult to keep silent
9. dislike deception and poor leadership
10. are naturally suspicious of those who "talk the talk" but fail to "walk the walk"
11. are open about their own faults
12. have strict personal standards and tend to be hard on themselves
13. are often the first ones to show a willingness to be broken in order to further what they perceive as a kingdom calling or direction

14. desire to be obedient to God at all costs

15. are loyal to truth rather than people

16. are willing to suffer for right

17. usually have only a few close friends

18. need to know where they're going—must have a "where" and a "why"

2. SERVER (MINISTRY/SERVICE)

"For even the Son of Man did not come to be served, but to serve..."
Mark 10:45

One of the unique qualities of those with the gift of service is a spiritual DNA that enables them to readily discern the practical needs of others and be inspired and motivated to fill those needs. Important necessities that would seem insignificant to others catch the attention of the service-gifted person. The  spiritual makeup of servers is such that they derive joy and fulfill-ment in knowing that their service frees up the person or group being helped, allowing them to be fruit-ful in the tasks that God has called them to do.

As a general rule servers are workhorses and not show horses. When there is a job to be done you will see a server show up first and leave last. Most ministers developed in their gifting are also driven by an attention to detail. Once someone with the gift of service sees a need their impulse is to promptly meet the need and if necessary work extra hard to complete the task. At times I have seen a server so motivated by his gift that he's able to fulfill the need regardless of weariness. Once he's become convinced of the importance of the undertaking, he will go the extra mile by spending whatever time or personal resources are necessary to get the job done. By doing more than what is expected, the minister knows it will not only please the person or group being helped, but is a genuine expression that his service is unto the Lord.

The tasks that attract a minister are usually immediate, practical needs. By contrast, a server's grace-package isn't particularly suited for long-range ventures. Projects involving long-range objectives or where there is little visible progress over time likely will be a source of frustration for most ministers. Also, though a server normally excels when working independently, it's not a good idea for him to be in charge of organizing or heading up a project for an extended length of time—unless the server also has a secondary gifting as a leader.

The minister's willingness to help out when he sees a need can result in an overcrowded agenda if he's not careful. This is because a server may have difficulty saying no when his services are requested, sometimes resulting in a schedule that is out of control. Also, I have found that if a server doesn't use wisdom, others may try to exploit him, knowing he feels a sense of obligation to help out. In such cases where his schedule has become overly hectic, it is the family that usually bears the brunt of the repercussions. This can cause an especially difficult conflict for a minister since family loyalty is very important to most servers.

While most serving-gifted individuals become involved in many activities, they usually will try to avoid being the center of attention. Also, since many servers aren't inclined toward public speaking, being thrust to the "center stage" will usually make the server uncomfortable and perhaps even embarrassed.

Because it is in the spiritual constitution of most well-developed ministers to be straightforward and honest, they invariably make able and trustworthy assistants who help with joyfulness, sincerity, and simplicity, without an ulterior motive or hidden agenda. A server can also be a true "armor bearer" when serving a leader. In fact, I have found that helping the leader through intercession, in addition to mundane tasks he fulfills, is where a server can particularly shine. Also, a server who is walking in the fullness of his gift will find authority and a special anointing when helping the leader through intercessory prayer.

Though he's truly fulfilling his gift when his service is "as unto the Lord," it is common for even a healthy minister to need to feel appreciated by those he's helping. Gratitude needs to be expressed and will confirm to the server that his work is necessary, important, and being blessed by the Lord.

The best example of a minister I have ever known is my wife Blanca, whose strongest gifting is serving. Highly developed in her gifting, she has a way of keeping her focus on the task at hand and getting things done, oftentimes going above and beyond. Though she has taught in large group settings, she is most comfortable working behind the scenes. Blanca's genuine smile results from a server's heart, which is without guile. Honest as the day is long, mighty in prayer, and faithful in service—what a blessing!

People with the spiritual DNA of a server:

1. have a heart for "doing"
2. are quick to see and meet practical needs
3. show love for others in deeds and actions more than words
4. will stay with something until it's completed and will do more than is required or expected—with gladness
5. like short-range projects
6. prefer doing a job rather than delegating it
7. feel their greatest joy in doing something that is helpful—especially manual projects, tasks, and functions
8. have an unusual ability to recall the likes and dislikes of people
9. are more interested in meeting the needs of others than their own needs
10. don't like being in the spotlight—like playing "second fiddle"
11. are often the "unsung hero"
12. need to feel appreciated
13. can be involved in too many activities because they have difficulty saying no to requests for help
14. have less difficulty with obedience than other gifts

15. desire to have and work best when there is clear direction
16. want to provide a means and make a way
17. are often drawn to care for and serve a leader
18. are true "armor bearers" when working in service to a leader

3. TEACHER

"And Jesus, when he came out, saw much people, and was moved with compassion toward them, because they were as sheep not having a shepherd: and he began to teach them many things." Mark 6:34

It is my experience as a teacher that those gifted with this particular spiritual DNA tend to have a deeper thirst and love for the truth than others. This means that a teacher who is developed in his gifting will normally be someone who desires to go beyond the obvious and the superficial and dig for truth—even when it may be difficult or inconvenient. As such, a mature teacher is definitely not the type to put his trust in second- or third-hand information—he wants to go straight to the source.

Because of a teacher's inner need to validate truth, a mature Christian with this gift will constantly compare what is generally accepted as true with what Yahweh Himself says. When a teacher hears a significant truth or opinion put forward in conversation or from the pulpit, his desire is to confirm the authenticity of what's been shared before adopting it. As such he is like the Bereans, of whom the Scriptures state, *"... they received the word with all readiness of mind, and searched the scriptures daily, whether those things were so."*[3] Anything that cannot be proved through Scripture, or confirmed directly by God through some other means, is seen as "subject to change," and a teacher will remain silent and unconvinced until it has been completely borne out.

A teacher is uncomfortable with highly speculative and/or subjective information and is particularly concerned that truth be presented in a balanced way. He is also alert to the danger of using personal experience as a foundation for truth. His preferred teaching method is always to start from Scripture and then illustrate it with an experience, rather than start from an experience and attempt to "proof text" it with Scripture. While a teacher isn't easily swayed, once a matter has been proven to him—when he "knows that he knows"—he'll withstand all types of pressure that come against him.

A teacher who is spiritually mature will move more slowly in judging matters than others because of his inclination to "weigh things" while listening and absorbing all that's being said and then drawing his conclusions. When in a group setting, he'll be hesitant to be one of the first to speak up, since he's processing and evaluating everything along the way. Because of his thorough style, when the teacher does share his views he'll usually do so in a manner that is well thought out, bringing to the fore details or factors that others won't have given weight to or even noticed.

When a teacher is speaking or writing he will usually do so in a systematic way where his presentation is laid out in an orderly sequence. A mature teacher won't "play with the truth" by misrepresenting the facts as perhaps others may do—the truth is far too important to him.

Unlike the prophet, who may come across boldly, the teacher is usually non-confrontational when presenting revealed truth. Because of this trait, as well as his non-critical and non-judgmental nature, many find the teacher to be an "emotionally safe" person. He must be on his guard, however, not to countenance or passively accept sin in others. Also, he needs to accept, and not shy away from, the responsibility of leadership when it is thrust upon him.

Yahweh created the teacher not just to validate truth but also to "experience" it. In fact, the teaching gift can only reach its highest fulfillment when the analytical, cerebral aspect of this God-given endowment is balanced with experiential knowledge received directly from the Lord. This happens when a teacher is spiritually mature enough to find the "secret place" of intimacy and fellowship with the Almighty. When he abides there, and is able to speak from the vantage of both types of understanding, a teacher has the ability to bless not only those directly benefiting from his teaching gift but also successive spiritual generations as well.

Mature teachers are essential to keep a church from wandering from sound biblical teaching. The role of this gift is critical to a local congregation staying on track and keeping from apostasy, especially in these last days in which few Christians are willing to "endure sound doctrine."[4] There are many well-known Christian leaders with the gift of teaching. Though you undoubtedly have your favorites, preferring one style or type of message over another, your main concerns in receiving this gift should be whether they are teaching a balanced message that is grounded in truth, providing you with a depth of understanding that is both engaging and challenging, and whether their message has the "seal of approval" of the Holy Spirit.

People with the endowment gift of the teacher:

1. are driven by a desire for truth and to clarify it for others
2. believe truth has the intrinsic power to produce change
3. are able to present truth in a logical, systematic way
4. are not confronters
5. are intellectually sharp and self-disciplined
6. tend to be reflective and slow to speak out
7. can bring out the deep things of God that have been hidden and delight to see "light bulbs" go off in others
8. solve problems by starting with scriptural principles
9. get offended when Scripture is inappropriately used out of context
10. feel concerned that truth is established in every situation
11. are "emotionally safe" and non-judgmental
12. validate truth by checking out the facts
13. require thoroughness
14. aren't easily swayed once they "know that they know" something
15. are uneasy with subjective truth
16. have a capacity to bring a generational blessing
17. have a primary calling to intimacy with God

18. have a secondary calling to delivering sound doctrine and truth to His people

4. EXHORTING (ENCOURAGING)

"Furthermore then we beseech you, brethren, and exhort you by the Lord Jesus, that as ye have received of us how ye ought to walk and to please God, so ye would abound more and more." 1 Thessalonians 4:1

Those with the endowment gift of exhorting are uniquely equipped to encourage, uplift, and inspire others. An exhorter has an upbeat, positive attitude and is people-oriented, which makes him the type of person to whom others are naturally attracted. Because of this and his other relational abilities, an encourager has an uncommon capacity to reach across barriers and connect with all types of people.

A healthy encourager is the one we all love to hear from in our times of discouragement, defeat, or confusion. He has the ability to speak to the heart of circumstances in a way that almost always brings hope, clarity, and direction. In this regard his gift bears some resemblance to certain aspects of the gift of prophecy. A key and almost uniform distinction between a prophet and an encourager, however, is that the former is not usually an optimist whereas the encourager will often be overflowing with optimism: "Hey, with God on your side how can you be defeated?"

I have observed that nearly every exhorter is the type of person who's "never met a stranger." It seems that an encourager can talk to just about anybody, anywhere, and therefore has a unique anointing to enter the marketplace to bring the gospel. Also, because of his relational skills, he has a unique ability to be a catalyst, inspiring and mobilizing people to take their place to serve the kingdom and realize their true potential in the body of Christ. Given the affable nature of this grace package, it is not surprising that some of the most successful evangelists, politicians, and salespeople are gifted as exhorters.

As a rule, an exhorter has a way with words, though not in the sense of using flowery eloquence. He's effective when he speaks because of his genuine empathy for others and also because he has the ability to discern their needs and level of spiritual maturity. Also, while a teacher tends to "aim for the head," reaching people through their mental faculties, an exhorter is much more inclined to "aim for the heart," reaching people most effectively on an emotional level. The encourager's favored style of sharing is demonstrative and entertaining, and most are fond of using broad, sweeping statements, sometimes without qualifiers. The encourager's underlying purpose in all of this will usually be to reach the most number of people "where they're at" and motivate them to grow to new levels in Jesus Christ.

Another significant contrast I have noticed between the exhorter and the teacher is that the exhorter tends to have a very different frame of reference when sharing spiritual truth. While a teacher's inclination is to use scriptural truth as a starting point and then illustrate or amplify it with an example or an experience, the exhorter usually begins with discoveries and insights he's made from his experiences and then validates or amplifies them by using Scripture.

Because the encourager is a "people person" who loves to see individuals blossom in their relationships and their spiritual development, an exhorter who's spiritually mature will usually make an excellent counselor. Since people are drawn to him by his openness and likeable nature, he has an extraordinary capacity to influence those he is counseling. The encourager, therefore, can speak much needed truth to counselees that is hard to hear but with a lower risk of offending and alienating them. As such, an exhorter oftentimes will be able to change hearts, minds, and lives in instances where other counselors lacking his gift package would fail.

The exhorter usually has both an inborn, intuitive sense that enables him to accurately evaluate the spiritual or life condition of others and the ability to recommend a clear, effective strategy of practical steps as a remedy (e.g., "You need to do 1-2-3 and then you'll get to where you need to be."). He will almost always avoid theoretical speculation or teaching that lacks a practical application. For him, it is results that count, and the value of any counseling or teaching he does can only be measured in terms of its implementation. In short, the encourager's spiritual makeup is geared toward helping to bring about change in others—intended to aid people along in their journey through life.

The exhorter's spiritual DNA also causes a spiritually mature individual to recognize the necessary role that adversity plays in spiritual growth and that every hardship brings not only suffering but also a resulting benefit. While an encourager will by no means wish for affliction to come anyone's way, he understands that trouble and trial are a basic part of the human condition and are key ingredients to bringing the believer to a higher level of spiritual maturity.

The gift-package of the exhorter provides him with the potential of being a natural servant-leader. He's likeable, a good communicator, and easily gains people's confidence. He has great insight into people's strengths and weaknesses. He's genuine and can be selfless in his concern for the spiritual welfare and development of God's people. As the encourager develops in his relationship with the One who made him the way he is, he will rise to be the full measure of blessing he's meant to be in the body of Christ.

People with the spiritual DNA of the exhorter:

1. are driven to see spiritual growth take place in others
2. are the type of people that "never met a stranger"
3. are attuned to people's feelings
4. enjoy and are good at personal counseling
5. are motivated to pick up the brothers and sisters when they are down and out, or dazed and confused.
6. are good communicators
7. are able to be transparent about themselves
8. make decisions easily and are spontaneous and flexible
9. are good at bringing reconciliation

10. usually have an end in mind and work toward it
11. love to prescribe precise steps of action to aid personal growth
12. encourage others to develop their personal ministries
13. tend to use Scripture to validate experience
14. are good at networking
15. prefer to apply truth rather than research it
16. have a unique anointing to enter the marketplace and bring the gospel
17. see application as the main reason for truth or facts
18. are good at inspiring and mobilizing people

5. SHARING (GIVING)

"And all the believers lived in a wonderful harmony, holding every-thing in common. They sold whatever they owned and pooled their resources so that each person's need was met." Acts 2:44-45 (MSG)

A Christian with the God-given gift of sharing will usually under-stand and appreciate the importance of contributing a portion of the goods and resources Yahweh has placed in their hands in order to be a conduit of His blessing. Because of their spiritual makeup, most givers will share cheerfully and generously from whatever is at their disposal, whether it's a morsel of bread, a straw bed to sleep on, a "widow's mite," profit from a real estate deal, or a portion of their stock portfolio. Even if a giver is the most humble yak herdsman in Mongolia or an indigenous tribesman from the Yana Yaku River in the Amazon region of Peru, he will share from that which the Lord has supplied. Evidence of this gift in a person's spiritual DNA isn't *what* is being shared, or whether it amounts to much or very little in society's eyes; what is important is whether

a person is not only willing but eager to be a vessel of blessing to others.

Though there seems to be a special anointing for increase on the giver, the gift of sharing is much more than the ability to increase and prosper as a result of applying the kingdom principles of giving and receiving. It is also a matter of the person's heart condition and his spiritual DNA. What I have observed is that those with the grace package of the sharer find no greater satisfaction and fulfillment than from being a blessing to those in need and benefiting the kingdom of God in their giving.

Because of the generous God-given nature of most sharers, they are often able to see material needs that others overlook and neglect. The giver will be moved to meet those needs through resources at his disposal or he will seek them elsewhere. It has been my experience that many givers prefer to do their giving "behind the scenes" so as to not attract attention to themselves. However, since most givers want to inspire others in their giving, and have an anointing to do so, when the giver finds a worthy cause, sometimes he may use the occasion to "go public" with his giving in order to motivate others. In this type of instance a sharer can be an excellent fundraiser, even if he doesn't have a flair for public speaking.

Though givers are generous by nature with their resources, I have found that many are also endowed with godly wisdom about sharing and how they manage their resources. As a giver operates according to the truth that Yahweh Yireh—the Lord who provides—is his source of provision, God honors that faithfulness and will alert him about the hidden agendas and motives of those seeking help. Because of this, a mature sharer isn't someone who can easily be manipulated, pressured, or deceived into giving. Along the same lines, if his giving involves donating to a ministry a sharer will weigh (and perhaps investigate) the soundness and integrity of the ministry and whether his resources will provide a good "return on investment." Also, once the resources have been given, he will want to feel a part of the ministry he's given to and will be alert as to how funds are being used.

Part of the giver's special God-given ability that enables him to increase is an extraordinary knack to make wise investments and purchases.

I have known several well-developed givers who seem to be able to prosper even in times and environments where most others fail. This is because someone with the true heart of a sharer—that is, someone God created to be that way—has a spiritual force (anointing, if you will) where resources seemingly are attracted to him. Time and time again Yahweh Yireh's favor will place a giver in the right place at the right time so that he can take advantage of opportunities, being blessed so that he in turn can be a blessing.

Someone with the spiritual DNA of a sharer is geared to give to needs not only in the immediate time horizon of the "here and now" but also over the long haul. In fact, a giver who is walking in the fullness of his gift has a "generational anointing" that enables him to bless future generations with his giving.

Because of a natural human tendency to look for security by amassing material possessions, a giver must maintain a constant heartfelt gratitude for the resources over which God has made him a steward and depend completely on the Lord as his source of security and supply. This only happens when he abides in the "secret place of the Most High" and sustains a vibrant relationship with his loving Father. By doing this a sharer will fulfill his potential in blessing others as well as the kingdom of God.

One of the greatest examples of a sharer I know is a good friend of mine, Bishop Bill Stevenson, who has proved what can happen when a person with the gift of giving operates in the faith and love of God. He grew up during the hard times of the Great Depression and wasn't able to go to school beyond the fourth grade after his father died; instead, barefooted, he hauled logs out of the snake-infested swamps of South Carolina to help feed his family. Despite this and many other disadvantages in life, he has managed to prosper beyond anything he could possibly have imagined in his early years—by giving.[5]

Responding to the call to be a pastor in his mid-forties, he eventually founded an inner-city church that has had a focus on giving and blessing those in need. As his ministry developed Bishop Stevenson started to train and send out many of his key leaders, who have planted very successful daughter churches. In other words, he has sown into their lives and selflessly released them to extend God's kingdom.

Because he has made giving a way of life, Bishop Stevenson has prospered personally—not only in finances but in health as well as in many other ways. The church he founded has demonstrated that a great deal can be accomplished for the kingdom of God when operating under the anointing of the gift of giving. Bishop Stevenson's ministry, as well as the numerous ministries that he has fostered, have exemplified a spirit of generosity and have served for decades as a beacon of light and hope in serving the needy. It has proved to be a conduit of blessing for thousands.

People who are gifted to be sharers:

1. believe God is the source of their supply
2. are motivated to provide resources—money, possessions, time, energy, and love—to help others and advance the kingdom
3. have a spirit of nurture
4. love to give without others knowing about it
5. hope that their gift is an answer to prayer
6. are willing to exercise personal thriftiness in order to give the most they can
7. are able to motivate others to give
8. handle finances with wisdom and frugality
9. are wise about their giving—not gullible and usually cannot be manipulated
10. are non-confrontational by nature and will go around barriers
11. like to keep their "options open"—are flexible and adaptable
12. have a wide range of competency
13. can work with a diversity of opinions and groups
14. are private about their life and family
15. have divine favor as well as natural business ability
16. have an ability to prosper even in adversity
17. have a "generational anointing"
18. need to maintain an "attitude of gratitude"

6. LEADING (PRESIDING)[6]

"And God blessed them, and God said unto them, 'Be fruitful, and mul-
tiply, and replenish the earth, and subdue it: and have dominion...'"
Genesis 1:28

A person with the endowment gift of presiding will usually have
an extraordinary God-given ability to visualize the future as well as
coordinate people and resources to achieve a goal. As a general rule a
well-developed organizer not only can see what's ahead but is capable
of developing strategies and implementing the means of getting there.

The key to understanding the gift of presiding is that the person
with it is a "born leader"—he "stands in front of the rest" to lead the
way. I have observed that whenever placed in a group setting, he will
emerge into a leadership role, whether it's organizing an office, planning an event, developing a project, or leading a church group.

A leader's personality is dynamic, and leaders tend to be methodical in
their work habits. He is also skilled at motivating others, having the ability
to persuasively promote a sense of purpose and vision, inspiring others
to move together with him toward achieving the goal he's presented.

Many presiders also have good insight into human nature, enabling
them to work with and through others and build a "team spirit." A well-
developed presider is good at delegating responsibilities to maximize effectiveness and can objectively assess
which tasks he must do himself and
those best done by other team members. His tendency is to remove himself from the nitty-gritty details of a
project in order to focus on coordi-
nating the overall effort. Quite often
he's graced with an intuitive sense of
"who fits where" that enables him to
position key players in the right place. Leaders also have the skill to
motivate people and push them beyond what they themselves believe

they are capable of accomplishing. Additionally, I have noticed that organizers are almost always able to maintain a continued accountability of team members.

Once a mature organizer commits himself to a venture, he's willing to endure a great deal of negative reaction to his leadership for the good of the project. In fact, a person with the gift of presiding is built to be under pressure and withstand it. Opposition may come from either "insiders" or "outsiders," but a person with this gift knows that without the continuous pressures that he must exert as a leader, the ultimate goal will not be achieved.

Loyalty from associates is very important to an administrator. Many prefer to use those who are trustworthy over others who may be more competent but less loyal. A leader needs to know who and what his resources are. Since the efficiency of the entire operation depends upon the faithfulness of team members, he would rather have fewer that he can count on than more that he cannot count on.

Because of his God-given abilities, a well-developed presider can make a difficult job look easy. Most are wired so that they can quickly assess problems and delegate responsibilities to the proper people to handle them and then make adjustments as necessary. Also, most leaders have a capacity for easing the effort required because of their methodical way of breaking down large and difficult undertakings into readily achievable objectives and assignments.

Authority and dominion are part of a leader's spiritual DNA. Because of this, a person with this gift should be keenly aware of the value of being under authority in order to exercise his own authority. A mature leader will recognize the importance of organizational structure and respect the limits of authority. An administrator will tend to stand aside until responsibility is delegated and not push for a position of leadership. When asked to, however, or in instances where there is a leadership vacuum, it is my experience that he will almost always be willing to step in and assume the responsibility for leadership.

Most leaders have a desire to complete their mission as quickly and efficiently as possible. Invariably the leader will find deep satisfaction when everything fits together and runs smoothly. Since he's wired to be goal-oriented, he loves to see a task, phase, or project come to a successful completion. Once that has happened most leaders will want to move on to a new challenge.

Those with the endowment gift of leading:

1. are able to envision the finished project
2. are natural and capable leaders
3. enjoy working on long-range goals and projects, and seeing all the pieces come together
4. need loyalty and confidence from those under them or over them
5. are task oriented - find greatest fulfillment and joy in working to accomplish goals
6. are able to be decisive
7. make jobs look easy
8. are able to set and maintain priorities
9. enjoy working with and being around people
10. see the need for organization as essential for proper functioning of a group or organization
11. know when to keep old methods going and when to introduce new ones
12. see the overall picture and clarify long-range goals
13. express ideas in ways that communicate clearly
14. enjoy delegating tasks and supervising people
15. are willing to let others get the credit in order to get a job done
16. try to fix problems without assessing blame
17. tend to be very busy
18. are normally "on top of" their schedule (manage their schedule well)

7. MERCY (COMPASSION)

"The Lord is good to all: and his tender mercies are over all his works." Psalm 145:9

One of the keys to understanding a person with a well-developed gift of mercy is that they are spiritually in tune with the heart of God. Those blessed with the mercy gift are attracted to and "feel" for people who are

emotionally hurting and have a strong desire to comfort and bring healing. Just as a server focuses on physical needs, those with the gift of compassion concentrate on giving empathy and comfort during times of distress. It is also typical for them to have a greater concern for mental pain than physical pain.

A mercy-giver has been given an innate God-given quality to discern and relate to the feelings of those around them. Often just by walking into a room they can sense the spiritual or emotional tone of a group or an individual, which is a trait they have in common with the endowment gift prophet. They will not only sense the spiritual and emotional atmosphere almost instantaneously, but at times they will become so empathetic that they will rapidly take on themselves the suffering and heartaches of those who are hurting.

Because a mercy-graced person feels genuine pity and compassion for people in distress, he is not only attracted to, but operates as a magnet for, those people. Individuals in anguish are drawn to mercy-givers and will easily confide in them because the compassionate person readily identifies with their pain and adapts to their feelings.

A caregiver is by nature tolerant and charitable in that his empathy helps him identify with where a person is coming from, even if he doesn't approve of the sin at the root of the person's plight. Caregivers are very hesitant to judge or criticize, and so tend to balance the prophet, who's often too hasty to judge.

Since compassion-graced people appear cheerful and outgoing, as might be expected, they are usually well liked and have many friends. Most mercy-givers, however, will have only one or two with whom they bond to the point of opening up with and becoming transparent. They are loyal even to those who are not much more than acquaintances. Because of their sensitivity to inconsiderate words and actions, a compassion-giver can become easily offended and react harshly toward anyone who disparages those they consider to be friends or acquaintances.

Since a mature mercy-giver is spiritually in tune with the heart of God, he also tends to have easier access to His throne room than those with other gifts. Because of their empathy with others and their access to the heavenly realm, it is my experience that many caregivers can be excellent intercessors. Some of the mercy-gifted also make outstanding worship leaders because of their keen ability to sense and change the spiritual atmosphere of their surroundings. Some even have the potential to sanctify the spiritual atmosphere.

Since the gift of mercy has the ability to sense genuine love, it carries a greater vulnerability to deeper and more frequent hurts from those who fail to demonstrate sincere love. This gift will find its greatest fulfillment when it is afforded the opportunity to lavish compassion and mercy on those who are hurting.

Mercy-gifted people:

1. are attracted to people who are hurting or are in distress and "feel" for them
2. have a desire to remove hurts and to bring comfort and healing
3. love to do thoughtful things for others
4. are intuitive and "soft" and are into hugs and touches
5. are magnets for people who are going through mental and emotional distress
6. usually look for the good in people
7. have a tremendous capacity to show love
8. sense the spiritual or emotional atmosphere of a group or individual

9. have a supernatural ability to love and care for others, even total strangers
10. desire to meet the sympathetic and emotional needs of the body of Christ
11. take care with words and actions to avoid hurting others
12. are deeply loyal to friends
13. often are closed to insincere and insensitive people
14. can be vulnerable in relationships
15. are ruled by the heart and not by the head
16. often have a problem with setting proper boundaries in relationships
17. sometimes avoid firmness and can be indecisive
18. grieve over broken relationships - desire to have Christians stop bickering and hurting one another

REFLECTING HIS GLORY

These seven awesome grace packages that Yahweh has placed on the earth are tremendous in their potential. When an individual is flourishing spiritually—abiding in the love of God and moving toward his destiny—he is in the process of realizing that potential and reflecting the glory of his Maker. There are, however, dark spiritual forces arrayed against such an individual that seek to rob him of all that our heavenly Father has planned.

Without the God-kind of love we may be able to accomplish our personal plans in life, but we will never even come close to developing the true potential of our gifting, nor will we be able to fulfill our purpose and destiny.

The capacity to walk in the *fullness* of our endowment gift resides in every one of us—contained in our spiritual DNA—but it exists only as a latent potential until it is developed as God has planned. The active ingredient in this process is the God-kind of love,[7] which is a force dwelling on the inside of everyone who is in God's family.[8] This vital, irresistible power is much more important to our spiritual development than fertilizer is to the growth of a plant. Without the God-kind of love we may be able to accomplish our personal plans in life, but we will never even come close to developing the true potential of our gifting, nor will we be able to fulfill our purpose and destiny.

If we are honest with ourselves, most of us need to acknowledge that up to this point in life we haven't realized our God given potential. The fact is that many in the body of Christ haven't even successfully identified their gifting, much less discovered their true purpose and destiny.

But what has been shall not be. Each one of us already has "what it takes." It's all inside, the love that's been shed abroad in our hearts by the Holy Spirit and the awesome potential of our endowment gifting!

Questions: Chapter Four

1. Each of the _____ gifts is in reality a
   God-given "grace package" that is determined by the
   _____ DNA with which person has been
   endowed.

2. A person with the gift of prophecy has in the core of
   his being an extraordinary capacity to discern spiritual
   _____.

3. A prophet's natural inclination is to place greater emphasis on his relationship with _____ than with those
   around him.

4. People with the gift of service have a spiritual DNA that
   enables them to readily discern _____
   needs.

5. The server's grace-package isn't particularly suited for
   _____-range ventures.

6. Because it is in his spiritual constitution to be straightforward and _____, the server makes an able
   and trustworthy assistant.

7. People gifted with the spiritual DNA of a teacher have a
   particularly deep thirst and love for the _____.

8. Anything that cannot be proved through _____,
   or confirmed directly by God through some other means,
   is seen by the teacher as "subject to _____."

9. God created the teacher not just to validate truth but also to "_____" it.

10. Individuals with the grace package of a teacher are essential for keeping the church from wandering from _____ biblical doctrine.

11. Those with the endowment gift of exhorting are uniquely equipped to _____, uplift and inspire others.

12. An exhorter has the ability to speak to the _____ of our circumstances in a way that brings hope, clarity, and direction.

13. An encourager is likeable, a good communicator and easily gains people's _____.

14. Sharers appreciate having the ability to be a _____ of God's blessing.

15. God honors the faithfulness of a giver who operates according to the truth that Yahweh Yireh is his _____.

16. A giver who is walking in the fullness of his gift has a "_____ anointing" that enables him to bless future generations with his giving.

17. People with the endowment gift of presiding have God-given ability to visualize the future, coordinate people and _____ to achieve their envisioned goal.

18. A key to understanding the gift of leading is that person with it is a "_____ leader."

19. _____ from associates is very important to
the administrator.

20. _____ and dominion are part of the spiritual DNA of the leader.

21. A mercy-giver has an innate God-given quality to discern
and relate to the _____ of those around
them.

22. One of the keys to understanding a person with the gift
of mercy is that they are spiritually "in tune" with the
_____ of God.

23. The mercy-giver has the ability to sense the spiritual
or _____ tone of a group or an indi-
vidual.

Chapter Five

GROWING IN GRACE

Becoming More Like Him

PEOPLE "WALKING AS TREES"

One of the great illusions of modern society centers on the actual spiritual condition of mankind. The underpinning of most human thought and endeavor in our age is illustrated by the cliché that "people are basically good." According to this naïve and mistaken understanding of human nature, as it's often reflected in popular music and culture, all a person needs to do to find true love and happiness is "let your heart be your guide," and as you "follow your dreams" you'll find fulfillment and contentment.

Sophomoric notions such as these are related to a basic worldview that sees each of us maneuvering through life as a captain of our own ship and master of our own fate. Accordingly, if God has any part in such a journey, it seems that His role is more like that of a deckhand than that of an admiral or even a navigator.

The illusions of our basic goodness as well as our ability to control our life and future stand in stark contrast with what the Holy Scriptures have to say. For example, speaking through the prophet Jeremiah, the

Lord declared that, *"The heart is desperately wicked and deceitful above all things, who can know it?"*[1] Jesus Christ also proclaimed that *"... out of the heart come evil thoughts, murders, adulteries, fornications, thefts, false witness, slanders."*[2] These plainly spoken truths are clearly at odds with popular opinion and culture. While the world is proselytizing the notion that a basic goodness resides in everyone Scripture warns us unequivocally that within unredeemed mankind is all manner of wickedness. The question is: whose report do you believe?

The truth of God's view on the subject was brought home to me a few years ago in an unforgettable way when I received a vision of how people truly are. I call this event the "twisted branches walking" vision, and this is what I saw:

> *I was looking down from a bird's-eye view on a residential neighborhood in a large city watching people as they went about doing everyday things. Many were walking—a few looked as if they were on their way to meet someone, others seemed to be on an important errand, and some were casually strolling along. There were still others who were relaxing and playing in a park. The strangest thing about what I saw in this vision was that none of these people who seemed so normal in what they were doing appeared in a human form. Every one of these "people" looked like a "walking tree branch"— all different sizes and shapes—each one covered by bark! The other notable thing about each one was that none of the "branches" was straight; each one was twisted to one degree or another—some being much more twisted than others. A few branches were so gnarled and warped that they were contorted in just about every way imaginable. One of the things that struck me most about what I saw was that not even one of the walking "tree branches" was close to being straight.*

This God-ordained vision seemed to last less than a minute, but when it was over I immediately realized He had shown me the reality of the human condition: that *everyone* is warped and twisted to some degree. There isn't a straight "branch" among us!

As I reflected on what I'd seen, it came to me—having been a carpenter for many years—that one of the peculiarities of wood (whether
a tree branch or a board) is that after it's been misshapen it *always* has a
tendency to return to a deformed shape, no matter how strong a force
is applied to it. In other words, wood doesn't have any *innate* capacity

to "go straight" once it's been warped. Even if a *huge* external force is applied, and even if it *looks* like it is straight, once humidity and moisture penetrate wood it will always display its *inherent* tendency, which is to revert to a twisted state.

How much like wood man is in his natural (unredeemed) condition! External pressure may bring outward compliance, but it has little effect where it really counts—on the inside of man. While social pressure, threats of punishment, and the force of the law can bring outward conformity to a norm, none of these can make the inner man "go straight." A person can *appear* to be someone worthy of emulation, to "have what it takes," but what is going on inside him is what really matters. As the Scripture says, *"...man looks on the outward appearance, but the Lord looks on the heart."*[3] How many shocking stories do we need to hear about fallen idols in Hollywood or the world of sports— or even in the church of Jesus Christ—before mankind realizes that appearance not only *can* be very deceiving, it *usually* is!

While there is no *external* pressure able to straighten out the "knots" and "kinks" on the inside of a person, there is an *internal* force available that can get the job done—at least for those who are truly born-again believers. The Holy Spirit abiding on the inside can take anyone who is "damaged goods" (and that includes everyone) and transform them such that the gifts, talents, and calling that God placed within them at the start are fully restored.

OPERATING ON ALL CYLINDERS

"For I say, through the grace given unto me, to every man that is among you, not to think of himself more highly than he ought to think; but to think soberly, according as God hath dealt to every man the measure of faith." Romans 12:3

Each one of us is a work in progress. No one has "arrived" at the place of reaching the full potential of their endowment gifting. While those who have been redeemed by the blood of the Lamb are indeed a new creation in Christ, and surely *"old things have passed away and...all things have become new,"*[4] this only marks the beginning of a process by which the Holy Spirit straightens the warps and kinks in our inner man. This work of the Holy Spirit has as its purpose the removal of every deformity within us so that we become *"conformed to the image of [the] Son."*[5] In other words, the Spirit of God uses the likeness of Jesus Christ, the perfect Man, as the pattern toward which He is transforming us—at least those of us who have given Him the liberty to do so.

But just what are these deformities on the inside of us? Most often they are soul wounds or strongholds that result from an unhealthy or malignant influence in our past. Some of them have lodged in our spirit while others dwell in our mind and emotions. Many result from false images and impressions that affected us while we were growing up. Others were caused by fears that latched onto us. Still others got passed down from the sins of a previous generation in the form of a generational curse. Most often these deformities dominate our thinking or the way we feel, causing us to have wrong attitudes and to react to situations in the wrong way. Whatever their origin, they have twisted us on the inside so that we are unable on our own to reach the potential God desires for each one of us—that we reach *"the measure of the stature of the fullness of Christ."*[6] Beloved, that is what God has in mind for you—and He's given you His Holy Spirit to make the way!

In the previous chapter we considered each endowment gift as it appears at its best, that is, when a person's grace package is fully developed to its potential—to *"the fullness of Christ."* The reality, however, is that most of God's people are operating in their gifting *far* below their potential. When this is the case, an array of negative traits and qualities—which are peculiar to each gift—become apparent. Just as there are positive characteristics associated with our spiritual DNA, there are also negative features when a person is not operating in his endowment gift as God intended.

Obviously each of us has his own unique spiritual journey, and where we are at any given time along the path is different from anyone else's. To a greater or lesser extent—depending on our own trail and where we are on it—we will display certain tendencies toward the negative or "unhealthy" qualities associated with our own particular gift package as well as positive ones.

Considering the downside of each endowment gift is important in several respects. It can help a person better pinpoint his strongest gift, especially in a case where two or three endowment gifts appear to be prominent. Another major reason for looking at the negative traits is that such an investigation can be extremely useful in evaluating a person's true spiritual condition. Each one of us needs to face our own personal reality. Too many of us are fooled into thinking that we are further along the road to spiritual maturity than we actually are. Many Christians are deluded into thinking they are walking closely with the Lord because they operate in what they call the "spiritual gifts"[7]—such as speaking in tongues or prophesying—when in reality they haven't even done the more important thing He commanded, which is to abide in Him.[8]

> *A true and accurate gauge of a Christian's spirituality is whether he is operating in his endowment gift in the way God intended.*

A truer and more accurate gauge of a Christian's spirituality, which is the closeness of his relationship with God, is the evidence displayed as he operates in the grace package of his spiritual DNA. If a person isn't using the endowment gifts he's been given as God intended, and the negative traits of immaturity and carnality are evident, then that person is clearly operating "under his own steam" and isn't abiding in Christ as he should.[9]

Recognizing a problem in our spiritual development is the first step to solving it. Yahweh wants our gifting to function like a well-tuned engine that's operating on all cylinders. But if we've been given a gift package "engine" with eight cylinders and we're only operating on two or three—with the rest misfiring—we are not only in for a bumpy ride in our spiritual journey, but smoke will be pouring out of our spiritual "exhaust," ruining the air for everyone around us! What we need to do is take a look "under the hood" of our grace package and work on fixing the misfiring cylinders of our endowment gift.

1. THE GROWING PROPHET

"Don't just pretend to love others. Really love them. Hate what is wrong. Hold tightly to what is good." Romans 12:9 (NLT)

A healthy prophet is known for his decisiveness and ability to quickly discern the heart of a matter. In an immature prophet this tendency may cause him to prematurely size up a situation and jump to a conclusion before he's given sufficient facts, which can in turn lead to bruised egos, hurt feelings and a loss of credibility.

A prophetically-gifted person can be painfully direct when correcting others, no matter who they're dealing with, which can be a problem. If you've ever been on the receiving end of an immature prophet who has acted without regard for your feelings, all you can say is "ouch!" If a prophet has "corrected" you in such a way that you feel condemned and judged, either you haven't equipped yourself properly with the helmet of salvation or the prophet has been operating in the flesh.

Unaware of the innate power of his endowment gift, a less developed prophet will come across many times as overly assertive and confrontational, appearing to be contrary by nature, taking the opposite side of an issue at the drop of a hat. Since he also tends to get emotionally carried away, all of these factors combined have the potential to create conflict and lead to "fireworks" at a social gathering or public meeting. Also, his strong desire to convey what he perceives as truth may be interpreted as his having little interest in listening to another person's point of view. Consequently, a growing prophet in such a setting will be viewed as a "loose cannon"—one who's impulsive, hardheaded, and contentious.

An immature prophet also may be too opinionated and too "black and white" about issues rather than being open to seeing all sides of a situation. This shortcoming can be taken as a form of intolerance toward seeing what most would consider a "partial good." Because of this inclination, he likely will get a reputation for being rigid and legalistic.

While being frank and outspoken, and able to name an evil for "what it really is," are positive attributes of this grace package, a prophet lacking in maturity may at times fail to make the proper distinction between the sin and the sinner. If he condemns both with equal vigor, I have found that oftentimes he'll come across as merely engaging in an angry tirade and fail to bring about the repentance and restoration that God desires. While it's vital to bring sin out into the open, no less essential is the ultimate purpose of that exposure: the restoration of the person being exposed. If a prophet is unsuccessful in this, he's failed one of the main purposes for which the gift was given.[10]

The need for growth in the prophetic gift is eminently displayed by Sam, a Panamanian friend of mine who has had frequent run-ins on the job with co-workers as well as with his boss. It seems that no matter where he has worked over the years he has managed to get himself in the "dog-house" because he couldn't keep quiet about his co-workers' sleazy life-styles. In fact, even though Sam is a good worker, he has been terminated from employment more times than I can recall. Why would anyone do such a thing—speak out knowing that it could cost him his job?

In his case, part of the answer is that Sam has a strong gift of prophecy and simply is not able to overlook dishonesty and corruption as others would. Being immature in his gifting, however, meant that he was unnecessarily abrasive and confrontational at times. Sam is still growing, as we all should be, and eventually came to realize that merely denouncing sin has not brought about the intended results: helping people to turn their lives around. The outcome of this understanding is that he has been able to walk in his gifting and maintain his principles while being better able to hold onto a job.

Another problem I have noticed with the prophetic gift is that since one of a prophet's innate abilities is to discern spiritual truth and expose sin, a carnal prophet may easily become pessimistic and negative in outlook. Invariably, the less healthy he is the more pronounced his pessimism and negativity will be. It can get to the place where such a prophet is unable to see the good in anything, or visualize a positive outcome.

The harsh judgment that an immature prophet has for others can end up boomeranging back on himself. The problem is that once he's locked into a negative mode, he tends to become extremely self-critical and feel worthless. In addition to this, such a prophet will also have difficulty finding or accepting forgiveness for himself, and the combination of these factors may well lead to a state of depression.

When dealing with an unhealthy prophet—one who's wallowing in pessimism—realize that because of ingrained patterns related to the immaturity of his gift, he won't be brought out of it just because a forceful effort is made to portray "the bright side of things." However, what I have found is that once he's had enough time to "chew on" what's been said to him, a growing prophet will likely see the truth of what's been spoken, realize the error of his ways, and climb out of his depressive pit.

Since a person with the endowment gift of the prophet is inclined to place greater emphasis on his vertical relationship with the Lord than on his horizontal relationships with people, one who's less developed in his gift may become socially isolated at times—even from family and others close to him. Clearly this can cause a strain in personal relationships and be a factor in his having to walk a "more difficult road" than others.

Problem Areas

Some of the negative tendencies and weaknesses of a prophecy-gifted person are to:

1. judge too quickly or too harshly
2. intimidate others by frankness and forcefulness
3. be insensitive to others since he's not a people-pleaser
4. be "bull headed"—becoming stubborn and uncooperative
5. try to cram "truth" down other people's throats
6. be intolerant of opinions and views that differ from his own
7. be sharp-tongued, mean-spirited and lacking compassion
8. react harshly to sinners, cut people off who fail
9. be impulsive or compulsive
10. become overzealous in personal evangelism to the point of being offensive

11. be hard on himself as well as others, be his own worst critic
12. be proud of his own rhetoric and persuasiveness
13. struggle with self-image problems
14. become pessimistic or negative in outlook and be subject to depression
15. be unforgiving and have difficulty finding forgiveness
16. be deceived into thinking he has all the answers
17. excuse his rudeness as "my gifting"
18. be hindered in close relationships

How to Improve

Ways for a prophet to experience growth:

1. View yourself not simply as a "truth teller" but also as a "restorer."
2. Meditate on how much God really loves and cares for you as an individual and has given you your unique gifting. Spend time abiding in Him.
3. Learn how to use your gift in love. Since "God is love," let His compassion and mercy lead you and guide you in your gift.[11]
4. Learn how to "build bridges" and improve your interpersonal skills by:
   a) considering other people's feelings
   b) being slower to speak and quicker to pray
   c) appreciating the value of others' perspectives since you do not have a monopoly on discerning the truth
   d) complimenting and encouraging others' progress and efforts
   e) understanding and appreciating the endowment gift of others
   f) developing healthy relationships with others, especially with those whose gifting balances yours, such as the gift of mercy

5. If you are prone to pessimism, avoid negative influences in your life like the plague. Immerse yourself in positive and uplifting activities that will benefit others as well as the kingdom of God.

2. THE GROWING SERVER (MINISTER)

"Love each other with genuine affection, and take delight in honoring each other." Romans 12:10 (NLT)

Those with the endowment gift of serving have a keen God-given ability to notice practical needs and take care of them. Many times others around them can be oblivious to those same needs because of their different spiritual DNA. However, when a need is so readily apparent to a server, he may develop resentment toward people around him who, in his judgment, walk right past those needs. While the immature minister assumes that others see what he sees, oftentimes this simply isn't the case. If you are not gifted as a server, and have been on the receiving end of a server's scorn for your presumed callousness, you know very personally the truth of this observation.

Servers are often placed in a position of responsibility because they are diligent workers. Once in that position, it is the natural tendency for a minister to give a helping hand or become involved in tasks that should be delegated to others. This inclination may cause him to be less effective because assigned tasks are not completed on schedule. A server who's lacking maturity may complain about being underappreciated and overworked, but at the same time he's unable to bring himself to accept help from others.

If a minister is assigned or asked to perform a task simply because he's a server and is therefore expected to enjoy doing it, he may feel exploited and react with resentment if he fails to remember that his gift and ability are from the Lord. Also, if the one he's helping is not making wise use of the server's time, the minister may lose the godly perspective necessary to complete the task in a positive frame of mind.

Because the server has an inner need to help, it is common for one who's less developed in his gift to inadvertently become a slave to the group, which may take his service for granted. However, the minister's natural sensitivity in such situations will cause him to feel slighted, and he may end up "wearing his feelings on his sleeves."

The minister's desire to help out and please others can cause an immature server to be the first in line to volunteer for many activities, leading him to become overworked and spread too thin to be effective. His zeal for service can also make him critical of others who do not share his enthusiasm and seem unwilling to take responsibility for doing their fair share of the workload. He will work tirelessly to meet a need but can become impatient with those who don't share his zeal and energy for the task at hand.

In some situations the minister's motives are likely to be misunderstood because of his eagerness to serve. Those around him may view him as "pushy" because of his strong desire to "get the job done" and move on. In his excitement to get things going, and in order to avoid red tape, he may fail to seek permission or proper authorization and bypass the channels of authority in a church or organization, which can be interpreted as rebelliousness or an unwillingness to submit to authority. In other situations the minister's keenness to serve is misconstrued as a desire for self-promotion. This is especially true in a case where he is assisting a pastor or church leader.

A less developed server may also unintentionally thwart the purposes of God or interfere with spiritual lessons He is teaching if he rushes headlong to meet every need he sees and doesn't seek the counsel of the Holy Spirit first. Certain needs and difficulties are intended by the Lord to bring about repentance in an individual's life, and if the minister jumps in to ameliorate those circumstances he's essentially working in opposition to God's purpose. This can be seen clearly, for example, in the case of the Prodigal Son: if an overzealous server had intervened to help make the wayward son's life more bearable while he was living with pigs, the server would've hindered the young man's return to his father.

I have observed that an unhealthy minister also may become so busy taking care of practical needs that he neglects his own relationship with Yahweh, confusing activity and service to the body of Christ with fellowship with God. When a minister becomes so overly involved in serving needs that his prayer and devotional life suffer, undoubtedly he'll be hindered in his spiritual development. This lack of balance can spill over into neglecting family responsibilities and neglecting those who are close to him—all in the name of serving the Lord. This same person will then wonder why there's no joy in ministry!

It seems that one of the greatest battles of a growing server is finding his true identity, affirmation, and approval in his Maker. If an immature minister looks to others and seeks to emulate their gifts, which aren't his own, he'll experience failure and frustration. Also, if he serves with the idea of being affirmed and approved by others, his efforts are likely to meet with disappointment. I have found that it's important for a minister to internalize the validity and worth of his own gifting and calling. He must appreciate and be grateful for the endowment gift that Yahweh has given him. Then he needs to learn to walk by faith in the authority and anointing of his God-given grace package. Though he may not be in the limelight, there is nothing second class about his gift of service. In fact, his gift is so worthy that it's truly the lifeblood of any ministry or organization.

Problem Areas

Some of the negative tendencies and weaknesses of a server are to:

1. be critical of others who don't help out with obvious needs
2. lack patience and become resentful toward others with a different gift package
3. be exploited by others because of his willingness to serve
4. fail to delegate responsibilities since he'd rather do it himself
5. get sidetracked with others' needs and may miss God
6. become too pushy or interfering in his eagerness to help out
7. find it hard to accept being served by others
8. be easily hurt when he feels unappreciated

9. fail to submit to protocol in his eagerness to get the job done
10. neglect God-given priorities
11. interfere with Yahweh's dealing and discipline with others
12. overemphasize practical needs and miss basic spiritual needs
13. be overly protective of family members when a threat is perceived
14. become overextended in his commitments and let his schedule get out of control
15. be sidetracked with others' needs to the detriment of his family's needs
16. become frustrated with long-term projects and goals
17. look to others for validation and affirmation rather than to Yahweh
18. fail to truly appreciate the value of his endowment gift

How to Improve

Ways to develop your serving gift:

1. Be content in the worthy role God has given you. If setting up chairs before a church service is what God has in mind for you, do not disparage its importance. If serving as an "armor bearer" for a leader in the church is God's intended responsibility for you, why would you want to do anything else?
2. Part of the maturing process for all of the endowment gifts involves a recognition and appreciation that each gift is as valuable as any of the others. When others don't appreciate your gift and fail to give you proper recognition, reject the temptation to take offense. Their attitude merely reflects their ignorance.
3. Value and cultivate good relationships, both in serving and in fellowship.
4. Refuse to entertain the negative mindset that others can't do the job as well as you. Be willing to be a "team player" and to

delegate tasks to others so that the job will be done efficiently.

5. Because you're aware of the importance of your gift of service, refuse to "take the bait" of becoming upset when others aren't as willing to pitch in to get the job done. It's better to encourage others to see practical needs and work with you than be offended.

6. Choose to be as diligent in seeking the Lord and studying the Word as you are in helping others. Don't put off your study of the Word of God, neglect your prayer life, or avoid your time of fellowship with other Christians. These combined with your role as minister will lead to a greater measure of fulfillment.

7. Continually remind yourself of the need to maintain godly priorities. It's okay to say no.

8. There's a multitude of opportunities for service. Seek God's wisdom and guidance so that you have clear direction as to which needs you are to become personally involved in meeting. Leave all the others for someone else.

9. Seek the Lord in this first, but if He should say "okay," volunteer to be a team member of a long-range project or mission in which your gifts can be fully used. This will enable you to experience long-term achievements.

10. In all things, make sure that your service leads people to praise God and not yourself.

3. THE GROWING TEACHER

"Never lag in zeal and in earnest endeavor; be aglow and burning with the Spirit, serving the Lord." Romans 12:11 (AMP)

Because of the unique abilities a teacher's been given, one who is lacking in maturity may be tempted to *"think of himself more highly than he ought"*[12] and be susceptible to the sin of pride. As wonderful as the knowledge and insight are that he's able to share with others, a teacher must always be mindful of the lurking danger to his soul, for as the apostle Paul noted, *"knowledge puffs up."*[13] It's far too easy for him to develop an inflated sense of self-worth and think, "Look at what I know and what an expert I've become!" Meanwhile, whether he's listening or not, the spirit of wisdom will be speaking to the teacher's heart to rein in his growing ego, for the knowledge and understanding that he imparts to others is not truly *from* him but *through* him.

Not long ago I attended a seminar given by a well-known teacher of biblical prophecy whose ministry is headquartered in Central America. He travels all over the world teaching about the signs of the end times, with his focus—from what I saw—primarily on the more sensational and fear-inducing aspects of the fulfillment of end-time prophecy. Though much of what he taught was either exaggerated or erroneous, he spoke with such great assurance and authority it was clear the gullible audience was won over by both his persona and the melodramatic audio/visual presentation that accompanied his teaching. However, as he stretched the truth to the point of breaking, I could hardly believe my eyes or ears. It seemed as if his exalted self-image prevented him from discovering anything but the most trite aspects of prophecy, and as a result he concocted a hyped presentation to evoke an emotional response from his listeners. Though this man is world-renowned as a teacher of prophecy, it was apparent that either pride or laziness had kept him from developing his true potential as a teacher, or else his gifting lies in another area. Either way, God's people are ill-served when this type of teaching occurs.

Another commonplace problem is that far too many teachers fall into the easy trap of developing a "doctrinal approach" to learning which inevitably leads to uninspired teaching. While the teacher may be able to master his subject due to thorough research and investigation, his "professional" attitude toward knowledge displays one glaring deficiency: he's neglected the key ingredient of inspiration—and that can only come from the One who is the source of all knowledge. An insufficiently developed teacher may be able to produce competent teachings using the staid doctrinal approach, in the sense that he is able to provide an accurate exposition of a particular subject, but he will lack the dynamism and freshness necessary to really grab the attention of his hearers, for such qualities only come from spending time in God's presence. When a teacher's approach to learning is purely cerebral, relying on intellect, his teaching will lack the manifest presence of God, and as a result he'll already have set one foot on the downward spiral toward dullness and boredom.

If the teacher should move even further down this declining slope he'll find that his teachings are not only dry and lifeless, but incapable of producing any lasting fruit. Though he was built to bring forth the deep truths of God and keep His people from error, this teacher will find that he's on a path that doesn't have enough to sustain even *himself*, nor will it be able to keep him "on track." Reaching this point in his spiritual journey should be a flashing red light warning him of danger ahead, for he's headed toward spiritual and doctrinal error and may ultimately end up operating his teaching gift without the "seal of approval" of the Holy Spirit—teaching error from the delusions of his own mind. I have known a few such teachers over the years, and their end has not been a pretty sight. In fact, sometimes their deception has led to very tragic consequences. This should serve a word of warning for all of us who are teachers!

I have also observed another difficulty for an unhealthy teacher that has to do with insecurities related to an inner sense of inadequacy or unworthiness. Even though he may have been used mightily by God to edify His people, the teacher may still be hindered in developing his gift because of a lack of confidence. This teacher's unease is usually displayed by the fact that he feels he needs "more" to be "truly" qualified—more academic credentials, more competence, and more affirmation. It's ironic that though he's the one viewed by others as "the expert," he doesn't feel that way at all.

At the very heart of this problem of insecurity is a lack of faith in the endowment gift he's been given by God. The insecurities which plague such a teacher are rooted in his over-reliance on his own effort and insufficient trust in the One who gave him his teaching gift in the first place. In fact, if he genuinely believes what Jesus Christ said, *"without Me you can do nothing,*"[14] then he'll find that he's able to operate in his gift with full confidence—but only if he is truly trusting in God. Once a teacher reaches such a threshold in his spiritual walk, he will be able to overcome his insecurity and jettison all the excuses that have hindered him, advancing more confidently toward his God-ordained destiny.

Another potential problem for an immature teacher is that he may not realize he hasn't been given his endowment gift so that he could live in an ivory tower, sequestered away from society. Rather, Yahweh equipped him with his analytical mind so that he might engage with society by bringing truth to bear on both the great and small questions of the day as well as the real-life struggles of those around him. I have noticed that immature teachers may be quite content to play the role of a passive observer, uninvolved in the issues that swirl around them, and fail to step forward and share the revelation and insight so desperately needed by others.

This tendency toward passivity is also a factor contributing to another potential weakness in the teacher who lacks maturity: the failure to confront others when it's called for. While meekness and kindness are part of the loving nature of Jesus Christ, we need to remember that at the right moment this same gentle Shepherd grabbed a whip, knocked over tables, and chased moneylenders out of the Temple, all the while denouncing them as thieves as they fled. As King Solomon wrote, *"For everything there is a season, and a time for every purpose under heaven."*[15] Yes, there's a time for patient and dispassionate discourse, but there's also a time when the appropriate word from the Lord is a stern rebuke and a cleansing of the house.

In order for this to happen it's imperative that the growing teacher find the spiritual fortitude to confront those who need confronting and deliver the unadulterated truth. This is truly where the "rubber meets the road."

How many thousands of lives would have been spared in Sodom if Lot had built up the courage to confront the sins of his debauched neighbors over the years he'd been living there! We'll never know because Lot chose the easy path of "getting along" with his neighbors instead.[16] Another striking example of a similar dynamic is found in the dysfunctional relationship between the high priest Eli and his two sons, Hophni and Phinehas. Surely Eli didn't first discover their wayward-ness when he was too old to do much about it.[17] No, he sat passively on the sidelines for many years, giving them free rein to carouse. As time went by his failure to confront their wickedness allowed it to grow with increasing malignancy. It was only when their immorality reached the apex of evil, bedding down with women who'd come to the Temple to bring their offerings to the Lord, that he finally found sufficient back-bone to rebuke them. But by then it was too late.[18]

The immature teacher often is full of excuses for his shortcomings, but if he's willing to persevere and overcome his failures he'll eventu-ally discover he has the potential to be a great source of generational blessing. One of the main reasons that teachers are held to a higher, more stringent standard than those with other gifts[19] is due to this very fact. Though God doesn't require him to do anything that's beyond his grace package, a teacher must learn to walk progressively in the light he's been given in order to develop his endowment gift to its full po-tential. As he continues to seek the Lord and walk by faith, he'll find that "manna" will appear at unexpected times, a heavenly provision by which he'll be able to feed and strengthen God's flock. At the same time, he'll experience an increase of anointing and authority such that he'll be able to bring blessing to succeeding generations.

Problem Areas

Some of the negative tendencies and weaknesses of a teacher are to:

1. develop pride in his intellectual ability, depending on human reasoning or understanding
2. neglect the practical application of truth
3. operate from the perspective of idealism rather than reality
4. get sidetracked easily by new interests
5. be "professional" in his relationship with God
6. tend to feel unworthy in the role of leadership

7. appear to be aloof and detached—lacking emotional warmth in reaching his audience

8. present a depth of research or level of detail that is unnecessary, resulting in a dull teaching style

9. present truth in an unbalanced way, taking it to an extreme

10. feel inadequate or unqualified, that he needs more credentials

11. be dependent on intellect instead of the Holy Spirit

12. be more concerned for the message than the response of the hearers

13. believe that spiritual truth can be better discerned through his own research rather than bestowed by revelation

14. be close-minded, legalistic, and dogmatic

15. resist valid ideas because they contradict his way of thinking

16. be passive and fail to take initiative

17. refuse to confront sin when it's necessary

18. exercise "selective responsibility"—letting certain responsibilities slide because of wrong priorities

How to Improve

Ways to grow in your teaching gift:

1. Acknowledge that all you "know"—whether it's from study, personal observation, or direct revelation—is not really "yours." It's not really *from* you but *through* you. By appreciating this truth you will be more capable of steering clear of the temptation of pride.

2. God wants you not just to validate truth but to "experience" it—in the context of intimacy with Him. Your calling first and foremost is to abide in Yeshua and find the secret place of your loving Father. Your secondary calling is to deliver truth.

3. Purpose to teach in a way that targets your hearers and their interests and provides them with a practical application of what you've taught.

4. Refuse to make excuses for yourself such as "I need to do more research," "I don't know enough," "I need a few more verses," or "I need to look at a few more commentaries." Realize that there will always be "something" that holds you back. Your excellence isn't so much in your competence but in your intimate relationship with Yahweh.

5. Take ownership of what you teach. Share only those truths you have thoroughly examined over time and found to be valid. If you are teaching something that has been revealed directly to you, then you obviously need to verify that it is in accord with the clear teaching of Scripture—not just a few "cherry picked" verses. Once a teaching has passed the "Berean test,"[20] do not go beyond what's been revealed to you into an area of speculation. Otherwise, you may become guilty of one of the worst failings of which the teaching gift is capable—propagating error.

6. If you've been guilty of shying away from confronting sin, repent. Too many of God's children will be damaged and lives destroyed if you are wishy-washy about such matters and unwilling to share the whole counsel of God. There is a time to call out sin for what it is, and you must build yourself up in the Holy Spirit so that you have the fortitude to proclaim the truth. Remember always that your motive is love and your purpose is restoration.

7. If you're so busy "pouring out" to your flock that your reservoir is dry because there hasn't been enough coming back in, it is time for you to rearrange your priorities and your schedule.

8. Take full possession of the "Promised Land" of your endowment by being willing to take on the role of a leader. Your spiritual DNA has given you the potential to be creative. Stretch yourself beyond your comfort zone and be willing to find truth in new areas. Do not become immobilized when you can't see the ultimate outcome of your efforts when you've only just begun. Be willing to step fully into your gifting.

9. It is excruciating to sit under a teacher who is dull and parrots clichés and platitudes. You are the one who's responsible to search the Scriptures and seek God—no one else can do it for you. Once you've done what you can do He will take the "dry bones" of your message and breathe life into it.

10. Be tolerant toward the ideas of other people—just so long as they don't undermine the clear teaching of Scripture. Learn to listen to and respect others' viewpoint, even if you don't happen to agree with them at the moment. You don't have a corner on *all* the truth—that's God's department. Just as the prophet Balaam should have learned, sometimes even a donkey can see more in the spirit realm and know more about the will of God than a supposed "man of God"![21]

11. Be diligent in your studies. One of the greatest shortcomings of some teachers is the failure to dig beneath the surface. Never merely regurgitate what others have taught—no matter how highly esteemed that teacher may be.

12. Avoid focusing continually on just one particular field of study as this may lead to imbalance.

13. Avail yourself of opportunities for Bible training. The greater your understanding the more your gift will be able to flourish.

4. THE GROWING EXHORTER (ENCOURAGER)

"Rejoice and exult in hope; be steadfast and patient in suffering and tribulation; be constant in prayer." Romans 12:12 (AMP)

An exhorter has a tendency to avoid heavy doctrinal teaching in favor of lighter, uplifting messages with an immediate or practical application. In the case of an immature exhorter, if there's an over emphasis on "seeing results," many times there will be a tendency to "play" freely with the meaning of Scripture—perhaps by taking verses out of context or misapplying or misinterpreting them—to get his point across. If an encourager compromises the integrity of the Word of God to achieve an objective, no matter how worthy, this clearly indicates a problem both with his heart condition as well as his priorities. Such a situation is dangerous not only to the exhorter's own spiritual condition but also to those he's influencing, because deceptive or unbalanced teaching and doctrinal error inevitably will be propagated and cause much harm. This is a common problem that applies to some immature teachers as well. However, because of the "itching ears" of many in the church,[22] in some cases it is not recognized for the danger it represents, and in other cases it is overlooked for the sake of not "making waves."

An immature exhorter may also have a problem keeping his priorities straight and persevering in challenging situations. If he is counseling and results do not appear as expected, perhaps due to the situation being more complicated and protracted than first anticipated, I have seen sometimes that an exhorter may lose interest in helping. In other words, he has become more intent on achieving a solution and seeing success with his counseling sessions than on being concerned about the person he is supposedly helping. Along a similar vein, a less developed exhorter may tend to hop from one project to another—jumping into a new endeavor without finishing an existing one. If this is the case, he may use projects to motivate others and then, when others are involved, find a better or more interesting venture. If this proves to be a pattern, those working with him likely will become frustrated.

One of the strengths of an exhorter is his ability to "connect" with people. His emphasis is more on eliciting an emotional response than an intellectual one. Part of this skill is verbal, and it is common for an encourager to carefully weigh his words and actions with the aim of achieving a response he's seeking. However, when his motives are muddied, an immature exhorter may not be above manipulating people's emotions by pulling on their "heartstrings" or by using some form of gimmickry—whether it is in preaching, everyday situations, or counseling someone. The intended effect is what is most important, and if he's carnal and lacks integrity, he may have fallen prey to the deception that the "ends justify the means." In such cases, the person with this grace package can be very effective and persuasive even though he's operating from less than pure motives.

It should be of no surprise then that if a carnal exhorter is sinking into the depths of a fallen spiritual condition, he's capable of a "moral flexibility" that most would shudder to even contemplate. I have found that for such an exhorter, slanting and distorting the truth or employing outright deception and trickery to maneuver people toward a desired result aren't out of the question. More than a few with this gift, both in and out of ministry, have chosen to pervert the prodigious talent and persuasive powers of their endowment gift for selfish ambition and ill-gotten gains. Such individuals seem to have a moral compass that can point in almost any direction, just so long as the ultimate destination of their scheming is "success"—that is, "success" in the way they'd define it according to their carnal understanding. Unfortunately, such manipulation has become commonplace in marketing and sales, politics, and even in some churches.

The people-pleasing tendency of some encouragers can lead to problems as well. Despite the fact that most exhorters appear to be confident, perhaps even overly confident, an unhealthy encourager may suffer from a range of insecurities rooted in a high need to please and to feel needed. Some can feel hurt by imagined or unintended slights and tend to "wear their feelings on their sleeves." Others may act out of insecurities related to a fear of rejection or loss of approval—being so dependent on others for attention, affection, and approval that they become addicted to positive affirmation. I have noticed that for this type of exhorter, who wants to be liked by everybody, there is a definite tendency to rely on "image management" (i.e., appearance) rather than substance.

As a general rule, when a less developed exhorter is thrust into a leadership role, it's likely he won't be guided by principle nearly as much as by consensus. What others think is highly important to him. In some cases he may even be the type to "put his finger to the wind" to see which way it's blowing before he moves in a certain direction. This tendency becomes especially problematic if such an exhorter decides to "play to the crowd" rather than seek the Lord and do what's right. Fearing others' opinions more than he does Yahweh's, being more interested in appearance than in truth, and being content to do what seems good can cause this encourager to lose his spiritual bearings and fall into a spiritual tailspin from which it may be hard to recover. This was a major part of the problem that contributed to the downfall of King Saul,[23] and it has played a part in the ruin of many others with the gift of the exhorter. As the Scripture says, *"Fearing man is a dangerous trap."*[24] The startling thing about a trap is that a person doesn't know he's in it until he's trapped—*and then it's too late!*

While most exhorters appear to be outgoing and self-confident, an unhealthy encourager may suffer from a range of insecurities rooted in a high need to please and to feel needed.

I have seen in the case of some unhealthy exhorters there is a tendency to be so busy interacting with and encouraging others that their primary family relationships may be neglected. Their spouse, children, or parents can find themselves on "indefinite hold" while they are out pumping up the world or socializing with friends.

Another danger for an immature encourager is that his need to please and be needed makes him particularly vulnerable to sexual predators, who zero in on these weaknesses by playing on his sympathies. In short, there may be a grave danger for an unhealthy encourager to fall into the trap of deception and drift into immorality if he's not aware of his particular vulnerabilities.

Problem Areas

Some of the negative tendencies and weaknesses of an exhorter are to:

1. use scriptures out of context in order to make a point
2. be inclined to become impatient when he doesn't see results
3. be too people-oriented and not sufficiently God-oriented
4. manipulate people's emotions and use deception for selfish gain
5. be slothful in self-development
6. jump into new projects without finishing existing ones
7. become overly self confident

8. "wear his feelings on his sleeves"
9. give up on a project or person that takes more time and effort than first expected
10. treat people as projects
11. be "cut and dried" in prescribing steps of action
12. present truth out of balance
13. set unrealistic goals
14. lead by consensus rather than seeking direction from God
15. fall into romantic traps
16. be so busy encouraging others that family life suffers
17. be inclined to oversimplify problems
18. drift into self-deception and sexual immorality

How to Improve

Ways for an exhorter to experience growth:

1. Recognize that you can only encourage others as you are open to the encouragement of the Holy Spirit.[25]
2. If you've resorted to "bending" the meaning of scriptures, making them say what they don't really say, repent. The truth and integrity of the Word is of utmost importance to our Lord[26]—and should also be of vital importance to you. Remember, if you sow deception you will reap deception.
3. When the apostle Paul was describing "love" in 1 Corinthians 13 the first attribute he ascribed to it is "patience."[27] There's a good reason for this: God wants you to demonstrate your love first and foremost by exercising your gift with patience and perseverance. Many of those whom you are seeking to help will change over time, if you're willing to work with them. Be patient with their slow progress and you will see a transformation—in God's timing.[28]
4. In counseling or working one-on-one with others, be careful to avoid:

   a) providing advice that isn't asked for. Proper timing and a receptive spirit are essential for the counsel you give to be received.

   b) giving "pat" answers. Nobody wants to feel like they're just "another project" that you're working on.

   c) sending signals that could be misinterpreted by someone of the opposite sex (being overly familiar or friendly or by touching or being physically too close).

   d) relying on your powers of persuasion instead of the Holy Spirit.

5. Take time to learn. You will have far more to encourage others with as you encourage yourself from the Word of God.[29]

6. As you reflect on the general tenor of your motives and actions, if you find how you think and what you do is based on feelings of insecurity—such as worrying about what others may think of you—then your primary need is to strengthen your relationship with your loving Father, the One who made you. You won't develop your gifting in a healthy way if you're walking in the fear of man. You need God's seal of approval—that's what matters.

7. Be a people builder. Your endowment gift of exhortation hasn't been given to you to make you popular or successful. Realize that God has given you your gift so that you can be of service to others and to the body of Christ. Fulfill your gift by "coming alongside others" to help, not for popularity or personal pleasure. Be ready to help in situations of difficulty, such as speaking a word of comfort to someone who's grieving or in despair, sharing "words of wisdom" with a rebellious teenager, or befriending a backslider and inviting them back to church.

8. If your responsibilities to your family have taken a backseat to your priorities outside the home, you need to repent—in other words, change your thinking and start doing things differently. Your primary ministry is to your spouse and family—and then to others. Spending too much time en-

couraging those outside the home while neglecting your family is unwise and can lead to many difficulties.

9. Appreciate your spouse's endowment gift and walk in harmony with it. Your grace package wasn't given for you to dominate others—especially your spouse.

5. THE GROWING GIVER (SHARER)

"Share what you have with God's people who are in need. Be hospitable." Romans 12:13 (GW)

While every Christian has been called to be a giver, God has endowed some with a special gifting and anointing to serve as vessels of provision and blessing to others, particularly to the body of Christ. This God-given capacity is an expression of *Yahweh Yireh*—the God who provides—manifesting Himself through the spiritual DNA of this gifting.

The endowment gift of the giver is tremendous in its potential when a person with this anointing learns how to walk in its fullness. In many cases once he attains a certain threshold of spiritual maturity a giver will realize that his grace package contains not only the desire and ability to be an instrument of blessing to others, but also a special capacity and anointing that cause him to prosper and obtain needed resources.

A major roadblock for an immature or carnal giver can be understood in terms of a lack of faith. If a giver is weak or incapacitated in his faith, he most certainly will have difficulty trusting the Lord as his source of provision. If this is the case, it has been my experience that there is little likelihood he will serve as the "conduit of provision" God intended for him to be. More likely, he'll merely prove to be a "clogged pipe" as he prospers. This type of giver will behave much like the rich man Jesus spoke of in a parable who tore down his barn to build a bigger storehouse so that he could store up "more" for the future.[30] A giver in such a spiritual condition needs to be convinced of the truth about the blessing of being generous, for *"There is one who scatters, yet increases more; and there is one who withholds more than is right, but it leads to poverty. The generous soul will be made rich, and he who waters will also be watered himself.*"[31]

The obvious key to increasing in his capacity as a sharer is developing a closer relationship with the Lord. As he grows in spiritual maturity because of this fellowship, he will be increasingly empowered to overcome his particular shortcomings. As he matures in the Lord, the sharer will come to realize that the resources placed at his disposal are there not only because God gifted him with special abilities, but that God Himself has been guiding his steps to prosper. This awareness, and the resulting gratitude toward Yahweh Yireh, will cause the giver to open his heart to greater levels of generosity than previously exhibited. He will then be able to see needs to which he was once blind and his gifting will flourish.

If a giver does not draw nearer to God there are very real dangers. Lurking in dark regions of the spirit realm are the twin hazards of fear and doubt. Each of these is capable of hindering, and perhaps even shutting down, the gifting of anyone with the spiritual DNA of the sharer. At some point fear may creep up on him, causing a sharer to become paralyzed in his giving because he feels his sharing will create a position of lack for himself. If he allows this fear to insinuate itself into his attitudes until it gains the upper hand, he will surely be stymied in the operation of his gift. Along a similar vein is the problem of a spirit of doubt. If a giver allows this enemy to sow uncertainty into his thinking, and he is unable to find complete assurance on the inside that his Father will supply for his every need, his potential to flow as a giver will be bottled up. Many worthy endeavors, anointed by God, have been unnecessarily limited because fear and doubt incapacitated the sharers who God ordained to supply such projects. If you have any doubts about it, just ask any pastor or missionary!

The obvious antidote for both fear and doubt is faith. By building himself up in the Word, and not letting it *"depart out of [his] mouth,"*[32] the sharer will find that he develops an overcoming faith that will pull down the twin strongholds of doubt and fear. By heeding the Word and exercising his gift of giving in an incremental way, he will grow in his capacity to be a source of blessing that will benefit God's people and advance kingdom purposes.

Another tendency in less developed sharers I have noticed is an insensitivity or indifference that results from a lack of compassion. This deficiency may become evident in a variety of ways. For example, in choosing an outlet for his giving, the less-developed sharer may be keen on giving toward the type of project that helps people tangentially but hesitates when it comes to directly helping people in need or alleviating human suffering. In other cases I have seen that a carnal giver may tend to place higher priority on the cost-effectiveness of what is being done rather than on whether it is meeting the real needs of people. Since there will always be a plethora of needs all around, in the end a giver who is motivated by the love of God will focus his efforts toward that which brings lasting benefit to people.

On the other hand, anyone with this grace package should not be moved in his giving by mere sympathy or he may fall prey to unscrupulous emotional manipulation. A mature sharer should have established criteria and guidelines that enable him to exercise godly wisdom in his giving. While a multitude of personal preferences may factor into the decision-making process of his giving, at its heart must also be the tried and true principles of Scripture. Questions such as these ought to be at the forefront of his thinking: Will my gift result in the "lasting fruit" of which Jesus spoke?[33] Will the resources I am giving be used effectively in fulfilling the Great Commission?[34] Are acts of mercy and kindness toward Jesus' brothers, the criteria by which the nations will be judged, fostered in my giving?[35] Above all else, when mulling over these and other questions concerning his giving, the sharer must purpose to "tune into" what the Lord is saying, being sensitive to His heartbeat and what moves Him at any given time.

Problem Areas

Some of the negative tendencies and weaknesses of a giver are to:

1. look to his possessions or money as his source of security, trusting in riches more than the Lord

2. use financial giving to get out of other responsibilities
3. want to "manipulate God"—that is, choose his offering like Cain
4. become proud in his ability to accumulate finances
5. find it difficult to be needy, to depend on anyone
6. fail to see that he is a steward of what the Lord has supplied
7. use possessions to try to control others
8. be cause-oriented and not people-oriented
9. pressure others to give
10. be too frugal at home with the family
11. upset family and friends with unpredictable patterns of giving
12. feel guilty about personal assets
13. measure spiritual success by material assets
14. use finances to gain recognition in the church
15. lack gratitude for what's been bestowed
16. become insensitive or indifferent to the needs of others
17. be focused more on temporal things rather than on the kingdom of God
18. fail to understand that he'll find security from his relationship with Yahweh

How to Improve

Ways to grow as a giver:

1. When you give, let it be done to please the Lord and not man. In the Sermon on the Mount Jesus said, *"When you give to the needy, do not let your left hand know what your right hand is doing."*[36] Do not look for accolades or even recognition from others. Do your giving quietly and without fanfare. Expect to receive a reward for your giving—but expect it to come from the Lord as He's promised in His Word.[37]
2. Realize your own neediness. The Lord wants you to be a generous giver for your own well-being.[38] We need to learn to

step back and view our way of living from God's perspective. You should give to others both because you are needy and also because you are indebted to Him for all that you have.[39]

3. Giving and sharing are heart issues. To understand what your heart values most, consider how you spend your money. Adjust your spending according to the priorities that God has given you.

4. You are "blessed to be a blessing." Put this into practice in your giving by doing it regularly and spontaneously as the Lord leads. Purpose in your heart to be open to unexpected needs that come your way, thereby allowing your faith and your gifting to flourish.

5. Be led by the Holy Spirit in all of your giving.

6. Give from whatever the Lord has blessed you with. If you have an abundance of food at a certain time of year, be an "angel of mercy" and bless a poor family in your church or community that is struggling to put food on the table. If there is a spare bedroom in your house, offer its use to a traveling evangelist or missionary.

7. Meditate regularly on scriptures which promise a blessing to the giver. It is more blessed to give than to receive. The Word makes it abundantly clear that there is no way you can "outgive" God. Whenever you give to the Lord—to His work or His people—He will make sure that sometime down the road of life you will receive an even greater return than what you gave.[40]

8. Guard your heart continually against the idolatry of materialism. Generosity has the liberating power of setting a person free from the idolatry of "stuff."[41]

9. In your way of living learn to live the truth that *"Godliness with contentment is great gain."*[42] Focus on being faithful in what God has called you to do and give it your all. Don't compare yourself with others—with what they have and you don't have. As your soul prospers in peaceful contentment your confidence in the Lord as your Provider and

your provision will also grow stronger.

10. A giver who has been entrusted with wealth needs to appreciate that he's been given a very privileged role in advancing God's kingdom. Be wise and think strategically in your giving.

11. You must rule your own house well. Communication and agreement with your spouse and other family members about your giving are essential.

12. If you are talented in the financial realm, be open to helping your church and its members become better stewards of their resources.

6. THE GROWING LEADER (PRESIDER)

"Bless them which persecute you: bless, and curse not."
Romans 12:14 (KJV)

People with the gift of leadership have traits that are essential in managing or supervising a project or an organization. For most with this gift package there is both a "take charge" and a "can do" attitude. The "take charge" mindset carries with it a significant potential for creating interpersonal conflicts within a group, particularly if the person doesn't use his gift with understanding. I have found that this is most likely to happen when a presider participates in a group in which he is not in the top position. If he has a strong personality that accompanies his gifting, as is often the case, his assertive demeanor is likely to be regarded by those in charge as a threat to their authority. For this reason, many who are less developed in their gift of leadership will find it extremely difficult to play "second fiddle." More than likely, such a position will prove to be more of an exercise in frustration than a beneficial use of his gifting—for himself as well as for those who are in charge.

When I was in my twenties, I worked several years on the mission field, where I witnessed an insurrection of several full-time mission workers against the head pastor, whose primary gift was mercy. The rebellion

was led by a staff member with a frustrated and immature gift of leadership. The disgruntled upstart sowed discontent among the staff, which
served only one purpose: to undermine the authority of the pastor. Stung
by such insubordination, and feeling less than total support from the
mission board of directors, the pastor resigned within a year. In retro-
spect, viewing the situation through the lens of the endowment gifts, one
of the main contributing factors was that a carnal leader chafed at serving
under the authority of someone with the gift of mercy. To be sure, other
factors were involved, but that was the essence of the conflict.

When a presider is in charge of an organization other hazards exist
as well. One of those derives from the fact that leaders tend to view situations in terms of the "big picture." Since a leader may be preoccupied
with developing a master plan and strategy, he may fail to adequately
consider the desires and feelings of those most affected. For example, in
an office setting, a leader will usually be the one who brings the vision
and the plan to the table, but if he is too focused on the project, and is not
sensitive to the needs of others involved, they may end up feeling more
like "pawns on a chessboard" than team members. Obviously this type of
dynamic will lead to frustration, disappointment, and dissension.

Another potential problem for an immature presider derives from
one of his special abilities. As a general rule, leaders have an extraordinary knack for understanding human nature—what motivates people,
what "makes them tick."[43] I have seen over the years that this skill can
be used either positively or in an exploitative way. What this means is
that a carnal leader may become quite adept at using people—manipulating them to achieve his self-defined goals or his own selfish ends
with little regard for the welfare of others. To him, the objective is what
is most important. In effect, the "ends justify the means." If such a tendency is left unchecked, the immature leader will eventually become so
morally bankrupt that he may resort to using emotional manipulation,
deception, or dishonesty and view it as merely part of the repertoire of
management "tricks" he uses to "get the job done."

Oftentimes a presider is a high-profile person who becomes the
emblem for a group or organization and, as such, he will become a

target for those opposed to the group's beliefs or goals. In most cases, the leader will have developed his ability to handle criticism and verbal attacks with composure by the time he's attained a position of prominence. Unfair attacks will usually leave him unflustered because, to him, it's all part of the job of being a leader. However, an undeveloped leader may have a deep-seated resentment lurking beneath the surface which causes him to seek revenge to even the score. Because the leader is personable and often skilled, even subtle, at manipulation, his retaliation will usually be done in a way in which the object of his scorn will be the last to find out. I know of what I am speaking—it has happened to me!

A presider is usually an excellent motivator and good at delegating tasks and responsibilities to others, but this can become a problem as well. An immature leader may decide to delegate tasks in order to evade a few personal responsibilities that are truly his own. If this tendency is unchecked, this manipulative behavior can lead to an abuse of authority and exploitation of others.

While most presiders tend to be future-oriented, it is ironic that one of the largest problems for a person with this gifting involves purpose. The leader will generally look at what he is doing from a utilitarian perspective—in terms of how productive he is or whether he is able to meet his goals and objectives. However, it is an uncommon leader who is willing to go *beneath* the surface and examine whether what he is doing is what God has called him to do. The leader has prodigious talents, but the question is, are they being put to use as God wills or as the leader wills?

Problem Areas

Some of the negative tendencies and weaknesses of a leader are to:

1. come across as arrogant or overly self-confident
2. view people as resources to be "used"—manipulate others to achieve his own self-defined goals
3. be inflexible—have difficulty adjusting plans so the Holy

Spirit is allowed to preside

4. become upset when others do not share the same vision or goal
5. stifle the vision of others by being overbearing
6. overlook major character flaws in others deemed useful to reaching his goals
7. develop callousness due to being a frequent target of criticism
8. respond to opposition or criticism by seeking to retaliate
9. make others feel belittled, alienated, incompetent, or inadequate
10. avoid personal responsibilities by delegating them to others
11. develop pride in his own abilities
12. abuse his position by exploiting and manipulating others
13. lose focus and interest in his job before it's finished because his attention is on the next project
14. have difficulty working under the authority of someone else
15. be more focused on overall objectives while ignoring the personal needs of team members
16. fail to appreciate God's purposes being fulfilled in the process of meeting a goal
17. fail to seek direction from Yahweh and then launch out where he desires to go
18. fail to develop a deep enough spiritual life to discern his true calling and purpose

How to Improve

Ways to grow as a leader:

1. As Yeshua advised His disciples in the upper room, "… *without me you can do nothing.*"[44] Any achievement you've been able to accomplish as a leader is a result of His greatness and generosity, not your own. To grow in your gifting requires your being able to come humbly before the Lord and depend upon Him.

2. Live each day with an "attitude of gratitude." It is the grace of the Lord that endowed you with your abilities to be a leader. Use your gifting in a way that continually says "thank you" to the One who made you.

3. Jesus washed His disciples' feet the night before He was crucified to demonstrate the new leadership style He had brought to earth. Let Jesus' attitudes, words, and actions be your guide as you lead others.[45]

4. Self-centeredness is not only wrong, it's also self-defeating. As you plan your future be as concerned about helping others fulfill their dreams and God will do likewise for you.

5. Follow Jesus' time-tested advice in all of your interpersonal relations: *"In everything ... treat people the same way you want them to treat you ..."*[46]

6. Let generosity of spirit be your hallmark—*"Give ... and it shall be given unto you ..."*[47]

7. Learn to be more of a listener and less of a talker. You're not an authority on everything.

8. Self-will is anathema to leading others. You may be able to impress others with your boldness and decisiveness, but in the end it's the Lord's opinion of your actions that counts. In all your decision-making let your heart's cry be, "Not my will, but Yours be done—in Jesus' name."

9. If you have been guilty of abusing your authority and mistreating others, ask the Lord for forgiveness and make it right with those you've abused. Without a healthy fear of Yahweh in this regard it is certain you will be unable to fulfill your destiny and potential.

10. The extent to which you are able to acknowledge your shortcomings and weaknesses will determine your potential to become stronger in those areas.

11. An especially wise investment of your time is getting to know the heart of the Father better, what is on His heart. This should be at the very top of your "to do" list.

7. THE GROWING MERCY GIVER (CAREGIVER)

"Rejoice with them that do rejoice, and weep with them that weep."
Romans 12:15

Integral to the spiritual DNA of the mercy gift is a strong desire to help remove the hurts of others. A caregiver's sensitivity and compassion causes suffering people to be drawn to him like iron filings to a magnet. If a mercy giver does not use wisdom and prudence in exercising his gift he will find that several dangers await him.

One of these risks stems from an immature mercy giver's tendency to become overly identified with people and their hurts, which can cloud his judgment. For example, failure to set proper boundaries when consoling a person of the opposite sex has the potential to create a situation where an improper relationship could develop. A caregiver who has identified too strongly with the person's suffering may find that a romantic sentiment starts to creep into their counsel. If this should happen, since he has emotionally over-invested in the person already, the potential for impropriety and the ensuing damage it will cause should never be underestimated. Over the years I have seen several good marriages severely harmed because of this very problem.

The tendency toward over-identification with suffering brings the possibility of other dangers as well. A mercy giver may become vulnerable to an unscrupulous person who preys on their soft-hearted nature. A caregiver must realize that not every person who comes to him with trouble has come merely for consolation. The regrettable truth is that to a scoundrel a mercy giver will be seen as naïve and gullible and therefore easily fooled. This type of "wolf in sheep's clothing" will deliberately misrepresent himself or his difficulties so as to manipulate a mercy giver, going to great lengths to "pull on the heartstrings" in order to obtain his selfish ends. Unfortunately, this type of situation is common, and I have seen it end up with very tragic consequences.

An immature caregiver's natural tendency to react to situations based primarily on feelings and emotions can be a problem in other ways as well. For instance, when consoling a person who is deeply hurting because of being abused or battered, a mercy giver may identify with the person's pain to the extent that he starts to pick up a torch for the person, even viewing him as a type of martyr. However, a mercy giver may be blinded by his emotions as well as his tendency to overlook sin and fail to see that the problem with the abusive relationship started long before the obvious physical or emotional damage began; it may be that the trouble stems from a lustful relationship that should never have been in the first place.

An unhealthy mercy giver can become so identified with the sufferings of those to whom he ministers that he will take on their burden in other detrimental ways. A caregiver may internalize the problems of the hurting and become subject to depression. In other instances, a mercy giver may become overly protective of those who are wounded to the extent that he gets defensive or even hostile toward friends or others who are less sympathetic to the person's plight.

A caregiver should be careful that in his desire to alleviate the pain of the hurting he doesn't end up enabling bad behavior or sin that created the harmful situation in the first place. By always wanting to rush in and "make things better" a mercy giver may become an enabler to a person who needs to make difficult but necessary changes in his life. In fact, a caregiver may be interfering with the chastening work of the Holy Spirit. Sometimes pain is necessary for spiritual growth or for change to occur.

As a rule a mercy giver is very friendly, tolerant, and non-judgmental. However, I have seen over the years that one who becomes proud of his compassionate nature may develop a critical spirit toward others who do not share their sensitivity. As with every endowment gift, the gift of mercy has its strengths and weaknesses and is not "better" than another. To become proud of one's compassion is to fall prey to vanity.

Problem Areas

Some of the negative tendencies and weaknesses of a mercy giver are to:

1. be overly sensitive and easily wounded in exercising his gift
2. fail to establish and maintain prudent boundaries with others
3. allow himself to be guided by his emotions
4. be emotionally vulnerable and easily taken advantage of or manipulated
5. become depressed or inwardly grieve because of empathy with others' problems
6. be indecisive, which sometimes reflects timidity
7. be open in showing affection, which may be misinterpreted by the opposite sex
8. be a magnet for disturbed individuals and misfits as well as rebellious types who have issues with authority
9. be highly sensitive to actions or words that might be hurtful to a particular group or individual
10. be overly idealistic and subjective which sometimes causes poor judgment
11. avoid confronting sin
12. be so accommodating and non-judgmental that he becomes an "enabler" of sinful behavior
13. feel unappreciated when those he's helped fail to express gratitude
14. become proud of his sensitivity and empathetic nature
15. close his spirit to those trying to bring correction to him or sever relationships with those deemed insensitive or harsh
16. interfere in the Holy Spirit's process of discipline
17. fail to be firm even if the Lord has told him to do otherwise
18. be more of a people-pleaser than a God-pleaser

How to Improve

Ways to grow as a mercy giver:

1. When providing emotional comfort and a shoulder to cry on the mercy giver must purpose to have Jesus at the center

of all he says and does. Having been designed to be an instrument of His compassion to a hurting world, a caregiver must remember at all times that he is to have the mind of Christ as well as display His heart.

2. A mercy giver must carry the burdens of others only long enough to place them in Yahweh's hands. The joy of the Lord is your strength, and in order to be effective a caregiver needs to keep his own emotional and spiritual tank full by developing a deep and consistent prayer life. Without a close relationship with the Father, a mercy giver who continually pours out to others will eventually experience spiritual burnout, suffer needlessly, and find his compassionate rescue efforts too often ending in failure.

3. In many situations timing is key. While the mercy giver's heart is to "jump in" whenever and wherever there is suffering, wisdom and spiritual discernment must come into play. Sometimes the best thing love can do is stand by and watch, painful as that may be.

4. When a wounded soul of the opposite sex comes your way, the best thing to do is refer that person to a caregiver of their same sex or counsel them with your spouse. There is just too much potential for your compassion to be mistaken for sexual or romantic interest—especially by those who are suffering—which can only bring greater problems to you both.

5. As a person equipped to lavish attention, love, and support on those in need, a caregiver will tend to be "soft" and intuitive by nature. However, there is no need for the mercy giver to be naïve. Jesus told us to be as wise as a serpent and innocent as a dove.[48] Be alert to the danger of pretenders who feign distress but are really predators who seek to take advantage of your good nature and desire to help.

6. Though your tendency is to try to spare other people's feelings, it is never a good idea to become a "slave" to their

feelings. There comes a time when the truth must be spoken to those who need to hear it. Confronting sin may be difficult for you, but it may be just what the person needs to be set free.

7. Be careful not to side with misfits and those who have a problem with authority. If you're not careful you may end up on the opposite side from where Yahweh wants you to be.

8. While being open and accepting of personal differences, caregivers tend to be less than charitable toward anyone whom they perceive as insincere or intolerant. Having a propensity to take offense in this regard, a mercy giver must be on his watch that unforgiveness does not creep into his heart. Rein in your feelings and make them heed the Word: *"Forgive and you will be forgiven."*[49]

9. Refrain from judging others who do not share the sensitivity that you possess. The body of Christ is comprised of many members, each with its own function. Don't close the circle with whom you're willing to work by developing a critical spirit. Seek to harmonize and balance your gift with others.

10. Guard against feeling unappreciated when others do not show or express appreciation for your compassionate efforts. In all you do, do it as unto the Lord.

11. Keep your focus on the Lord and not on man. If you are a "people pleaser" your efforts will continually come up short and end in disappointment. However, if you're a "God pleaser" your gifting will find its true fulfillment.

SETTING THINGS STRAIGHT

While it's true that every believer has been given *"... exceeding great and precious promises"* in order to be a *"partaker[s] of the divine nature,"* that nature is only characteristic of those who have also *"... escaped the corruption that is in the world through lust."*[50] In other words, carnal Christians, those who are not completely sold out to Yahweh and walking with Him, are going to manifest a corruption of the spiritual DNA that He has given them and will display their gift in a distorted and diminished manner. The antidote—a form of "gene therapy" if you will—for this unhealthy condition is to learn to walk in the God-kind of love. To do so we must be willing to learn how to abide in His presence. By so doing, we will experience a supernatural work of restoration, one that is able to transform the twists and distortions in our nature and return us to the pattern Yahweh planned from before our birth.

Most of us have a long way to go to realize anywhere near the full potential of our grace package. We are like the "twisted branches walking" I saw in the vision I shared earlier. If it seems to you that you have too far to go to become anything close to "straight," don't be fooled by the enemy that you simply don't have "what it takes" to improve. That, my friend, is far from the truth.

Each one of us needs to begin by being honest about the facts of our own spiritual condition and avoid the deception that comes when we look at ourselves through rose-colored glasses. However, even when those facts are negative, the good news is that there is a spiritual truth that overrides those facts—one that enables you to be the overcomer God has always intended for you to be. If you indeed are a child of the Most High God, one who's made Jesus Christ the Lord of your life, you've been equipped with the most powerful force in the universe: "... the love of God [that's been] shed abroad in [your] heart by the Holy Ghost."[51] This irresistible force within is the same one that Scripture says "... never fails."[52] It never comes up short and never comes up against anything it can't outlast or overcome; in other words, it cannot be defeated!

Once you've grasped the awesomeness of this truth, and that it is a spiritual law which governs the entire universe, you will realize that whatever condition you are in, you do have "what it takes." The grace, anointing, and authority of your endowment gift will flow, even flourish, when you abide and walk in the God-kind of love. Your gift will come to reflect the glory for which it's intended. You will be a living testimony to the unveiling of the mystery "... that's been hid from ages and from generations ... which is Christ in you, the hope of glory."[53]

Questions: Chapter Five

1. What do you think are some of the major "kinks" or "twists" on the inside of you that have come from your upbringing or your past?

   _____

   _____

   _____

   _____

   _____

2. How much man is like wood in his _____ (unredeemed) condition!

3. Each one of is a "work in progress". No one has " _____ " at the place of having reached the full potential of their endowment gifting.

4. The "deformities" inside of us are soul wounds or _____ that result from an unhealthy or malignant influence in our past.

5. A major reason for looking at the negative traits is that such an investigation can be extremely useful in evaluating a person's _____ spiritual condition.

6. Recognizing a problem in our spiritual development is the

first step to _____ it.

7. A prophet who's lacking maturity may act without regard
    to the _____ of others, which can
    feel condemning and judgmental.

8. A carnal prophet may have a strong tendency to become
    _____ and negative in outlook; the
    more unhealthy he is the more pronounced his pessimism
    and negativity will be.

9. An immature prophet may have difficulty finding or
    accepting _____ for himself, which
    lead to a state of depression.

10. A less developed server may develop _____
    toward people around him who, in his judgment, walk
    right past obvious needs.

11. An unhealthy minister also may become so busy taking
    care of practical needs that he is _____
    toward his own relationship with the Lord.

12. One of the greatest battles of a growing server is finding
    his true _____, affirmation and approval
    in God.

13. A teacher who's lacking in maturity may be tempted to
    "think of himself more highly than he ought" and be
    susceptible to the sin of _____.

14. One difficulty for an unhealthy teacher has to do with
    _____ related to an inner sense of
    inadequacy or unworthiness.

15. If a teacher genuinely believes what Jesus Christ
said, "without Me you can do nothing," then he'll
find that he's able to operate in his gift with full
_____ —but only if he is truly trusting
in the Lord.

16. An exhorter has a tendency to avoid heavy doctrinal
teaching in favor of lighter, inspirational messages with an
immediate or practical _____.

17. An immature exhorter may tend to have a problem with
perseverance and keeping his _____
straight.

18. When an immature exhorter's motives are muddied, he
may not be above _____ people's
emotions by pulling on their "heartstrings."

19. If a giver is weak or incapacitated in his faith he will most
certainly have a problem _____ the Lord as
his source of provision.

20. The twin hazards of _____ and _____ are
capable of hindering, and perhaps even shutting down,
the gifting of the sharer.

21. Another tendency of the immature sharer may be manifested in terms of insensitivity or indifference, which
results from a lack of _____.

22. Many who are less developed in their gift of leadership
will find it is extremely _____ for them to
play "second fiddle."

23. If a leader is too focused on the "big picture" and not _____ to the needs of team members, they may end up feeling more like "pawns on a chessboard."

24. An immature leader may decide to delegate tasks in order to _____ a few personal responsibilities that are truly his own.

25. An immature mercy giver may become overly _____ with people and their hurts, which can cloud his judgment.

26. The mercy giver should be careful that in his desire to alleviate the pain of the hurting he doesn't end up enabling bad behavior or _____ that created the harmful situation in the first place.

27. If not cautious, a mercy giver may become _____ to an unscrupulous person who would seek to prey on his soft-hearted nature.

28. One antidote for the unhealthy distortions and twists in our nature is simply to learn to walk in the _____ of love.

Chapter Six

SEVEN ENDOWMENT GIFT PORTRAITS

The Giftings Displayed by Bible Characters

BIBLE CHARACTERS COME TO LIFE

Our loving Father is interested in relationship. He isn't way "out there" in some remote corner of the universe with a giant "do not disturb" sign as some deists have foolishly theorized. Far from it. He's made Himself available and He is involved. After making the heavens and the earth, before He sat down to take a rest, Yahweh decided to fashion a being much like Himself as His crowning touch. Because of this being's similarity to his Maker, he would be able to relate to Yahweh personally. So God made His man, Adam, and wife Eve, and before long they went on daily strolls together in the cool of the day.[1] You see, the man wasn't made just to occupy the top spot on the planet—ruling and reigning over the rest of creation—but also to be a friend, someone the Lord could relate to closely. It was "good," even refreshing, to walk about and converse with His junior partner. That's our relational God.

The Book which our Maker has given us reflects His keen desire for interaction, filled with hundreds of stories about the experiences of men and women and the ups and downs of their relationships with Him. In the pages of Scripture we meet flesh-and-blood sons and daughters of Adam in their various struggles, triumphs, and failures. Through their lives we learn a great deal about how they related to their Maker. We read about the precious few who earnestly desired to know Yahweh and learn of His ways as well as the many who were content to live in ignorance. We discover that while some wholeheartedly sought to please the Lord, others were indifferent or rebelled against Him. But at its very heart the Bible shows us that God not only cares for us but has actively pursued our relationship.

Aren't you glad our heavenly Father didn't just provide us with a rulebook, an "owner's manual" filled with do's and don'ts? How boring and lifeless that would be—and how unlike our God, who is the Author of life. Such a book wouldn't do much to inspire us. However, the great God we serve chose to provide us with a Book filled from cover to cover with stories concerning almost every human condition and insight imaginable. There are tales about mighty exploits and teachings that reveal the secrets and mysteries of the ages. The Scriptures recount narratives of godly and wise men and women as well as naughty, foolish, and wicked ones. In its pages are panoramic accounts of the rise and fall of nations and civilizations as well as an eagle-eyed view from heaven of what is in store for all mankind as history unfolds.

With the exception of our Savior, each one of the persons portrayed in the Bible had strengths and weaknesses and character issues like us all. Even the most exemplary were mere mortals in need of a Redeemer. For example, Elijah, a great and holy prophet, is described in this way: *"Elijah was as human as we are."*[2]

Each and every one of Adam's descendants has been endowed with special gifts from his Creator. We discover through the Scriptures that all have been just like ourselves, with attitudes and actions typifying a particular endowment gifting. In this chapter, as we look at seven characters from the Bible, one for each of the gifts, and consider what made each of these individuals "tick," a deeper understanding will emerge. Their motives, attitudes, and abilities will become clearer in light of the spiritual DNA of their gifting. As we view them in terms of their inner nature, new insight will be gained regarding their outward behavior. We will be able to relate to each one better as the real-life people they were.[3] We will also come to appreciate their spiritual condition as well as the nature of their God-given assignment.

Like ourselves, each of these Bible characters was chosen by his Maker to fulfill a purpose which, of course, He knew about well in advance. Yahweh gifted these individuals according to His purpose, supplying them from His providential storehouse—a place where the future and all destinies are known. Each lived at a particular time and place to fulfill specific tasks. Their unique gifts and calling intersected with their divine destiny, and because of that they discovered their true purpose. By their examples, we can see that God has a plan and a destiny for us all.

1. PETER, THE PROPHET[4]

A primary attribute of an endowment gift prophet is the uncommon ability to discern spiritual reality and verbalize it. As such, a prophetically gifted person is equipped by their spiritual DNA to see into the spirit realm with greater facility than others. Of the twelve disciples Jesus chose to accompany Him throughout Galilee and Judea, it was Simon Peter who was the first to declare with certainty that the One he had been following was in fact "... *the Messiah, the Son of the living God.*"[5] Upon hearing this declaration from Peter's lips, Jesus acknowledged its truth and observed that Peter had received this revelation from "... *My Father in heaven ... [and] did not learn this from any human being.*"[6] Peter indeed was an endowment gift prophet who was used by the Lord in a special way to set in motion a spiritual movement that has continued to spread until this very day.

Because of his persuasive ability as a prophet, Simon Peter boldly proclaimed such a convicting message on the day of Pentecost that a flood of new believers was swept into the kingdom of God.[7] His message was compelling not only because of the "baptism of fire" he received but also because his prophetic endowment gift made it possible for him to tie together spiritual truths that had been hidden for the ages and make them known to the multitude. His preaching was so convincing that within a matter of days, despite intense persecution from the authorities, the church burgeoned to many thousands. Due to the powerful anointing upon his prophetic gifting, Peter became the early church's chief spokesman.

The audacity with which Simon Peter preached was displayed again a short while later to the ruling council, the Sanhedrin, when he daringly charged them with responsibility for having put their Messiah to death. The inner drive that impelled Peter on such a bold course, proclaiming truth to power without regard for the consequences it might bring upon his head, was the spiritual DNA of a prophet.

At times Peter displayed impulsiveness, but once he became committed to a course of action he was not dissuaded by adversity or opposition. A prime example of this was when he and the other disciples were crossing the Sea of Galilee in the dead of night and he saw Jesus a short distance from the boat coming toward them, walking on the water.[8] As the others cowered in fear thinking it was a phantom, Peter shouted out to the Master saying, *If that is really you, call me to come to you.* After Jesus told him to come ahead, Simon Peter jumped out of the boat and started walking toward Jesus. It wasn't until he looked down at the waves churning beneath his feet that he lost his nerve and began to sink into the water. Jesus reached down, grabbed his hand, and then they both climbed into the boat.

In this incident Peter demonstrated what a man is capable of doing with his eyes "fixed on Jesus." With his feat that defied the laws of nature, Peter showed his wholehearted trust in the One who called him and a willingness to take risk, regardless of the consequences. This combination of boldness mixed with obedience is a trait of the gift of prophecy.

Peter's shortcomings are never glossed over in the Gospels. He is portrayed with his foibles and his virtues, in moments of weakness as well as triumph. The overall picture that emerges is that first and foremost Simon Peter was a God-pleaser. In fact, his daring impetuosity stemmed mainly from his passion to do right in the eyes of the Lord and his utter loyalty to truth. Except for brief instances where his faith failed, Peter was willing to put everything on the line because of his complete commitment to Yahweh. This was demonstrated time and again, such as when Jesus finished teaching a hard saying that many of His followers misunderstood, causing them to abandon Him. After most of Yeshua's followers left, He asked the Twelve if they wanted to go as well. Characteristically, Peter spoke up for all of the disciples and said, *"Lord, to whom shall we go? You have the words of eternal life."*[9] Peter was the disciple who recognized the value of truth and was uncompromisingly devoted to it. The truth personified in Jesus Christ had earned Peter's undying loyalty.

Simon Peter's actions and attitudes make sense in light of the vertical orientation that is an essential feature of the spiritual DNA of a prophet. Time and again Peter showed his primary point of reference was upward toward God rather than horizontal toward man. The high esteem Simon Peter held for the God-nature in Yeshua caused him to recoil at the mere thought that the Messiah might be harmed. Ironic as it may seem, it was Peter's awe for the Holy One of Israel that caused his outburst and rebuke of Jesus when the Lord explained that, as the Messiah, He needed to suffer at the hands of the religious leaders and be put to death.[10]

In a similar manner, Peter's appreciation and reverence for the Master, as well as his own sense of unworthiness, caused him to refuse to allow Jesus to wash his feet in the Upper Room.[11] For the Lord to take on the humble role of a servant was more than Peter's mind could fathom. However, once Jesus informed His eager disciple that his rejection would disqualify him from being part of what the Lord was doing, Peter changed his tune completely—asking the Master to wash his hands and his head as well! In this episode we again see the spiritual DNA of Peter's gift of prophecy: an extraordinary desire to please the Lord, an extreme sensitivity toward missing God's will, and a willingness to change course quickly to come into alignment with the purposes of God.

Simon Peter also revealed an ability to be open about his own faults, though, like many prophets, he struggled to receive forgiveness. Having been proven wrong after doubting Jesus' advice to launch out into the deep waters to fish, Peter fell to his knees before the Lord and confessed his sin.[12]

However, on another occasion Simon Peter found great difficulty accepting his failure. He had denied the Lord three times the night Jesus was arrested, just as Yeshua predicted, and Peter's guilt was so overwhelming he despondently left the ministry to which Jesus had called him and returned to his former life as a fisherman. Jesus understood how hard it was for Simon Peter to receive forgiveness and emotional healing. In order to encourage him and start the process of restoration, Jesus went to the lakeside where he was fishing and asked Peter three times if he loved Him—once for each of Peter's denials the night of his arrest. Once Simon Peter affirmed his love for the Lord three times he started on the road to recovery. Peter grew stronger and would never again be dragged down by guilt or shame. He moved on to fulfill the great destiny to which Jesus had called him—to be "the rock"—bringing an enduring legacy of strength to all who would follow in his footsteps.

Other Biblical Prophets:

- ❖ John the Baptist: Luke 3:2-20, 7:18-29; Matthew 21:32
- ❖ Anna: Luke 2:36-38
- ❖ Mary: Matthew 1&2, Mark 6:3, Luke 1:26-56, Acts 1:14
- ❖ Ananias: Acts 9:10-17, 22:12-16
- ❖ Hosea: Hosea 1-14
- ❖ Jeremiah: Jeremiah 1-52
- ❖ Isaiah: Isaiah 1-66
- ❖ Jonah: Jonah 1-4

2. MARTHA, THE SERVER[13]

Nearly every Christian is familiar with the story of Martha inviting Jesus into her home and being overly concerned with taking care of Him and the disciples. Through this experience we can gain much insight into the gift of the server, though mostly by means of Martha's need to grow in her gifting.[14]

It is not by accident that this episode is preceded in the text by an account of a conversation between Jesus and a scribe concerning the implications of following the Great Commandment—to love Yahweh and our fellow man.[15] In that exchange the self-absorbed expert in the Law of Moses inquired about the significance of the second half of the command, to *"love your neighbor as yourself."* In response, Jesus shared the Parable of the Good Samaritan with him, which vividly portrayed to the rule-bound scholar the real essence of the command he struggled to grasp. The main point of Jesus' parable was that "love of neighbor" involves genuine compassion and generosity toward anyone who comes across our path, even if sacrifice is required or social boundaries need to be crossed. A person's love for neighbor will reflect his love for Yahweh, and what the Lord desires from us is that His boundless "God-kind" of love be manifested in our attitudes and actions toward everyone with whom we come in contact.

Having illustrated this truth regarding the Great Commandment, the Gospel writer Luke then continued along with the same idea by describing the attitudes and actions of Martha and Mary, two sisters who were good friends of Jesus.[16] Once Jesus accepted Martha's invitation to come in, she realized that very shortly her many houseguests would need to be fed, so she did what a server normally would do in such a situation—she got busy, very busy. Martha was a "doer," and therefore she wanted to demonstrate her affection for her friends by preparing a meal and making them feel at home. She did what was normal to her—that is, operating in her gifting.

At the same time Martha was getting things ready, Mary was comfortably seated at Jesus' feet, listening to His every word. According to the social norms of the times, Mary's actions were highly inappropriate. First of all, as a woman, her place was in the kitchen preparing the meal and not sitting with the men listening to Jesus. Also, since women were actively discouraged from learning in Bible times, she was breaking that stricture as well. In short, Mary was out of place to be sitting listening to Yeshua share secrets of the kingdom and not helping her sister take care of their many guests.

It didn't take long for Martha to come to the end of her rope with her sister. As a woman with the gift of ministry she viewed acts of service as a true demonstration of love. How uncaring could Mary possibly be? She wasn't even willing to lend her own sister a hand! However, from Martha's frustration, as well as Jesus' reaction to it, it is clear that mixed in with her self-pity was also what we could call "gift projection"—that is, Martha was trying to impose the attitudes and concerns of her gift of service on Mary. All of Martha's pent-up frustration spilled out when she bitterly complained to Jesus, *"Lord, do You not care that my sister has left me to do all the serving alone? Then tell her to help me."*[17] Think about it: Martha was actually accusing Yeshua the

Messiah, a trusted friend, of not caring *Himself!*

Jesus, attempting to reassure Martha of His loving care for her, began His response by repeating her name, *"Martha, Martha...."* By doing this, He was addressing an insecurity that many servers have—the need to feel appreciated. In repeating her name Yeshua was simply saying, "Martha, I *do* appreciate you."

Jesus then addressed another weakness in Martha that is common to those who are endowed with the gift of service—to become fretful about the task at hand. He observed that she was *"anxious and troubled about many things."*[18] Martha had focused so much on what needed to get done that she was in danger of losing sight of the purpose for her service, which was to make Him and the other guests feel at home. It is ironic that by inviting the Prince of Peace to stay in her home, she had gone into a state of turmoil and become anything but peaceful.

At this point Jesus took Martha to task for having misplaced priorities as well as trying to impose them on her sister. Jesus told her, *"There is only one thing worth being concerned about. Mary has discovered it, and it will not be taken away from her."*[19] Though she cared a great deal for Jesus, Martha had let her activity come between them. Her accusatory tone also indicates that she was at the point of being spiritually exhausted. The "cares of this world" had taken over her mind and heart. She had run out of patience and was resentful.

However, as Jesus indicated, despite the seeming urgency of the tasks of the moment, godly priorities would not be cast to the wind. Mary, who in all likelihood was endowed with the gift of compassion, would not be kept from her time with the Lord.[20] She would be allowed to operate in her own unique gifting, and there was no need for her to become frazzled like her sister. Mary, who was in awe of Jesus, could continue replenishing her "spiritual batteries" in His presence because she had discovered the *"one thing worth being concerned about."*

Martha, like so many with the endowment gift of serving, had gotten off track when she allowed her busyness to interfere with her relationship with the Lord. He was the one being served, and therefore she should have had His interests in her heart more than her own need to serve. Though it can't be denied that there was much to do, if she had truly appreciated who it was under her roof, Martha would have taken some time to enjoy Yeshua's presence and thereby entered into His rest.

However, Martha's tendency to be headstrong was apparent as she sought to force-fit Mary into the mold of her own gift of service. It is clear that Mary's spiritual DNA was very different from that of her sister and so, no matter how exasperating Martha found it to be, Mary would respond to having unexpected houseguests according to the gift within her. After all, Yahweh had given Mary her unique spiritual makeup for His purposes as well.

Luke gives the example of Martha and Mary to amplify the point Jesus made in the Parable of the Good Samaritan. This episode shows us how the Great Commandment is to be manifested in everyday life. The contrast between the sisters' attitudes and reactions to the same situation dramatically reveals the importance of how the Lord must be at the heart of all we do. By loving Him first, we are then able to fulfill our calling to service. No matter how noble and self-sacrificing our service appears to be, if it doesn't flow from a love of God, then it will be in vain.

Other Biblical Servers:

❖ Philip (the "Deacon"): John 1:43-45, 6:5-7, 12:21-22; Acts 6:5, 8:5-40, 21:8-9
❖ Peter's mother-in-law: Matthew 8:14-15
❖ Phoebe: Romans 16:1-2
❖ Ruth: the book of Ruth
❖ Stephen: Acts 6:1-7:60
❖ Dorcas: Acts 9:36, 39

3. EZRA, THE TEACHER[21]

Ezra[22] was a "man of the Book," a priest and scribe born during the Babylonian captivity of Judah several decades after Jerusalem was sacked and burned by Nebuchadnezzar's armies. Early in Ezra's life, following a decree issued by King Cyrus of Persia which allowed the

Hebrews to return to Jerusalem, Zerubbabel had led a large caravan of his fellow Jews back to Judah to rebuild the Temple. The Lord had another plan for Ezra at this time, however. Rather than returning to his ancestral homeland with the first wave of returnees, Ezra spent many years in the land of captivity studying the Torah, learning the ways of Yahweh, and compiling a complete set of the sacred Scriptures.[23] It was only after he had finished his task and was adequately prepared that the Lord enabled him to return to Judah.

Ezra was a seeker after truth from his earliest years. As he grew in his understanding of the Holy Scriptures and developed his ability as a teacher, he established a reputation for wisdom, dedication, and integrity—so much so that his renown spread to the court of King Artaxerxes of Persia. After the way was paved for Ezra in such a manner, when the time was propitious, he requested backing from the king to lead a second band of Hebrews back to Jerusalem.

King Artaxerxes responded to his petition with such a degree of goodwill it could hardly have been expected; the king endorsed the mission of the *"scholar of the Teaching of the God-of-Heaven"*[24] by issuing an official decree so favorable that, among its conditions, it allowed for the financing of the expedition as well as furnishing the Temple with nearly four tons of gold and twenty-five tons of silver[25]—some of which came from the king's own treasury. Certainly, as was noted so often concerning Ezra and his ministry, *"the hand of the LORD was upon him!"*[26] Such should be the testimony of anyone who has matured in their endowment gift and is walking in their calling.

The Scripture informs us that Ezra was *"a ready scribe,"* one who had devoted his life not only to the study of the Torah but also to explaining it to others.[27] His quest for understanding and seeking God's ways caused him to walk in favor with both God and man. Because of this, he was able to persuade some five thousand men, women, and children from all walks of life to pull up their roots and trek nine hundred miles across the wilderness, a journey that would take four months, to return to the place where Yahweh had intended to bless His people: Israel.

Rounding up such a group was no small feat because, after the decline and fall of Judah and having several generations immersed in the pagan ways of Babylon and Persia, only a tiny remnant of Hebrews retained even a slight understanding of the Law of Moses and the ways of the Holy One of Israel. Though the Temple in Jerusalem had been rebuilt, the people of God—"the apple of His eye"[28]—were still far removed from Him in their hearts and their minds.

It was for this reason that Ezra had been prepared and commissioned to bring about the second phase of the restoration process begun by Zerubbabel some sixty years earlier. Through the endowment gifting of the teacher, Yahweh had chosen to set His people free from their corruption, waywardness, and idolatry. Ezra was to be the primary instrument of restoring the remnant that settled back in Judah. The development of the teaching gift within him required decades to reach maturity. It entailed his not only being conversant with the writings of Moses and skillful in expounding on the rest of the sacred Scriptures, but it also involved understanding the heart of God so that His people would be able to escape the condemnation that held them in bondage.

The significance of Ezra's ministry as a teacher can be truly appreciated only when the pivotal role he played in Jewish history is considered. No longer would Yahweh choose to speak to Israel through His prophets.[29] From Ezra's time forward the gift of teaching would be the key method by which He corrected and sustained the Hebrew nation.[30] By using Ezra to help restore His people, the Lord was ushering in a new way of bringing about the necessary change in them—through the ministry of teaching.

The impact of Ezra's instruction on the people of Judah proved to be profound and long-lasting. As the extent of the returned exiles' waywardness became increasingly apparent to Ezra, the heart-rending grief he felt was exposed before the congregation as he tore his garments, pulled out his hair, and wept in agony before the Lord, pleading their case before Him. A huge crowd gathered at this spectacle, and the entire assembly was not only moved to tears of repentance, but each took a solemn vow to change his ways—and did so.[31]

At a later time, as Ezra led the people in praise and worship, the congregation was moved to respond by raising their hands high to Yahweh and then falling to their knees with their faces to the ground in worship. Then, as Ezra and Nehemiah opened the Scriptures and expounded on them, the people realized the scope of their sinfulness and started to weep before the Lord.[32]

Because it was the Feast of Tabernacles, Ezra and Nehemiah admonished the congregation to wipe their tears and rejoice in the Lord since it was supposed to be a time of thanksgiving. Once the people understood, they were so moved by the teaching that each returned to his home, fashioned a booth from branches, and celebrated for seven days as prescribed by the Law of Moses. Considering that the children of Israel hadn't done so for many hundreds of years, since the time of Joshua, it was clear that the remnant of God's people was now entering into a true spiritual awakening.

A more difficult part of the restoration process required Ezra to deliver a strong word to the congregation that would cause much pain but would lead to repentance and spiritual healing. Many, including priests and Levites, had taken wives from among the heathen that inhabited the land. This clearly violated an injunction contained in the Law of Moses[33] which was intended to preserve Israel as a people holy unto the Lord. Yahweh did not mince words about their wickedness as He spoke of how the Hebrew land of promise had become *"... a polluted land, polluted with the obscene vulgarities of the people who live there; they've filled it with their moral rot from one end to the other."*[34]

Ezra, like most endowment gift teachers, found it hard to confront this sin even though it was obviously eating away at the moral fiber of God's people. However, the Lord brought Shechaniah, an encourager, to Ezra's side at this trying moment with the result that Ezra found the strength necessary to confront Judah's moral decadence.[35] He delivered a message to the entire congregation, telling them they must covenant together to *"put away"* (i.e., divorce) their foreign wives and children—or they themselves would be removed from the midst of the congregation.

While such a covenant agreement caused unimaginable grief to the affected families, it was a necessary, painful measure that would help to bring about the spiritual restoration of the people of God.[36] The result of their obedience was that the Hebrew nation was strengthened and the moral blight that plagued the land was virtually eradicated.

With some help, Ezra demonstrated that he could be courageous as well as diligent and insightful. He proved to be as committed to righteousness as he was to wisdom. Because of his ardent desire to instruct the Hebrew children in the ways of the Lord, he became their true "spiritual father." His exemplary role as a teacher was the result not only of the trying times in which he lived but also the unquenchable thirst for truth within him. Ezra was endowed with an extraordinary teaching ability, and he understood that he would have an enduring impact on the people he loved as he taught through both words and deeds.[37]

Ezra clearly demonstrated the importance of the teaching gift in the process of restoring God's people and bringing about revival. Furthermore, we also see in him the potential this endowment gift has to impact future generations. The teaching gift of Ezra proved to have a lasting effect on the natural seed of Abraham, the Hebrews. As we, the spiritual seed of Abraham, come to appreciate and give due honor to the qualities Ezra displayed as a teacher, the church itself will be impelled toward the prophesied "restoration of all things"[38] which will hasten the Lord's return.

Other Biblical Teachers

◈ Solomon: Proverbs and Ecclesiastes
◈ Luke: Gospel of Luke and Acts
◈ Thomas: John 20:24-29
◈ Apollos: Acts 18:24-28 and 1 Corinthians 3:6
◈ Aquila and Priscilla: Acts 18:1-3, Romans 16:3-5, 1 Corinthians 16:19, 2 Timothy 4:19
◈ Timothy: 1 & 2 Timothy; Acts 16:1-3; 1 Corinthians 4:17, 16:10-11

4. BARNABAS, THE ENCOURAGER

Barnabas is first introduced in Scripture shortly after the day of Pentecost when the church in Jerusalem had just dramatically mushroomed to about five thousand new believers.[39] During this great outpouring of the Holy Spirit a number of the saints who owned property sold some of their possessions to take care of the needs of the poor in the rapidly growing congregation.[40] In the midst of this, Scripture mentions only one person who sold his land, referred to by name: *"Joseph, the one the apostles nicknamed Barnabas (which means "Son of Encouragement"). He was from the tribe of Levi and came from the island of Cyprus."*[41]

From this first mention of Barnabas we discover that he was actually "Joseph of Cyprus," an apostle with a Levite background who was so highly thought of as an encourager that the other apostles gave him the name "Son of Encouragement"—a nickname that would stick with him for the rest of his life.[42] Undoubtedly Barnabas was cited in regard to the collection for the poor not only because of the outstanding example he set for others by selling his property, but also because of his persuasiveness in exhorting others to do so as well.

We see from various episodes elsewhere in the book of Acts that Barnabas proved to be a trailblazer for the early church, one whose gift was to always uplift and encourage believers wherever he went. He was used mightily by the Lord as a key leader in the development of the church at Antioch as well as a missionary in Asia Minor and on the island of Cyprus. Barnabas also played a key role in the spiritual development of his cousin John Mark[43] in addition to mentoring and encouraging the apostle Paul.

The Scripture tells us that Barnabas was *"full of the Holy Spirit and strong in faith"* and that many were brought to the Lord through him.[44] Though much of his ministry was done in the face of opposition and persecution, the gift of encouragement within Barnabas not only enabled him to persevere and overcome hostility but also to help others do so as well. It appears that these qualities were evident to the elders of the church in Jerusalem, because when it was time to send a leader to head up the fledgling church in the key city of Antioch they chose Barnabas.[45] As it turned out, the apostles chose wisely because shortly thereafter the congregation there grew so significantly that it became second only to the church in Jerusalem in its influence.

Time and again Barnabas demonstrated a trait that is typical of the endowment gift of encouragement—a genuine concern for the spiritual development of others. For example, when Saul returned to Jerusalem after his dramatic Damascus Road conversion, many disciples were leery of him because of his fierce opposition to the church in days gone by and the suffering caused by his deeds. However, Barnabas took Saul "under his wing" and spoke to the apostles in Jerusalem about the genuineness of Saul's conversion. In short order they accepted Saul among their company and he went out with them preaching in the name of Yeshua.[46]

Several years later, as the burden of duties of the burgeoning church in Antioch escalated, Barnabas reached out to Saul again, this time to bring him from Tarsus, Saul's home city, to Antioch to join the growing ministry team he was developing. Under Barnabas' skillful guidance and encouragement, Saul and the entire leadership of the church flourished—so much so that after four years of mentoring, the church at Antioch was able to send out a missionary team, making it the first church outside of Jerusalem to do so. As the church leaders were fasting and ministering to Yahweh one day, the Holy Spirit instructed them to separate Barnabas and Saul to serve the Lord in a work He was calling them to: a missionary journey to Asia Minor and Cyprus.[47]

As Barnabas and Saul set out on that first missionary trip they took Barnabas' young cousin John Mark, who was from Jerusalem, with them to help. We are not told why, but during the journey John Mark decided to leave them and return to Jerusalem.[48] This incident caused a great deal of friction between Barnabas and Paul, which became evident when it was time to launch out on their second missionary journey about three years later.[49] Barnabas, the endowment gift encourager, wanted to give his cousin a second chance, an opportunity to redeem himself by coming along to help. However, Paul took a sterner attitude: *"John Mark failed us before and therefore he cannot be trusted a second time."*[50]

As an encourager, Barnabas was focused on John Mark's potential and was inclined to believe that his cousin would do well in ministry under his guidance. The dispute became so sharp that it caused a temporary rift between the two apostles. Though they had planned to retrace the steps of their first journey, to see how the saints in each city were faring, instead Barnabas headed to his home island of Cyprus with John Mark at his side while Paul ended up going on a much more extended journey—through Syria, Asia Minor, all the way to Macedonia, and even to Athens—assisted by Silas and the young Timothy, whom they picked up along the way.[51]

Obviously Paul's second missionary journey opened up a tremendous door for the kingdom of God for it was on this trip that the Good News of Jesus Christ was delivered for the first time in Europe. At the same time, under the tutelage of Barnabas, John Mark became an evangelist who later wrote the Gospel of Mark, which is a legacy for the entire church and stands as a testimony not only of its author, John Mark, but also to the encouragement and mentoring he received from Barnabas.[52] In fact, even though there is no "Gospel of Barnabas" in the Bible, it is fair to say that he and his gift of encouragement had a hand in the writing of about half the New Testament; of its twenty-seven books, thirteen were penned by the apostle Paul and one was written by John Mark—both of whom experienced the indelible imprint of the ministry of Barnabas on their lives.

The apostle Barnabas fulfilled his own personal destiny as an endowment gift encourager and was greatly used in many ways to advance the kingdom of God. In the case of his relationship with Paul, he was instrumental in helping pave the way for a ministry that would not only bring the gospel to Asia Minor, but also to Europe—and even to the very heart of the empire in Rome. In a sense, because Barnabas unselfishly allowed Paul to "stand on the shoulders" of his ministry, Paul was enabled to reach far higher than he would have been able to do otherwise.

Barnabas was a mighty weapon in the Lord's hand because he walked in humility and lived an extraordinary Spirit-filled life.[53] Part of his legacy is the vivid example he gave us of what it means to abide in the God-kind of love and walk in His power. As an encourager Barnabas continually looked out for the spiritual well-being of others the Lord had placed around him and was able to overcome strife, obstacles, adversity, and much persecution. He demonstrated a kingdom-mindset and made sure that in his doings the Lord received all the honor and glory. Barnabas lived up to the good name others had given him, and his example is one that all of us would do well to follow.

Other Biblical Encouragers (Exhorters)

- ❖ Silas: Acts 15:2-40, 16:25, 17:4,10-15; 1 Peter 5:12
- ❖ Titus: 2 Corinthians 2:13, 7:6,13-14, 8:6-23, 12:18; Galatians 2:1,3; 2 Timothy 4:10; the book of Titus
- ❖ James: James 1:1-13
- ❖ Aaron – Exodus, Leviticus, and Numbers

5. ABRAHAM, THE GIVER

The story of Abraham begins in Genesis when he had already reached seventy-five years of age. At that time Abram[54] was living in Mesopotamia where he received instruction by Yahweh to leave his father's house and the land of his kindred. He was to go *"to the land that I will show you"* and there he would become a *"great nation"* to be used as an instrument for the blessing of all mankind. So it was even before Abram had set foot in the land of Canaan that he received an assurance—an unconditional promise—from the Lord that, *"I will bless you and make your name great; and you shall be a blessing ... and in you all the families of the earth shall be blessed."*[55]

Is it possible that Abram could have comprehended the staggering promise he received from Yahweh? Not likely, because the magnitude of the word and its far-reaching ramifications were beyond human reasoning or capacity. However, because of his trust in the One who had given him the promise, Abram would prove time and again throughout his life that he was "blessed to be a blessing." In fact, the "father of our faith"[56] would provide an example of generosity for all who are givers, whether or not their predominant endowment gift is sharing.

Not long after Abram arrived in Canaan a severe famine spread across the land which forced him, along with his wife Sarai[57] and others, to go to Egypt to find sustenance. However, even during this time of hardship, the Lord caused Abram to prosper. As it turned out, Abram found favor with the Pharaoh such that when he returned from Egypt he "... *was very rich in livestock, in silver and in gold.*"[58] Even in the midst of adversity the knack of the endowment gift of giving to be "at the right place at the right time" caused the blessing of prosperity to come Abram's way.

The eternal covenant of blessing that Yahweh made with Abram was the source of his great faith in God's provision. The record of Abram's dealings with everyone around him—his generosity of spirit—can be understood best in light of his belief in the great promise he had received.

For example, when Abram returned to Canaan he had so much cattle that a problem arose between his herdsmen and those of his nephew Lot because there wasn't enough grazing land for both herds. In order to avoid conflict, Abram generously suggested that Lot choose a portion of land for his herd to graze on first, and *afterward* Abram would select grazing land elsewhere from what was left. This kindly attitude of Abram toward his nephew can be appreciated when we understand that he looked to Yahweh as his source of supply. And so Scripture records that Lot set his eyes on the rich, well-watered Jordan Valley[59] and took his herd down toward Sodom. After Lot departed the Lord *Himself* instructed Abram to "lift up [his] eyes" and said that as far as he could see in every direction the land would be his possession and the possession of his posterity forever.[60] This incident provides a clear contrast between the self-will of Lot, which ultimately ended in destruction, and the abundant, eternal blessing that God had in store for Abram and for all those who, to this day, share his faith.

Abram's trust in Yahweh and the "attitude of gratitude" that it engendered was evident in his response to nearly every difficulty he faced. Later on, when Lot was taken captive by an army led by King Chedorlaomer, Abram armed more than three hundred servants from his household to rescue him. He led them, along with a large army of warriors, into battle against Chedorlaomer and his allies. Abram pursued his enemies a great distance and the Lord gave them into his hands. He slew the enemy kings, rescued Lot, and returned victoriously with the plunder of the defeated kings.

Upon his return Abram used the triumphant occasion to honor Yahweh. At the victory celebration he gave a tithe of the spoils of war to his principal ally, the priest-king Melchizedek, and turned over the rest of the loot to the men who fought at his side as well as the king of Sodom. Abram refused to take any of the plunder for himself and used the event to declare publicly before the assembled heathen that it was the *"most high God, the possessor of heaven and earth"* that gave him the victory.[61] He wanted everyone to know that his own military genius had not brought about the successful outcome, but rather the Lord with whom he had entered into a covenant. Yahweh had kept His word; Abram was able to bless his allies with riches and his enemies were defeated. Abram's confidence was not in his own abilities nor in the riches he obtained but in the provision of his promise-keeping God.

Hospitality is another notable attribute of many endowed with the gift of sharing. In his ninety-ninth year,[62] one afternoon shortly after he received the promise of a son through Sarah and his name was changed to Abraham (i.e., *"father of many nations"*), he was sitting in front of his tent when the Lord appeared to him. While seated in the Lord's presence, Abraham looked up and saw three strangers a short distance away. The Scripture implies that at the moment Abraham beheld the three strangers he left the Lord "hanging," for it says he *ran* to greet the visitors and humbly bowed before them.[63] This must have been quite a scene for this ninety-nine-year-old man running to greet three strangers.

We are not told what the Lord shared with Abraham, but evidently, whatever it was, caused a great eagerness in him to host these visitors. Since it was in the heat of the day, Abraham invited them to refresh themselves, and once they consented, he, along with Sarah's help, hurriedly put together a grand feast for his guests. Though Abraham had many servants who could have helped prepare a meal, he personally picked out a fatted calf, had Sarah make bread, put the meal together, and served it himself. The strangers were not the only ones to be blessed that afternoon, however. As the meal was finished, one of them gave Abraham a prophetic word about his wife—that at the same time in the following year she would be holding a newborn son in her arms! Sarah, who was long past childbearing age, did in fact conceive a son, Isaac, the long-awaited "child of promise," as foretold.[64]

Though the Lord had blessed Abraham with wealth and many possessions throughout his life, he was content to live as "a stranger and sojourner"[65] in the land God had given to him for an inheritance. He showed a peculiar lack of interest in the comforts that the world around him had to offer. Though Abraham certainly had the resources to "settle in" and build a palace for himself and his family in Canaan, his way of life reflected the "other-worldliness" of his heart. He *chose* to dwell in a tent—as would his son Isaac and his grandson Jacob as well.[66] It was only when Sarah died, and he needed a place to bury her body, that Abraham actually came into possession of a plot of land in Canaan, when he bought a cave from one of his Hittite neighbors.

From the time that Abraham received the promise of blessing in Mesopotamia he had the heart of a pilgrim. He set his affection and his eyes beyond the horizon of this life, toward the heavenly city *"whose builder and maker is God."*[67] During his journey here on this earth Abraham had become a *"friend of God"*[68] and he valued this friendship above all else.

Other Biblical Givers

- ❖ Barnabas: Acts 4:36-37
- ❖ Epaphras: Colossians 1:7, 4:12; Philemon 23
- ❖ Zacchaeus: Luke 19:1-10
- ❖ Mary of Bethany: John 11:1-12:8
- ❖ The poor widow: Mark 12:41-44
- ❖ Believers of Macedonia (2 Corinthians 8:1-7)

6. NEHEMIAH, THE LEADER

The story of the rebuilding of the broken walls of Jerusalem provides the dramatic backdrop for one of the most outstanding examples of the gift of leadership found in Scripture.[69] It was a time of great discouragement for Israel. Even though a remnant of Hebrews had managed to return to Judah from exile during the seventy long years since King Cyrus of Persia issued a decree allowing them to return to Jerusalem, the city's charred gates still lay rotting, and its walls were heaped in ruins.

At this time Nehemiah,[70] a Jew who had been elevated to one of the highest positions in the Persian Empire, heard of the plight of his fellow countrymen in Jerusalem. He was serving in the trusted capacity of cupbearer in the court of King Artaxerxes in the Persian capital of Susa. The news of the suffering of the Jewish remnant in faraway Jerusalem grieved Nehemiah so greatly that he wept. It was then that he decided to dedicate himself to a time of seeking the Lord through fasting and prayer. This time of consecration proved to be the key to the incredible story of the rebuilding of Jerusalem's walls.

After four months dedicated to prayer, it was clear that Yahweh's hand was upon Nehemiah as a leader. The Lord gave him sufficient courage so that when the time was right he was able to bring the matter before King Artaxerxes. The king was so moved by Nehemiah's appeal that he consented to his request for a "leave of absence" from the royal court so that he could lead the rebuilding effort. Furthermore, the king agreed to send documents along with Nehemiah that would ensure safe passage to Judah for him and his entourage as well as to provide timber for the project, which was to come from the king's own forest.[71]

It is clear that Nehemiah was not only a leader with a vision but also one with a plan. In short order he enlisted the backing of the most powerful monarch on earth in rebuilding Jerusalem's walls. Though he had never even seen Jerusalem, he would be traveling there with enough materials to ensure the project reached completion. He had laid out his plan before Artaxerxes so successfully that the king even sent horsemen from his own cavalry to protect Nehemiah and his party on their journey.

Upon his arrival in Jerusalem, Nehemiah displayed great wisdom and ability in his planning and motivational skills. After his first few days there, he discreetly surveyed the broken-down walls around the city under the cover of darkness prior to letting anyone know the purpose for his visit. Nehemiah took this surreptitious approach so as not to alert the citizenry and leaders of his intention to rebuild the walls of the city, for if they had known they certainly would have tried to marshal a host of arguments against him. After assessing the magnitude of the rebuilding effort, Nehemiah went before the inhabitants of Jerusalem to share the vision and plan that had been birthed within him. Though he had only just arrived from faraway Susa, Nehemiah spoke to them of "our" problem and of the shared effort it would take to remove the disgrace that the broken walls represented. He presented the vision for restoring the walls so effectively that the people responded resoundingly: *"Let us rise up and build!"*[72]

As an endowment gift leader, Nehemiah also proved to be brilliant in organizing the work effort. He wisely divided the huge job of rebuilding the wall into small sections, making various families, neighborhoods, workers from the provinces, interest groups, and tradesmen responsible for building the particular gate or wall section most related to their own interests. Because of his keen insight into human nature, he was able to foster a team spirit within each group and integrate that camaraderie into a sense of higher purpose for the overall project. Nehemiah's motivational and organizational skills succeeded in recruiting almost the entire citizenry of Jerusalem and its environs[73] in the construction work, including some of the women.[74]

As a godly endowment gift leader, Nehemiah took on his role in restoring the walls as a direct assignment from the Lord. Just as his own personal involvement had been preceded by consecrated prayer, the actual construction would have to be sanctified as well. He enlisted the high priest Eliashib along with the other priests to consecrate the overall endeavor and to begin the rebuilding. Their work assignment was to build the Sheep Gate—through which animals used in the Temple sacrifices passed—as well as the adjacent section of wall. It is evident that uppermost in Nehemiah's mind was the notion that the whole project was to be a *holy* endeavor, and as such it had to be built on the solid foundation of godly principles and priorities and its labor needed to be sanctified.

Nehemiah's efforts to restore the viability and strength of Jerusalem as a city-state drew opposition from many quarters. Sanballat, the governor of Samaria, was indignant from the first day Nehemiah set foot in Jerusalem because he realized that Nehemiah had come to look after the interests of the children of Israel, a people he despised.[75] The effort to rebuild the city's walls initially was greeted with mockery by Sanballat and his cohorts, but their scorn soon turned to panic when it became clear that the endeavor was proceeding at a rapid pace. It was then that Israel's enemies banded together to create as much trouble as they could and, if need be, to fight against Jerusalem.

In the face of opposition Nehemiah, as a mature endowment gift leader, proved to be unflappable. He never wavered from his sense of mission and refused to be delayed or driven off course from his purpose. Nehemiah countered every move of his enemies with prayer, and the Lord gave him a plan: he set up a round-the-clock guard duty against them, and during the day, with half the skilled men and laborers working with a tool in one hand and a weapon in the other, the other half stood guard watching their backs.[76]

For every scheme the enemies of the children of Israel devised against them, Nehemiah was given the necessary discernment and understanding to foil their attempts at treachery. They began a concerted campaign to dishearten everyone engaged in the building of the wall, but Nehemiah continually spoke words of encouragement to the workers and bolstered their confidence, reminding them that God's hand of protection was over them. When Sanballat saw that his every move was failing, he then invited Nehemiah to come meet with him outside of Jerusalem—which, of course, the man of God flatly refused. Nehemiah, steadfast in his calling and sure in his authority, responded to

Sanballat by saying, *"I am engaged in a great work, so I can't come. Why should I stop working to come and meet with you?"*[77]

The work of Yahweh went on as the people of God continued in their task. Jerusalem was strengthened as her walls were rebuilt. The walls that had been nothing but rubble for so many years were completed in just fifty-two days! Strong and impenetrable, Jerusalem would no longer be vulnerable to her enemies nor embarrassed by her weakness.

Nehemiah proved to be a mover, a shaker, and a doer. Everything he did had the hand of God all over it. He demonstrated the characteristics of the endowment gift of leadership from start to finish. The walls of Jerusalem stood firm and tall once more.

Other Biblical Presiders

❖ Joseph: Genesis 30-40
❖ Deborah: Judges 4-5
❖ David: 1 Samuel 16-31, 1 Kings 1-2, 1 Chronicles 10:13-30
❖ James: Matthew 13:55; Mark 6:3; Acts 12:17, 15:13, 21:18; 1 Corinthians 15:7; Galatians 1:19
❖ Jairus: Matthew 9:18, Mark 5:22-43, Luke 8:41-45

7. THE GOOD SAMARITAN, MERCY GIVER

The story of the Good Samaritan provides a revealing portrayal of the endowment gift of mercy in action. Jesus told this parable to illustrate the simple message that God requires each one of us to treat the needy and afflicted with kindness and compassion, without reservation or partiality.

An expert in the Law of Moses had just asked of Jesus who is included in the category of a "neighbor" in God's command to "love your neighbor as yourself."[78]

Jesus replied and said, "A man was going down from Jerusalem to Jericho, and fell among robbers, and they stripped him and beat him, and went away leaving him half dead. And by chance a priest

was going down on that road, and when he saw him, he passed
by on the other side. Likewise a Levite also, when he came to the
place and saw him, passed by on the other side. But a Samaritan,
who was on a journey, came upon him; and when he saw him, he
felt compassion, and came to him and bandaged up his wounds,
pouring oil and wine on them; and he put him on his own beast,
and brought him to an inn and took care of him. On the next day
he took out two denarii and gave them to the innkeeper and said,
'Take care of him; and whatever more you spend, when I return I
will repay you.' Which of these three do you think proved to be a
neighbor to the man who fell into the robbers' hands?"

(Luke 10:30-36)

In this account both the priest and the Levite purposely chose not to involve themselves in the plight of a battered and bleeding fellow countryman who was lying on the road half dead. By making their way around him and passing on the other side of the road, each showed just how shallow and meaningless his spiritual beliefs were. Clearly, while each man had "head knowledge" of the Lord through the Scriptures, both the priest and the Levite had hearts that were far from His.

It was only the Samaritan, a member of a despised sect of "half-breed" Jews, who was moved with compassion when he came upon this pitiful scene. The Samaritan's heart went out to this stranger who had been so badly beaten, stripped of his clothes, and left to die by robbers. The gift of mercy within him caused the Samaritan to become so concerned about the wounded man's well-being that he went far out of his way to make sure he would be safe and restored back to health.

To be sure, the Samaritan had previously made his own plans for that day. He was on a journey and certainly did not anticipate having it interrupted by such an awful scene. However, his response to the dire need in front of him was to feel compassion. It welled up within him so much so that he put aside his own agenda and decided at that moment to sacrifice his own plans in order to help the stranger in distress. The first thing he did was to meet the most immediate need in front of him, which was to bandage the man's wounds. The Samaritan found some cloth as well as oil and wine among his provisions, and with them he treated the stranger's injuries.

His schedule for the day was now in ruins, and he had given some of his goods for the man's treatment. At this point the Samaritan decided to give up his own personal comfort as well. The wounded stranger needed to be brought to a safe place to recuperate, which meant that the Samaritan would now have to give up his own personal transportation and let the injured man ride. He put the man "on his own beast" and walked alongside to steady him until they reached an inn.

At this point the Samaritan nursed the wounded stranger overnight and gave the innkeeper the equivalent of two days' wages so that the injured man could continue to heal there at the inn. This was all done for a person who was unknown to him until the previous day!

The example of the Good Samaritan shows that there is a cost to exercising this gift of mercy. The empathy he felt caused him to serve the man in distress in a sacrificial way. The priest and the Levite had allowed themselves to be ruled by the cold calculations of the head. Not so with the Samaritan; he was ruled by his heart and was willing to do whatever was necessary to remove the suffering and restore the well-being of the afflicted. If it cost him his time, comfort, goods, and even his finances—so be it! If it meant caring for someone from another culture or religious group that despised his own—so be it! This is the gift of mercy in action.

Other Biblical Mercy Givers

- ◈ John the Apostle: The Gospel of John and 1, 2 & 3 John
- ◈ Hosea: book of Hosea
- ◈ Jeremiah: Books of Jeremiah and Lamentations; called by some "the weeping prophet"
- ◈ Ruth: book of Ruth
- ◈ Dorcas (Tabitha): Acts 9:36
- ◈ Onesiphorus: 2 Timothy 1:16-18

Questions: Chapter Six

1. The Book our Maker has given us reflects His keen desire for _____.

2. Each one of the persons portrayed in the Bible had strengths and _____ as well as character issues like us all.

3. Each one of the characters in the Bible was chosen by their Maker to fulfill a _____ which, of course, He knew about well in advance.

4. **Peter** demonstrated a combination of boldness mixed with _____ which is a characteristic of the gift of prophecy.

5. The impetuosity that Peter displayed so frequently stemmed mainly from his passion to do right in the eyes of the Lord and his utter _____ to truth.

6. Simon Peter also revealed an ability to be open about his own faults, though, like many prophets, he had difficulty _____ forgiveness.

7. **Martha** was a woman with the gift of ministry who viewed acts of service as a _____ demonstration of love.

8. Jesus addressed a _____ in Martha that is common with those who are endowed with the gift of service—to become fretful about the task at hand.

9. Martha, like so many with the endowment gift of serving, had gotten off track when she allowed her busyness to interfere with her _____ with the Lord.

10. **Ezra** had been a seeker after _____ from his earliest years.

11. As Ezra grew in his understanding of the Holy Scriptures and in his ability as a _____, he also developed a reputation for wisdom, dedication, and integrity.

12. Ezra demonstrated the importance of the teaching gift in the process of restoring God's people, bringing about revival, and impacting future _____.

13. **Barnabas** proved to be a trailblazer for the early church, one who left behind believers who were uplifted and _____ wherever he went.

14. Time and again Barnabas demonstrated a trait that is typical of the endowment gift of encouragement—a genuine concern for the spiritual _____ of others.

15. Barnabas had fulfilled his own personal destiny as an encourager and had been greatly used by the Lord in _____ the kingdom of God.

16. **Abraham**, "the father of our faith," provided an example of the way of _____ for all who are givers, whether or not their predominant endowment gift is sharing.

17. Abraham showed a peculiar _____ of interest in the comforts that the world around him had to offer.

18. Abraham's hospitality to three strangers resulted in him being blessed with a _____ that in a year's time Sarah would give birth to a son for whom they had waited so long.

19. It is clear that **Nehemiah** was not only a man with a vision but also one with a _____.

20. Nehemiah displayed great wisdom and ability in his planning and _____ skills.

21. Nehemiah proved to be brilliant in _____ the work effort of rebuilding Jerusalem's walls.

22. The **Good Samaritan's** heart went out to the _____ who had been so badly beaten, stripped of his clothes and left to die by robbers.

23. The example of the Good Samaritan shows that there is a _____ to the exercise of this gift of mercy.

24. The Samaritan was ruled by his heart and was willing to do whatever was _____ to remove the suffering and restore the well-being of the afflicted.

Chapter Seven

A PORTRAIT OF PERFECTION

Jesus Christ and the Endowment Gifts

*J**esus Christ is worthy of all praise!* Whether or not you have arrived at
the realization that He indeed is *"the way, the truth and the life,"* as
He said,[1] has no bearing on the excellence of who He is and always
will be. There is none like Him—nor will there ever be. He is magnificent beyond compare.

Pondering the awesomeness of Emmanuel—"God with us"—brings
us rapidly to a place of understanding. Yahweh, the Lord of the Universe,
is not the unmoved Mover of the philosophers but is the Almighty One
who cares enough to have sent us His only Son. Yeshua came to us with
outstretched arms, wanting to embrace us and lavish His warm-hearted
affection upon us.

Jesus also lived to please His Father. Willing to serve eternal purposes, He came to us in humility in the form of a simple man. Born
to peasants, He was right at home with the common folk. The Father's
plan involved His suffering at the hands of the unrighteous and dying
in ignominy and shame. That was alright with Him because He believed in us and, most of all, because He cared.

How was Jesus able to live a life so full of wisdom, grace, and mercy that we read about in the Holy Scriptures? Assuredly, He was appointed to His earthly mission *"before the foundation of the world,"*[2] but how did the Son of Man live to such matchless perfection? After all, did He not "empty Himself" by giving up His divine privileges when He was born as a human being?[3] The excellence of His character and the purity of His motives are certainly of divine origin, but they were accomplished by the *man* Christ Jesus. Every aspect of His character was formed by the spiritual DNA within Him. The great difference between our Savior and the rest of mankind was the *measure* of grace that was upon Him. To operate in perfection in all seven endowment gifts as He did is supernatural—beyond the capability of mortal man. Fortunately for us, He was transparent about the way He lived. He was sensitive to the voice of the Father at all times and submitted His will to His Father's plan. Through His spiritual sensitivity and obedience Yeshua developed the giftings within Him to *full* maturity.

It is intriguing how characters portrayed in the pages of the Bible grow in depth when viewed in terms of their endowment gifts. Even the so-called "heroes" of our faith are depicted in the Scriptures with "warts and wrinkles," letting us know they really were as human as ourselves. Abraham, for example, was great in faith and generosity of spirit, but suffered from momentary lapses in judgment which caused conflict and hardship that endures to this day. In Yeshua, however, we come to view and understand what each gift looks like when fully operated and empowered by the Holy Spirit. Contrary to all other personages, whose imperfections grow larger when examined more closely, the magnificence of Jesus' persona becomes even more resplendent. As we gaze through the lens of Scripture at His endowment gifting we discover a truth that is simply amazing. Jesus operated in each gift to perfection!

If we reflect upon the awesomeness of this insight for even a moment we shall come to a greater appreciation of who the Son of Man really was. It was humanly impossible for anyone to have traveled along such an arduous path and blessed so many along the way and to have done it without fault. Though legalists and nit-pickers were quick to point out areas in which He seemingly broke the Law—such as performing miracles on the Sabbath and touching an "unclean" leper—He was merely showing us all how absolutely *huge* the heart of God really is. Our heavenly Father's love is far beyond the limitations of our puny imagination. Though some find perverse comfort in the mistaken notion that Yahweh is most concerned about mankind's adherence to a list of "do's and don'ts" delivered by Moses, Yeshua revealed that the greater purposes of Yahweh are all centered on His love. The astounding truth is that Jesus revealed this by simply operating in His endowment gifting!

The eyes of our understanding are enlightened. As we look at the perfection with which Jesus operated in all the endowment gifts, we find incontrovertible proof that He was Emmanuel. None other than God in the flesh could have accomplished such a feat. In fact, the human mind is incapable of conceiving of such a character as perfect as Jesus the Messiah. If we were to search the entirety of literature and drama throughout all of human civilization, as well as the annals of history, no other person would shine as brightly as the Nazarene called Jesus. And yet, still more amazing was that He never even once pointed to His own perfection. Instead He gave all the honor and glory to Yahweh, His Father.

The divine inspiration of Scripture is also attested to by the accounts of Yeshua operating in each of the gifts to perfection. The Gospels record at least seven instances for each of the seven gifts. Since the Gospel writers undoubtedly had no knowledge of the endowment gifts when they were writing, it is evident that the Holy Spirit Himself inspired them to include these particular incidents in Jesus' ministry. Through their accounts we find that Yeshua did what is humanly impossible—operate in all seven gifts to perfection.

1. JESUS THE PROPHET

> "... for the testimony of Jesus is the spirit of prophecy."
> *Revelation 19:10*

Everything Jesus Christ did was *spiritually* discerned. According to His own testimony, He never initiated anything based on His five natural senses. Whatever He saw and heard in the spirit realm—*that* was what He did.

Everything was based on His relationship with Yahweh. According to Yeshua's own words, *"... the Son can do nothing of Himself, unless it is something He sees the Father doing; for whatever the Father does, these things the Son also does in like manner."*[4] In short, the Son lived in a continual state of dependency, relying on His Father's direction. He lived and ministered by following the initiatives of heaven. His was a totally different way of being.

Yeshua, as an endowment gift prophet, had "spiritual radar" that was ready at all times to discern the hearts of men. The Gospels describe numerous occasions when He read the minds of His disciples as well as the thoughts of the Pharisees and Sadducees, who were His implacable foes.[5] He also had the ability to sense when others were drawing from His anointing, such as when He was in the midst of a throng and a woman with an issue of blood touched Him and was instantly healed.[6]

Jesus never backed off from controversy when the truth was at stake. He confronted hypocrisy head-on, such as when He called the scribes and Pharisees a *"brood of vipers"* and *"whited sepulchers."*[7] Even in the last few days of His ministry He faced wickedness in a way that was bold and audacious. As the Messiah threw the peddlers and moneychangers out of the Temple for turning His Father's *"house of prayer ... into a den of thieves ..."*[8] He overturned tables and chairs with a whip in His hand. The Lion of the tribe of Judah had no qualms about standing up for His Father's good name—especially when He came against religious pretense and corruption.

Jesus was a bright light shining in the darkness. Through His very presence lies and deception were exposed. The forces of darkness plotted against Him, seeking His demise, simply because He was the Light. The religious leaders targeted Him with their intrigues. Time and again they schemed to destroy His reputation and His very life, even being so foolish as to claim that His power was demonic.[9] But Jesus the Anointed was the matchless champion of the spirit realm who plots and prevailed every time. The words He spoke o' powers of darkness, for truly He was the Word made He conquered even the forces of death and hell.[11]

The crowds, seeking a touch or a sign, followed Jesus wherever He went. Through it all, the Master maintained a heavenly perspective during the rise of His popularity by never departing from the narrow way. At times the throngs demanded His attention, yet Yeshua was still able to find respite and solitude.[12] When it became necessary, He secluded Himself to commune with "Abba," for His Father was also His best friend. Among His twelve disciples there were three—Peter, James, and John— whom He chose to accompany Him at special moments. However, at His greatest hour of need, in the Garden of Gethsemane, these three failed Him miserably. All He asked for them to do was support Him in prayer during His time of tribulation.[13] This proved to be too much for His closest friends, however, for within an hour they were fast asleep.

It was the gift of prophecy in Yeshua that caused His fiercest opposition. Having the darkness of their wicked hearts exposed was too much for the religious imposters to handle. Instead of receiving the Truth, they chose to strike back by sending their own Messiah to an agonizing death. In reality, however, Yeshua went of His own free will for His suffering had been ordained by the Father. Our loving Savior embraced suffering for our sake. He extended His grace because of our need for forgiveness.

2. JESUS THE MINISTER

"...the Son of Man did not come to be served, but to serve, and to give His life as a ransom for many." Mark 10:45

The prophet Isaiah provided a clear message to Israel that its awaited Messiah would come as a suffering servant. Yahweh announced through the prophet that *"... (the) Righteous One, My Servant, will justify the many ..."* but would also be *"... despised and rejected of men."*[14] This astounding revelation concerning the Promised One of Israel was clear enough, but was one that few were able to grasp: the Messiah was to come as Yahweh's servant but would be rejected by the very people to whom He was sent.

The circumstances of Jesus' birth foreshadowed both the humility that would characterize His life and ministry and the unyielding rejection He would experience at the hands of the leaders of Israel. He came into this world in a lowly stable in Bethlehem because, as the Scripture records, there was no room at the local inn that night.[15] This humble start for the promised Messiah was an early indication that the only begotten of the Father would live and minister as a true servant but would find little accommodation during His sojourn. It also hinted at the process Yahweh would use to develop the gift of service in Him, training the Son of Man in meekness and submission as He grew as well as sensitizing Him to the needs of ordinary people along the way.

It is clear that Jesus was geared toward helping those He ministered to in down-to-earth ways and never sought recognition for Himself or the approval of man. He was trained in practical skills by working with His hands as a carpenter—learning the trade of Joseph His stepfather.

When the Master taught, His emphasis was always on a pure and simple way of living, with His life being a primary example. The qualities of humility and simplicity were also the basis of His teaching when He addressed the multitudes. At the Sermon on the Mount, near the very start of His ministry, He spoke about how blessed it is to be "... *humble in spirit ... meek ... merciful ... [and] pure in heart.*"[16] As Jesus finished His message He wanted to make sure that His words, though contrary to a worldly or selfish point of view, were not taken as lofty idealism but rather as a wise and solid foundation on which to build one's life: "*But anyone who hears My teaching and doesn't obey it is foolish, like a person who builds a house on sand.*"[17] The vain philosophies and supposed wisdom of this world have very little in common with the simple yet enduring truths that Yeshua imparted. In the end, when all else fails, it is His words that will remain.

The Master coached His disciples and others on the importance of self-denial and humility and frequently pointed them toward His own servanthood as an example. His life was open for them to see, and He invited His followers to *"Take my yoke ... and learn of me ..."*[18] The yoke Jesus spoke of was His submission to the Father's will and His readiness to be directed by Yahweh. Many other traits of the endowment gift of ministry are symbolized by a yoke as well, but the basic idea Yeshua was sharing with the Twelve is the notion of ministry as humble service.

One sign of a true minister is obedience, the measure of which is whether a person is seeking his own will or that of another who is above him in authority. Yeshua modeled submission to the Father continually. One day He brought out a startling revelation about Himself to a crowd in Capernaum concerning His origin and purpose: *"I have come down from heaven, not to do my own will, but the will of him who sent me."*[19] The Son of Man was on a mission that had been ordained in heaven, and hearing and obeying His Father's voice was the means by which He would accomplish that assignment. Finding the Father's will and purpose in every circumstance was of paramount importance. Though Yeshua's obedience was tested time and again, He was found faithful and true in all ways. Even when faced with His ultimate challenge, submitting to the suffering and shame of the cross at Calvary, the Messiah was victorious because of His obedience as a servant—one on a mission from above.[20]

There is a right and a wrong way to do almost anything, including operating in your gifting. Yeshua never imposed Himself or the gifts within Him on anyone in need who was reluctant to receive from Him. For example, He asked a crippled man at the pool of Bethesda, who had been waiting there many years for his healing, *"Are you willing to be made whole?"*[21] Of course, in this instance and many others, the Master's willingness and ability to deliver and heal was never in doubt. However, at times the unbelief of those in need was able to block the Lord's capacity to help.[22] The wisdom of the Son of Man's approach contains a lesson for all with the endowment gift of ministry: never let your eagerness to help take precedence over an intended recipient's willingness to receive.

Jesus Christ lived His life as He taught: the way to greatness is through service to others.[23] Though His fame spread far and wide due to the mighty wonders He performed, Yeshua never sought the limelight for Himself. His motive was always to glorify His Father and to help people in need. At times He would even minister in secret so as not to attract attention, instructing those who had been healed to tell no one. There were even occasions when the Master ministered incognito so that the healed person didn't even know by whose hands he had been made well.[24]

The importance of service was portrayed dramatically by the Master one night just before He was crucified. Yeshua and the twelve disciples were gathered to share supper in the Upper Room. Knowing He would have just a few hours more to be with them, Jesus chose to share an experience they would never forget. Just before dinner, He stripped to His waist, poured water into a bowl and, with a towel in hand, began to wash the feet of each one of the disciples.[25] This was certainly a most startling and awkward turn of events for His followers—Rabbi Yeshua taking on the lowly role of a servant!

This surprising portrayal of servitude forever shattered any lingering illusion the disciples may have clung to about the nature of serving Yahweh. The Messiah's example was intended to make an indelible imprint on their minds about a lesson He had stressed throughout their time ministering together—that He had not come to be served but to serve.[26] And yet, even after the Twelve had witnessed Jesus sacrifice His own needs so often for the sake of others, and saw that personal gain had no place in His agenda, this scene still left them in a state of shock.

The Master's lesson was so intimate and personal that the reality of service was now starting to dawn on each of them: selfishness, personal ambition, and strife would have to be rooted out of their hearts. This realization was alarming but at the same time brought liberation concerning their view of the Messiah. From that night forward those whom He had chosen would never be able to forget that "Yeshua ha Meshiah" was also "Yeshua the Servant"—and that they were called to serve as well.

3. JESUS THE TEACHER

He taught truth concerning the kingdom of God and eternal life

"You call me 'The Rabbi' and 'The Master,' and rightly so, for such I am." John 13:13 (WNT)

The endowment gift of teaching in Yeshua's life was simply astounding. At the age of twelve, when most children would be outside playing, Jesus was found by His parents instructing the leaders of Israel at the Temple in Jerusalem![27] The Gospel of Luke records that just after the Passover, a time when some of the great teachers of Israel were gathered at the Temple, Jesus was seated in their midst *"… listening to them and asking them questions…"* and that *"… all who heard Him were astonished and overwhelmed with bewildered wonder at His intelligence and understanding and His replies."*[28] This episode of young Jesus "teaching the teachers" was so remarkable that it is the only incident in the Messiah's growing years recorded in Scripture.

Jesus had been on a quest for truth from His earliest years. At the very start of His ministry, after having been tested by the devil in the wilderness, He stood up in the synagogue in Nazareth and read a portion of Scripture from the book of Isaiah, which said:

The spirit of the Lord is upon me, because He has anointed me to preach the gospel to the poor. He has sent me to proclaim release to the captives and recovery of sight to the blind, to set free those who are oppressed, to proclaim the favorable year of the Lord.[29]

At the conclusion of His reading the Son of Man told the congregation, *"Today this Scripture has been fulfilled in your hearing."* Clearly Yeshua had been searching the Scriptures over the years to discover the truth about His calling. Sometime during that pursuit He had come to a dramatic conclusion concerning who He really was. From that point forward, the authority with which He taught and the truths of His message were so compelling that oftentimes His listeners were in awe of His teaching. For example, even in Yeshua's hometown of Nazareth, where He was met with much skepticism because people knew Him merely as the son of Joseph the carpenter and Mary, they wondered, *"Where did He get all this wisdom...?"*[30] In fact, that was a common reaction. His teaching was so remarkable that, as He went from town to town in Galilee teaching in synagogues, amazement was the most common reaction.[31]

Even in Jerusalem, where He was forced to stay out of public view because the religious leaders were plotting to kill Him,[32] Scripture records that as He taught, *"The Jews then were astonished, saying, 'How has this man become learned, having never been educated?'"*[33] Though they were bitterly opposed to Him, the leadership could not deny the wisdom and understanding by which He taught. In fact, Nicodemus, a member of the ruling Sanhedrin, came to Yeshua one night and said, *"Rabbi, we all know you're a teacher straight from God."*[34] However, despite such a humble admission, the religious establishment proved to be incapable of understanding that the source of His authority and power was the inherent truth of His teachings, the gifting with which He'd been endowed, and His close relationship with Yahweh.

One of the most obvious aspects of Jesus' ministry was His knack for attracting a crowd. Whenever He held a special teaching event, such as the Sermon on the Mount,[35] thousands would walk from near and far to come out to hear Him. The Master had an incomparable ability to capture the heart and imagination of the people. Because of His unique insight and special gifting He imparted the most elusive and esoteric truths in such a down-to-earth way that simple farming folk and tradesmen could grasp its meaning. For example, when Jesus spoke of the invisible realm of the kingdom of God, He illustrated His point with things from everyday life with which common people could relate. He spoke of household items such as salt and leaven and used animals such as sheep and goats to illustrate His point. His stories were about activities familiar to everyone—sowing and reaping, threshing, casting a net, and receiving wages.

The apparent simplicity with which the Master taught was deceptive, however, because His instruction usually contained unfathomable truths that needed to be searched out. For example, Jesus' parables invariably had several levels of meaning, with the deeper truths intended only for those who came near to Him, such as His twelve disciples. From this we see that one of His purposes was to draw people to the truth. The wisdom of Yeshua's teaching methods can be better appreciated when it is understood that His stories customarily directed the hearer toward the truth but required the listener to become engaged such that he would be able to draw his own conclusions.

The aspect of Jesus' teaching ministry that infuriated the Pharisees most was that He refrained from judging immorality.[36] Unlike the religious nit-pickers of His day, the Nazarene's primary focus was on issues of the heart rather than outward behavior. His teaching went to the root of sin rather than to its leaves and fruit. He modeled fairness with everyone, taught mercy, and reserved His condemnation for religious hypocrisy and oppression. However, as hard as they tried, the fastidious religious leaders of Israel were unable to refute His teaching. They were confounded at every turn because, as He told them, *"… My teaching is not My own, but His Who sent Me."*[37] Yeshua exposed the pretense of their self-righteousness for all to see and denounced the heavy religious bondage they had imposed on God's people. His honesty was intolerable and so they sought to silence the Messiah and His band of followers forever.

By definition, a rabbi, or teacher, must have at least one disciple or learner.[38] As was the custom among the teachers of Israel in His day, Rabbi[39] Yeshua handpicked the disciples who would follow Him. Interestingly, the twelve young men He chose were ones who had been overlooked or rejected by other rabbis.[40] It was upon these, who had left everything behind to follow Him, which Yeshua poured out most of His time and effort.[41] To this committed dozen He shared the hidden meaning of the parables that were veiled to others.

Jesus had so much to share because of the closeness of His relationship with the Father. He employed every opportunity as a teaching moment, modeling for His disciples the very essence of His teaching. They lived side-by-side and learned every day by His example, His instruction, and even by His rebukes.[42] The Master was able to impart life-changing teaching to His disciples such that they, and every spiritual generation since that time, were willing to go to the ends of the earth to deliver His message.

4. JESUS THE ENCOURAGER

He encouraged His disciples and all He came in contact with to grow in spiritual maturity.

Jesus' ability with words was renowned. Large crowds showed up whenever news got out that He was going to be speaking. One day when Yeshua was in Jerusalem the ruling priests and Pharisees decided to clamp down on His growing influence over the people by having Him arrested and brought to the Temple for questioning. When the Temple police who were sent to arrest Jesus came back empty-handed, the exasperated leaders questioned them about their failure. Embarrassed, the Temple officers offered up the excuse, *"Have you heard the way he talks? We've never heard anyone speak like this man."* The confounded authorities responded sarcastically, *"Are you carried away like the rest of the rabble?"*[43] By failing to bring Jesus to their superiors at the Temple, the police had proved the remarkable impact Jesus' words had on almost everyone.

Yeshua encountered all kinds of people as He ministered, including the demon-possessed, unsavory tax collectors, women of ill-repute, and lepers. He treated all of them with kindness. His friendliness toward sinners and social outcasts even caused the religious leaders to accuse the Messiah of being a sinner Himself.[44] Though many of those He ministered to were shunned by their neighbors and classified as "sinners" by religious folks, Jesus proved to be a friend to all.

For example, one day as Yeshua was traveling through Samaria He stopped at a village where He met a local woman drawing water at the village well.[45] Jesus engaged her in a conversation, though according to the customs in those days it was highly inappropriate for a Hebrew man to talk with a Samaritan woman, especially in public. They discussed spiritual matters and problems in her life, and Jesus provided her with godly counsel. However, when His disciples came by and saw them engaged in a discussion, Scripture says *they were shocked. They couldn't believe he was talking with that kind of a woman.*[46] The Master, being the type of person who "never met a stranger" and nonjudgmental by nature, wasn't fazed in the slightest by their reaction. He was more concerned about the woman's spiritual well-being and helping her change the course of her life than He was with fitting into the mold of social conformity or being pressured by the expectations of His disciples.

Everywhere Jesus went, and in almost everything He did, He demonstrated a concern for the spiritual development of those around Him. Whether preaching at a public gathering, counseling one-on-one, or in a small group setting, Yeshua continually helped people reach a higher level of spiritual understanding. Just one of many examples was when Nicodemus, a member of the ruling council, came to the Master under cover of darkness seeking spiritual guidance. Jesus was open and honest with Nicodemus and gave him a basic lesson in the ABCs of the kingdom of God. He explained in detail the need to be born again, taught him about the Father's love for mankind, and outlined many other key aspects needed to understand the ways of Yahweh. This spiritual leader of Israel was raised to a totally new spiritual level because of this one secret nighttime counseling session, and from that point forward Nicodemus became a secret follower of Jesus.[47]

When a person is discouraged, an encourager will be stirred into action to help bring about a remedy. When Yeshua predicted to Simon Peter that he would deny Him three times the night He was arrested, Peter boldly proclaimed, *"Even if I have to die with You, I will not deny You."*[48] As we all know, the Lord's words proved to be true. Peter ended up profanely calling on God as he falsely claimed that he didn't even know his friend Jesus, and his disavowal almost immediately produced great humiliation and a deep wound within him. The Scripture merely informs us that *"he wept bitterly,"*[49] but we know from Peter's later actions that he suffered from overwhelming shame. His bravado and self-confidence had collapsed into a heap of self-recrimination and guilt.

Apparently his remorse gnawed at his conscience day and night because it wasn't long before Simon Peter made up his mind to go back to his former trade of fishing. Evidently he figured that by doing so he could leave his disappointment and failure behind. However, Yeshua was not going to leave His friend in such a state of confusion and regret. As an encourager the Messiah came to Peter while he was fishing and asked him three times—once for each denial—whether he loved Him. Of course, Peter's love for his Lord was never in doubt despite his terrible failure the fateful night of the Master's trial. Jesus forced Peter to affirm his love so that he could begin his journey on the road to recovery.

Jesus displayed a matchless ability to take spiritual truth and put it in a nutshell so that it could be remembered and put to use. Some of His guidance came in the form of practical steps to develop spiritually. Other advice provided basic pointers by which His followers could develop godly priorities. These are just four from a multitude of examples:

◈ The model prayer Yeshua gave His disciples, which begins with *"Our Father who is in heaven…,"* was intended to provide a pattern for prayer.[50]

◈ Jesus' guidance to *"seek ye first the kingdom of God and His righteousness…"* gave a simple two-point summary of how a follower should prioritize the issues in his personal life.[51]

◈ The Master's instruction to *"have faith in God,"* *"speak to the mountain"* with steadfast trust, and walk in forgiveness provided guidelines for activating faith which, when employed, will overcome intractable problems.[52]

◈ The Great Commission provided a mission statement for Yeshua's followers, as well as the general principles by which God's kingdom is to be advanced.

Throughout His ministry the Messiah gave positive exhortations intended to break down the barriers of carnal thinking and to challenge all who heard Him to a grow to higher level of spiritual maturity. One of the greatest examples recorded in Scripture was at the Sermon of the Mount where He encouraged God's people to *"... love your enemies ... do good ... bless ... give ... lend ... be merciful ... judge not ...."*[53] The "friend to all" has an encouraging word for every one of us. What a friend we have in Jesus, our encourager!

5. YESHUA THE GIVER

He gave Himself as "a ransom for many" and gave continually as He ministered.

Sharing was a way of life for Yeshua. The Son of Man gave of Himself and everything He had because of the spirit of generosity within Him. The Lord was so dedicated to giving that He didn't even have a place of His own to find respite in all His comings and goings. Jesus said, *"The foxes have holes and the birds of the air have nests, but the Son of Man has nowhere to lay His head."*[54] The Messiah was constantly aware that His stay here on earth would be brief, and so He didn't give temporal things a moment's thought. His attention was focused on fulfilling His mission.

Our Savior told His disciples He only did those things He saw His Father do.[55] Yeshua saw His own life here on earth as a gift from God to mankind. He told Nicodemus that *"God so loved the world that He gave His only begotten Son...."*[56] Jesus was speaking of Himself as the Son who had been given by God. The Father had given Him to anyone who is willing to receive Him.

During Yeshua's time on earth He poured out His life for us all. He gave us His everything until His very last breath while hanging on a cross. He gave His own back, having been whipped, for our healing and offered up Himself as a sacrifice. He had given His own life to be a ransom for many. Salvation was now available for us all.

Scripture tells us that the Son of God willingly gave up everything for our benefit. The apostle Paul wrote, *"For you know the grace of our Lord Jesus Christ, that though He was rich, yet for your sake He became poor, so that you through His poverty might become rich."*[57] Our worthy Savior did this for humanity, which does not even deserve it. Truly this was the God-kind of love in action—giving lavishly to those who merit nothing.

By His life and actions Yeshua provided us with a model for giving. He also taught us about giving. He said that accumulation of "stuff" was for non-believers.[58] He instructed His own to *"lay not up for yourselves treasures upon earth…but lay up for yourselves treasures in heaven…."*[59] The dilemma everyone must face is that *"no one can serve two masters…You cannot serve both God and money."*[60]

Jesus left us with both His words and His deeds to follow. He spoke of the *"… deceitfulness of riches"*[61] and taught that we should give with a pure motive, one that God could smile upon. When we share what we have with those in need, it shouldn't be done to be admired by others, "tooting our own horn," nor should we let our left hand know what our right hand is doing. When a person gives as unto the Lord, He is the One who will reward us.[62]

The type of generosity our Savior taught can only be understood in light of the magnitude of the gift we have received. The parable that illustrated this point was about a man who was forgiven a huge debt that he could never repay.[63] Each one of us who has received the free gift that came down from heaven—the salvation of our Lord Jesus Christ—is as that man. "For-give-ness" is at the very heart of the message of the Good News. It is essential for us to appreciate the immense generosity of which we are the beneficiaries. With hearts filled with gratitude we ought to give to others according to the same grand measure by which we have already been "for-given." Stinginess on our part reflects a lack of true appreciation and will result in our own sorrow and loss.

Yeshua referred to His standard of generosity several times in His message at the Sermon on the Mount. If a follower really heeds the Master's words, it's clear he will need to tap into the God-kind of love to put Jesus' standard into practice: *"Give away to everyone who begs of you [who is in want of necessities], and of him who takes away from you your goods, do not demand or require them back again.*"[64] Jesus' stance toward the needs of others and our own possessions is 180 degrees opposite to the world's system and the view of most Christians. Nonetheless, our Lord gave it as an instruction for anyone who would follow Him: give freely and expect nothing in return.

Fortunately Jesus did not leave it there. Just a few verses later Yeshua promised: *"Give, and it shall be given to you, good measure pressed down and shaken together and running over, they shall give into your bosom. For with the same measure that you measure, it shall be measured to you again."*[65] The insight from combining both of Yeshua's statements is that we're to give with a pure heart but know that our giving is not in vain. There is a recompense for giving, and it is measured out according to the measure by which we have given.

When Yahweh's anointing operates through someone endowed with the gift of sharing, He has a way of making provision even when a source of supply isn't apparent. One day Jesus and His disciples decided to relax from their hectic schedule and go off to a remote countryside spot to take a break.[66] However, word started to spread round about that Yeshua was nearby. It wasn't long before a huge crowd, more than five thousand, showed up. They wanted to hear the Master teach. Though this unexpected multitude ruined His plan to take a rest, Yeshua felt compassion for those who had come out to hear Him. He gave an impromptu teaching that lasted until late in the afternoon.

After He was done speaking the people were hungry and there was no nearby place to get food. The disciples asked around and found that very little was at hand—just five loaves of bread and two fishes that a boy had with him. Undaunted, the Savior took the loaves of bread in His hands, lifted them up to God, and blessed them. Jesus then broke the bread into pieces and handed them to the disciples, who in turn doled out the bread among the people. Jesus repeated the process by doing the same with the two fishes. When everything had been handed out the people ate until they were full—all five thousand of them. Then the disciples collected the leftovers and filled twelve baskets with them! The multiplication witnessed that day shows that, no matter the circumstance, when the power of God is working through a giver the need *will* be met.

The endowment gift of giving that Jesus Christ demonstrated was not only for those days in which He ministered on the earth. Yeshua Himself was in fact the ultimate endowment of the Father to every one of us. Through Him all the promises of God are yea and amen.[67] Because of Jesus we experience a generational blessing as *"...the true children of Abraham. [We] are his heirs, and God's promise to Abraham belongs to [us]."*[68] Yet, even more than that, the "complete package" of our gift includes the privilege for us, His spiritual sons and daughters, to enter into God's presence and live with Him in eternity. Truly the impact of Yeshua's endowment gift of giving is to all generations and for all time.

6. JESUS THE LEADER

He took dominion and authority over everything that opposed kingdom purposes.

Yeshua's dynamic personality was as compelling as the truths He revealed. The majority of people He addressed were like many in our day—lukewarm with self-centered interests. But they also wanted to experience more in their lives. The Messiah's engaging presence had a way of shaking up those around Him. His vibrant persona was imprinted with the "seal of approval" of Yahweh's Spirit, and signs and wonders followed wherever He went.

Yeshua was equipped by His gifting as a leader to get things done. He was a man of action on a mission from heaven. Today's popular image of Him falls far short of the reality of His commanding presence. He lived in an age without electronics and sound systems and yet His booming voice was loud enough to be heard by a crowd of more than five thousand.[69] He had such staying power that He could hike long distances on the dusty trails of Judea and Galilee and no sooner arrive at His destination than an expectant multitude would be gathered to hear Him preach. Except for setting aside time for rest and prayer, the

Son of Man never let fatigue dictate His agenda or interfere with taking care of the people's needs.

Jesus presented His followers with a compelling vision that was never intended for the fainthearted. The plan He set before them called for active involvement on their part. They were to leave the comfort of their surroundings and go into the whole world to preach the Good News of God's kingdom. Furthermore, the Master's mandate required personal sacrifice from each one who would go forth in His name. It would have a daily cost, for He said, *"If any of you wants to be My follower, you must turn from your selfish ways, take up your cross daily, and follow Me."*[70] But His vision involved great rewards as well: the promise of His Spirit, being filled with the fullness of God, abiding in His presence now and in eternity as well as rewards beyond our imagination or comprehension.[71]

Part of the leadership endowment gift involves organizing and administering. Yeshua never did things just "any old way," haphazardly leading His followers onward. His great purpose required a plan and an organization that involved His followers at their various levels of commitment. First the Savior shared His vision, the Good News of God's kingdom, with the multitudes. From this crowd He selected seventy for special training and sent them out two-by-two into the towns and villages of Galilee, proclaiming the gospel of the kingdom.[72]

More familiar to us than the seventy, however, are His twelve disciples.[73] Jesus chose these individuals to be His close associates, the ones with whom He devoted most of His time and effort. They lived with Him, and He shared special secrets with them, training them in every way. These were to be His leaders in advancing God's kingdom once He was taken from their midst. Within the twelve disciples, there was also a group of three, the ones with whom He would share special life-changing experiences and revelation as well. The three—Peter, James, and John—were His "inner circle" of friends. They accompanied Him on extraordinary occasions, such as when He went up on a mountain and was transfigured, as well as when He travailed in prayer at the Garden of Gethsemane.[74]

So each of these groups—the three, the twelve, the seventy, and the multitude—formed concentric circles around Him. Their level of access to Him and intimacy with Him is what defined them. The outermost circle was the crowd that received His teachings and general message. The second circle was comprised of those willing to serve and follow His lead. Inside that circle were the chosen twelve who were to one day lead the church. The innermost circle was the special group of three who were closest to His heart and to whom unique revelation was given.

Authority and dominion are part of the spiritual DNA of a leader. Yeshua demonstrated His authority over wickedness, the forces of nature, and the power of spiritual darkness throughout His ministry. A prime example was when He came face-to-face with those who were desecrating the Temple grounds by turning it into a carnival.[75] The sacrilege of the hawkers and moneychangers despoiling His Father's house filled Him with indignation. And so Yeshua made a whip and drove them out in a tumult from the Temple grounds. As He overturned their tables the peddlers fled in fear, and not one dared to pick up even a single coin of the hundreds that scattered everywhere. The Son of the Most High had taken charge!

An even more telling instance of Jesus' dominion was when nature itself was forced to bow its knee to the Master's authority. One night Yeshua and the Twelve were on the Sea of Galilee when suddenly a fierce storm came up out of nowhere.[76] The wind howled and the waves pounded relentlessly, one after another, raging so high that the boat was in danger of sinking. The ferocity of the storm put the disciples into a state of panic, but Jesus was fast asleep during all the commotion. Fearing for their lives, the disciples roused the Master wanting Him to do something—anything. And He did do something: He spoke. He rebuked the wind and spoke to the waves, *"Peace, be still!"*[77] No sooner did He utter those words than the angry winds and the turbulent waves subsided in obedience. Jesus and the disciples continued on their journey, now across a tranquil sea. The malevolent force behind the storm had been compelled to cease and desist. Such was the Jesus' authority.

By early the next morning Yeshua and His group reached Gadara, on the other side of Galilee, and were immediately challenged by another startling encounter as they landed.[78] A naked madman, tormented by unclean spirits, came at them menacingly as they reached shore. This demented soul had terrorized the whole region for years with his ranting. He was possessed by foul spirits that compelled him to dwell among the tombs of Gadara's cemetery wearing no clothes. The Savior stared at the man with great intensity and demanded, *"Come out of the man, you unclean spirit!"*[79] A crazed demon snarled back, *"What business do we have with each other, Jesus, Son of the Most High God? I implore You by God, do not torment me!"*[80]

By such a response, begging Jesus not to torment him, we see that the depraved spirit ruling the man immediately recognized Jesus' authority over him. In fact, the demon had been reduced to a pitiful state at the mere sight of Yeshua's authority. In short order, he and the host of demonic spirits with him were sent hurtling, and the man who had been tormented for so long was restored to his right mind.

7. YESHUA THE MERCY GIVER

"For we do not have a high priest who cannot be touched with the feelings of our infirmities...." Hebrews 4:15 (MKJV)

Yeshua couldn't have been more different from the world into which He was born. The Son of Man was warm and caring! It was as if every feature of His spiritual DNA had been infused with a spirit of compassion. At the very center of our Savior's being was the endowment gift of mercy, which caused Him to care *deeply* about people and their myriad afflictions. His heart of compassion impelled Him to go forth to bring wholeness to a blighted world. On the other hand, the heartless taskmaster that holds this world in his death grip is relentless in his oppression and iniquity. The *"god of this world"* wreaks disease, death, and destruction wherever he reigns. His story is one of cold-blooded schemes and tales of woe.

The agenda for Yeshua's earthly ministry was ordained in eternity. Mercy from on high had set His course. The plan was spoken into being through the prophet Isaiah eight centuries before the Nazarene proclaimed His charge:

> *The Spirit of the Lord GOD is upon me, because the LORD has anointed me to bring good news to the afflicted; He has sent me to bind up the brokenhearted, to proclaim liberty to captives and freedom to prisoners; to proclaim the favorable year of the LORD....*[81]

Jesus was anointed to show the Father's heart to a people Yahweh had every intention of blessing. When the Son rolled up the scroll in His hometown synagogue after reading Isaiah's prophecy and announced its fulfillment in Himself, a movement was set in motion that the enemy would never be able to stop or detain. On that fateful day in Nazareth the train of faith had left its station. Fueled by compassion, Yeshua attained its initial purpose by the time He completed His earthly journey. This same train of faith will one day reach its ultimate destination—bringing the Good News of God's kingdom to the ends of the earth.

At one with the Father's purpose, Yeshua was continually moved with compassion. When Jesus approached the village of Nain in Galilee, He saw a woman near its gate leading a funeral procession for her only son.[82] Moved with compassion at the sight of the mother's grief, the Savior gently reassured her in a comforting tone, *"Do not cry."* The pallbearers stopped in their tracks. Jesus touched the bier saying, *"Arise, young man!"* Tears of sorrow turned to shouts of joy as the lad sat up and started speaking. Yeshua had felt a mother's pain, and the Source of love had His way that day.

Children always occupied a special place in Jesus' heart. They were drawn like lambs to the manly strength of the Good Shepherd, longing to be picked up and embraced in His loving arms. At times little ones would eagerly seek a place on His lap, to which Yeshua would cheerfully consent. Scripture records that His disciples tried to prevent parents from bringing their little ones to Him, treating the children as if they were nothing more than a nuisance. According to their frame of mind, the Master was on a heaven-sent mission. He had a message to deliver to the people, and that was the really important business at hand. However, Yeshua countered their small-minded notions:

> But when Jesus saw, He was much displeased and said to them, Allow the little children to come to Me and do not hinder them. For of such is the kingdom of God. Truly I say to you, Whoever shall not receive the kingdom of God as a little child, he shall not enter into it.[83]

Jesus viewed children as far more than a pesky annoyance to be tolerated. He valued them for their innocent ways as well as their example of wide-eyed, expectant faith. Youngsters were deemed by the Master as worthy, and in His arms they received validation as well as a warm-hearted embrace and blessing.

The Gospels record the Messiah's extraordinary compassion toward women as well. During His time, women were subjected to second-class treatment across the board. In many ways the religious establishment made a female's plight even harder. Yeshua's heart went out to these mistreated daughters of Abraham. The Scripture makes it clear that whenever a situation arose in which He had an opportunity to alleviate a woman's suffering, even though His actions caused Him to go against the prevailing customs and traditions, He always opted for mercy. Jesus was ruled by a heart of compassion, and for that He came to be despised by the religious sticklers of the day.

One example of this occurred on a Sabbath when Jesus was invited to teach at the synagogue in Capernaum.[84] As He faced the congregation expounding on the Torah He noticed a woman in the back hunched over from a crippling condition. She was doubled so far over that she couldn't even look up. The Master's heart went out to her for the pain and humiliation she was suffering. At that moment He decided enough was enough—He would bring an end to her affliction. Interrupting the lesson, He called her up from the women's section at the rear of the synagogue. As Yeshua laid hands on her He declared, *"Woman, you are freed from your sickness!"*[85] At that very instant she received her healing and for the first time in eighteen years she stood upright. Immediately she started to praise the Lord and broke out into a boisterous celebration.

However, the leader of the synagogue and others eyeballed what had happened and were far from pleased. Jesus had healed her on the Sabbath, and according to them He had violated the Law of Moses by "working" on the day of rest. But Yeshua would have none of their foolishness. He put them to shame by pointing out that while they saw nothing wrong with watering an ox or donkey on the day of rest they were filled with indignation when a daughter of Abraham was set free because her deliverance came on the Sabbath. They could only hang their heads.

The Gospels are filled with a multitude of examples in which compassion welled up within the Messiah as He went throughout Galilee and Judea. For example, He was moved with great sympathy at the pathetic sight of a leper who crawled before Him on his knees begging to be healed.[86] Though lepers were supposed to avoid human contact because of being deemed "unclean" according to the Law, Jesus reached out with compassion and the man considered "untouchable" by the Law immediately received healing at the Master's touch.

In another instance, after Jesus' friend Lazarus died, Mary threw herself at His feet weeping at the loss of her brother. As other mourners sobbed in the background and Mary was totally distraught, the emotionally charged moment brought tears to Yeshua's eyes. It was as if the Lord of love could not look upon grief without that grief becoming His own. *"When Jesus saw Mary weeping, and the Jews weeping which came with her...Jesus wept."*[87]

Yet another instance is mentioned in the Gospels, near the very end of His ministry, as Jesus came toward Jerusalem for the last time and gazed at the city, considering its fate. He pondered the terrible devastation that lay ahead for the City of David for not having recognized the hour of her visitation.

Jerusalem, Jerusalem, who kills the prophets and stones those who are sent to her! How often I wanted to gather your children together, the way a hen gathers her chicks under her wings, and you were unwilling.[88]

The Messiah had poured out His heart and was willing to give His life for the people to whom He had been sent, yet they failed to even recognize Him! The Gospel writer Luke records, *"And when he was come near, he beheld the city, and wept over it."*[89] It was a tragedy that needn't have been. Jesus' mission throughout His course had been determined by a heart of compassion. He was love personified, and yet they couldn't perceive who He was! Even as He hung from a cross His heart still went out for others: *"Father, forgive them for they know not what they do."*[90] In a cruel world of misery and hardheartedness, Jesus showed us what fills the heart of the Father—*compassion*!

Questions: Chapter Seven

1. The great difference between our Savior and the rest of mankind was the measure of _____ that was upon Him.

2. As we look at the perfection with which Jesus operated in all of the endowment gifts we find incontrovertible _____ that He was Emmanuel.

3. The divine inspiration of Scripture is attested to by the accounts of Yeshua operating in each of the gifts to _____ .

4. Yeshua, as an endowment gift **prophet**, had "spiritual radar" that was ready at all times to discern the _____ of men.

5. Jesus never backed off from controversy when the _____ was at stake.

6. It was the gift of _____ in Yeshua that caused His fiercest opposition.

7. The promised Messiah's humble start, being born in a lowly stable in Bethlehem, indicated that the only begotten of the Father would live and _____ as a true **servant**.

8. The Master frequently coached His disciples on the importance of self-denial and _____ and pointed them toward following His own servanthood as an example.

9. One sign of a true minister is _____ ,

the measure of which is whether a person is seeking his own will or that of another who is above him in authority.

10. The episode of young Jesus "**teaching** the teachers" was so remarkable that it is the only incident in the Messiah's _____ years recorded in Scripture.

11. The apparent simplicity with which the Master taught was deceptive because His instruction usually contained unfathomable truths that needed to be _____ out.

12. The aspect of Jesus' teaching ministry that infuriated the Pharisees most was that He refrained from _____ immorality.

13. Yeshua was an **encourager** who encountered all kinds of people as He ministered—including the demon-possessed, unsavory tax collectors, women of ill-repute, and lepers— and He treated all of them with _____.

14. Everywhere Jesus went, and in almost everything He did, He demonstrated a concern for the spiritual _____ of those around Him.

15. Jesus displayed a matchless ability at taking _____ truth and putting it in a nutshell so that it could be remembered and put to use.

16. By His life and actions Yeshua provided us with a _____ for **giving**.

17. The type of generosity our Savior taught about can only be understood in light of the magnitude of the _____ we have received.

18. Yeshua referred to His standard of _____
    several times in His message at the Sermon on the Mount.

19. Yeshua was equipped by His gifting as a **leader** to get things
    _____.

20. His great purpose required a plan and an _____
    that involved His followers at their various levels of com-
    mitment.

21. Yeshua demonstrated His _____ over
    wickedness, the forces of nature, and the power of spiritual
    darkness throughout His ministry.

22. Within the very center of our Savior's being was the endow-
    ment gift of **mercy**, which caused Him to _____
    deeply about people and their myriad afflictions.

23. At one with the Father's purpose, Yeshua was continually
    moved with _____.

24. The Messiah had poured out His heart and was willing to
    give His life for the people to whom He had been sent,
    yet they failed even to _____ Him!

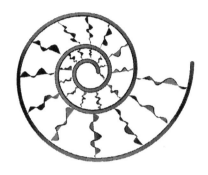

PART THREE: HIS PURPOSE

"For God saved us and called us to live a holy life. He did this, not because we deserved it, but because that was His plan from before the beginning of time—to show us His grace through Christ Jesus." 2 Timothy 1:9 (NLT)

Chapter Eight

THE GIFTED CHURCH

A Mosaic by Design

"For as the body is one, and in it are many members; and all those members of the body, though many, are one body; so also is the Messiah." 1 Corinthians 12:12 (MNT)

The body of the Messiah was designed to be interconnected and interdependent. Each member has been gifted with a particular spiritual DNA that enables him to perform a needed function in the body. An elemental part of Yahweh's plan is for His people to depend on each other for the general well-being of the church—Jesus Christ's body here on earth. No one among the followers of Jesus Christ is capable of supplying every function needed by the church. That basic truth is obvious, but the implications of this truth are not entirely understood or appreciated by many. To get a clearer picture of what the Lord has in mind for His people let us first consider what ministry is intended to look like in a local assembly of believers.

BODY MINISTRY—THE WAY GOD DOES THINGS

"Each one should use whatever gift he has received to serve others, faithfully administering God's grace in its various forms." 1 Peter 4:10 (NIV)

The church is supposed to function just like a physical body, with the various parts comprised of believers who are gifted for a particular area of service. The gifting within each individual member—personality, talents, and anointing—should complement that of others and contribute to the well-being of the overall body. Though much can be determined by what is seen on the outside—for example, a person's behavior as well as obvious talents and interests—just as important is what is on the inside. Most of God's children are grossly undeveloped in terms of their potential. They are truly "diamonds in the rough," something like the "golden Buddha" of the following true story:

> *In a temple near Thailand's ancient capital there once stood an enormous clay statue of Buddha. Though crude in appearance, it had been cared for over several centuries and became revered for its longevity. In the mid-1950s the nine-foot high statue was being moved by heavy equipment to a new location. During the process it slipped and fell to the ground and a crack appeared in its side. Immediately a monk ran to the statue and took a flashlight and shined it into the crack. As he peered inside, what he saw was the brilliant reflection of gold! Inside this clay statue was one of the largest and most radiant golden statues ever created in Southeast Asia. Over the passage of time people had simply forgotten that the golden buddha had been covered with clay to keep it from being stolen by an invading army. Today, now that it's been uncovered, the five and a half ton statue shines with a brilliant luster as pilgrims visit it from all over the world.[1]*

Are we the redeemed not worth much more than this pagan idol?

And yet the potential within many of us goes largely unnoticed and unappreciated. We have a wealth of innate resources that is undiscovered because most of us are unwilling to scratch beneath the surface of our "clay" exterior. For the most part, we focus on the obvious and look through a rearview mirror at our past to determine what we are capable of and where we are headed. We look at the natural rather than look inside to see what has been placed there supernaturally. For these reasons, most of us live far beneath our personal potential, and because of it the body of Christ suffers.

According to Paul's letter to the church at Ephesus, the fivefold leadership of the church—the apostle, prophet, evangelist, pastor, and teacher—has been given to the body by Yeshua to equip the believers *"to do the work of the ministry."*[2] The primary role for a pastor, therefore, just as with the other "equipping gifts," is training—getting the people of God ready to do His work. In fact, preparing believers for a life of service is right at the top of the job description for a pastor. While preaching and other activities are important, they simply are not the Lord's highest concern or priority.

WHAT DOES THIS BODY LOOK LIKE?

The responsibility for training people begins with knowing and understanding them—their motivations, background and life experiences, spiritual maturity, gifts and talents, personality, and strengths and weaknesses. What a grand mosaic God has created! It has a multitude of shades and colors, each one having its place and bringing spiritual depth to the intricate masterwork on earth called the "body of the Messiah."

This supernatural mosaic is as diverse as the colors in a rainbow with each gradation representing an aspect of the spiritual DNA Yahweh has distributed throughout His body. After all, diversity is a concept that our Creator God initiated. The biodiversity we see in the natural world is merely a reflection of the intricacy found in the spirit realm. The church has been designed to operate in the awesome potential shown to us by the Master while ministering here on earth as the Son of Man.

The array of giftedness in His body and its potential is far beyond our limited comprehension and in many ways is waiting to be released.

Another image of the church which emerges from Scripture is that of the bride of Christ. For instance, the apostle Paul admonished husbands to love their wives "... *just as Christ loved the church and gave Himself up for her.*"[3] Also, in Revelation we catch a glimpse of the marriage feast of the Lamb when the church will be as a bride clothed in fine white linen.[4] With these images in mind, a diverse church that is both the body and bride of the Messiah, we will now consider the part each endowment gift has in fulfilling God's purposes.

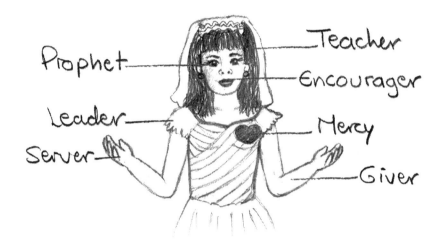

The endowment gift **prophet** brings the eyes of spiritual discernment to the body. Those who operate in this gift are like a "canary in a coal mine" for God's people when it comes to spiritual hazards. They sniff out hypocrisy and hidden sin and are not quiet about it when it is discovered. Double-standards will never make it past the bright eyes of the prophet. A local body without this gift is vulnerable to anyone who may try to infiltrate the church with a hidden agenda. The prophet will not shy away from issues that others would rather just "sweep under the rug." When injustice is encountered, the mistreated will normally find that the vocal advocate in their corner is an endowment gift prophet.

If this gift is underappreciated or misunderstood the congregation is likely to become lax in regard to sin and self-examination. Church discipline will suffer as well. If the prophet is willing to be a team player and walk by the leading of the Holy Spirit, he will serve as a cleansing agent that is able to purify the body. Contamination and corruption cannot exist when this gift is in operation. When the need arises, the grace of the prophet will be able to remove the debilitating power of sin and a healthier, stronger body will emerge. One reason that surveys in the United States and elsewhere have shown a minimal difference in the behavior of Christians when compared with the world is that we, the church, haven't given the prophet his proper place.

The endowment gift **minister** (server) serves as the hands of the body. The practical things that need to get done in every congregation—from the smallest to the greatest—will languish without these "good hands" people. In fact, a ministry simply cannot thrive, nor even survive, without those who are willing to "pitch in" and take care of whatever needs to be done. Right at the start of the early church the need for servers was understood by the apostles and "...*seven men of honest report, full of the Holy Ghost and wisdom...*" were appointed so that the church would continue to flourish.[5] Those three attributes—honesty, being Spirit-filled, and walking in wisdom—are proof-positive that the gift of service is a far higher calling than is generally appreciated. We may think of "waiting on tables" as an insignificant task, but the Lord thought so highly of it that He chose from among those seven servers the first martyr of the church, Stephen. He preached such a convicting message to the religious establishment in Jerusalem that some of them, enraged, picked up rocks and stoned him.

While the gift of ministry can be symbolized by the hands it is also true that this gift functions also as the lifeblood of any local assembly. As every leader knows, without the person behind the scenes "taking care of business," chaos will likely reign. A local church must learn to elevate service just as Yeshua did at the Upper Room when He washed His disciples' feet. Leaders must recognize the vital role played by these "unsung heroes" or the work of the entire ministry will be greatly hindered.

The endowment gift **teacher** serves as the brain for the body. This gift keeps the church on a firm foundation when it comes to the Word and sound doctrine; the body is edified and able to reach new heights. The positive impact of the teacher is maximized when he is able to both discern the heart of God and impart His counsel with integrity, wisdom, and understanding. A true teacher is a seeker of truth who is most effective when he is not only able to receive fresh insight and revelation but can then convey that knowledge in a way that changes hearts, minds, and lives. To accomplish this, the teacher must have the ability to reach God's people "where they are at" and move them onward to greater understanding. Since this gift has influence over the direction the body is headed, it is critical for the teacher to maintain godly priorities, hear from Yahweh, and walk in integrity. Humility and obedience may be an issue for some teachers because of the tendency, noted in Scripture, for the possession of knowledge to result in an inflated ego.[6] Because of the perilous times in which we live, the teaching of stale formulas and principles, no matter how well they are packaged, is insufficient for the proper feeding of God's flock.

> *Because of the perilous times in which we live, the teaching of stale formulas and principles, no matter how well they are packaged, is insufficient for the proper feeding of God's flock.*

The **encourager's** role in the body is represented by the mouth because of the expressiveness connected with this gift. The positive attitude and outlook of the exhorter are crucial in getting the body through difficult times. An effective exhorter is not only able to lift the spirits of those who feel overwhelmed by circumstances, but he can impart an overcoming attitude that leads to victorious living. According to the encourager, no mountain is too high to conquer and none of life's problems is too big to hold us back when God is with us. The persuasive abilities of this gift can be instrumental in bringing about real change in people's hearts and lives, especially if the encourager is seen as genuine. His friendliness can be contagious and will help draw those who feel less connected to the body into closer fellowship. As such, the people orientation of the encourager is one of the key elements in fostering a warm, caring community. Without the encourager a local church will come up short in its ability to nurture personal spiritual growth.

This gift is also a necessary element for overall church growth and expansion. Since there is a tendency for those with this gift to get "off-track" by allowing subjective standards and emotions to get the upper hand in their lives, it is important for this gift to be balanced by the teaching gift, which will keep the encourager from wandering into the wilderness of deception and error.

The **giver** serves as the arms of the body. This vital gift fosters a spirit of generosity and enables the church to receive and share provision. The anointing upon the giver attracts and frees up resources to be used for kingdom purposes. If it were not for this gift the body would be severely hampered in reaching out and extending itself to those in need. The value of sharing for the health and growth of the church was demonstrated many times in the early church as recorded in the book of Acts. For example, just after the day of Pentecost, when three thousand were saved, we read:

> *And all the believers met together in one place and **shared** everything they had. They sold their property and possessions and **shared** the money with those in need. They worshiped together at the Temple each day, met in homes for the Lord's Supper, and **shared** their meals with great joy and generosity—all the while praising God and enjoying the goodwill of all the people. And each day the Lord added to their fellowship those who were being saved.*[7]

In these four verses the word "shared" is mentioned three times along with "great joy," "generosity," and "goodwill." It is clear that the heartfelt camaraderie experienced by these new believers was an essential ingredient contributing to the explosive growth of the emerging church. How different are the values and mindset of present-day believers when compared with what *should* be our role model for church growth! While many contemporary leaders tout "new paradigms" for extending God's kingdom, we can be sure that these verses from Acts and other similar verses are not there just to occupy space. The gift of giving was meant to affect the body more profoundly than currently is the case. As the people of God seek for an ever-elusive "revival" perhaps we would be better served seeking for a restoration of gifts and qualities that have been lost—including a truer understanding of the gift of sharing.

The gift of **leading** in the body is symbolized by its shoulders. The shoulders represent strength and responsibility. For example, in referring to the coming Messiah, the prophet Isaiah said, "...*and the government shall be upon His shoulder....*"[8] Essential to the presiding aspect of this gift are dominion and authority. The gift of leading and its anointing impart both of these qualities to the body. While every believer has been given authority by the Messiah,[9] a specific anointing for governance is infused into every aspect of the leader's spiritual DNA. A dynamic leader is especially gifted to impart vision and is geared toward thinking strategically, both of which are necessary qualities in advancing God's kingdom. In this sense, the gift of leading is crucial for establishing new works and can foster the development of an apostolic anointing within the body.

Without the direction provided by the leadership gift a local assembly will tend to wander about aimlessly looking for its purpose and lose its sense of mission. The organizational abilities of this gift are crucial in accomplishing whatever goals the Lord has set before the church. It's one thing to have a vision but quite another to take the necessary steps in getting there. At this time Yahweh is emphasizing the need to restore apostolic authority and leadership to His church. Those with the gift of leading are breaking new ground that ultimately will usher in the return of our Lord.

The gift of **mercy** serves as the heart for the body. The corporate expression of God's presence in the community, the local church, is to be firmly "*rooted and grounded in love.*"[10] Compassion is the expression of Jesus' love for the lost and hurting. It is the healing power of mercy that brings wholeness to His body. It is for the sake of mercy that the local assembly reaches out to minister to the downtrodden, outcast, wounded, and forlorn. A physical body is unable to function without a heart, and it is the same with a congregation. Without a vibrant presence of the gift of compassion, a local church will either be on life support or will pass away. Yeshua warned the church at Ephesus that it was in danger of having its lampstand removed because it had left its first love.[11] The first love for every believer and the local assembly must always be a love of the Father and a love for one another. Without mercy and compassion a church can appear to be successful—even growing in membership as well as in programs and activities—but it will still fall far short of the purpose for which it was created.

Yeshua's entire ministry flowed from compassion, and so should it be with the local church. Without this grace the atmosphere of a congregation will lack warmth and be unable to produce lasting fruit. The "perilous times" that the apostle Paul spoke of[12] are upon the world. Let the gift of mercy be given preeminence in the body.

GOOD AND VERY GOOD

The whole body of the Messiah functioning together in harmony is the obvious goal of the church. From the very beginning of time the Lord has displayed a special favor toward those things that are His as they reach a state of fullness or completion. The first chapter of Genesis describes each phase of creation. He spoke light into existence, and when it was done Scripture records that *"He saw that it was good."*[13] And so it was at each step along the way—after each part of creation came into being, the Lord "saw that it was good."

At the very end of this process came the culmination of God's handiwork: Adam and Eve. Having been made in His image and likeness, they were to have dominion over all creation. At this point, now that Elohim's work had reached its fullness, the Bible tells us, *"…God saw **everything** that He had made, and behold, it was **very good**."*[14] When everything was together in its entirety the final result was not just "good," it was "very good." Creation in its fullness was more than its parts. It was greater than the sum of all that had preceded.

The Genesis account displays an enduring principle related to God's pattern of blessing: a greater degree of favor rests upon fullness than upon its components.[15] It is the same with God's new creation as well. Every believer is a new creation in Christ Jesus.[16] Each one is a member of the Lord's body and a constituent part of the whole. As the individual member develops in his gifts and contributes to the overall functioning of the body, it is declared by Yahweh as "good." For example, when a prophet discerns a spiritual threat and brings it to the attention of the local assembly, God declares that to be "good." As a member with the endowment gift of mercy reaches out and ministers to the homeless, the Lord also declares that as "good." And so it is with each member contributing his gifts and talents in fulfilling God's purposes. Furthermore, as the members work together in harmony, God declares it to be *very good.* There is a special anointing that comes with this type of unity and harmony. This truth was expressed in a psalm recorded by King David:

> *Behold, how good and how pleasant it is for brothers to dwell together in unity! It is like the precious oil upon the head, coming down upon the beard, even Aaron's beard, coming down upon the edge of his robes.*[17]

This special corporate anointing, symbolized by the oil running down Aaron's beard as "brothers dwell in unity," is a key to understanding both the dynamic growth and power exhibited in the early days of the church. Luke informs us in the book of Acts that just after the day of Pentecost the new believers felt a "sense of awe" and were of "one mind," and as they met *"…the Lord [continued]…adding to their number day by day those who were being saved."*[18] Unity produces the results for which we are all longing!

HE BECOMES WE

> *"By this, love is perfected with us, so that we may have confidence in the day of judgment; because as **He is, so also are we** in this world." 1 John 4:17 (NASB)*

Yeshua provides us with the perfect example of the gifts operating in harmony. Obviously each of the seven endowment gifts was integrated into His persona in such a way that the right gift took prominence at the appropriate moment. This is how it should be in the church. For example, when sin rises up in the body the other gifts need to make way for the prophet to bring a proper diagnosis of the spiritual malady. Once genuine repentance occurs, the gift of the encourager and the mercy giver should come to the forefront to help bring about restoration. For long-term recovery the teacher may be needed to keep things on track. In other words, each gift works together in a harmonious way for the well-being and wholeness of the body.

Jesus not only supplies us with the model for all the gifts working in unity, He also supplies the anointing to get the job done. Though the seven endowment gifts are resident within the various members of the body, they still must be manifested to be of any use. The Holy Spirit will move upon one believer in one way or at a different time than He may move on another believer. The two major factors in this are the person's spiritual DNA and their level of maturity. In other words, there is an interaction between the gift within them, the level of spiritual development, and God's anointing.

The spiritual maturity of the believers will significantly affect how the Spirit is able to move in a congregation. If a believer is a spiritual child or adolescent then he will be of limited use in ministering in his gifting. The spiritual child will be more preoccupied with receiving a touch of the Holy Spirit than with fulfilling God's purposes or serving others in the body. He will enjoy the presence of a corporate anointing but will tend to seek after experiences or manifestations rather than be used by Yahweh for the good of others. His focus will be more on self, and if he stays in this arrested state of development he will become part of the perpetual "bless me club" within the church.

Others who move beyond this immature condition will enter a stage of spiritual adolescence in which they desire to be used by the Lord but have mixed motives. The primary hindrance for such a person is that he operates in a way that meets his own personal needs as much as, if not more, than meeting the needs of others. This person also is likely to have quite a few personal problems that remain to be dealt with or even recognized—perhaps emotional wounds, character issues, or a poor self-image. Not having been set free from strongholds and hurts will result in a situation in which a believer may desire to serve but is limited in his capacity to do so.

The highest level of anointing and service will be found among those who have worked their way through most of the problems of their spiritual adolescence and have come out on the winning side. They are moving on toward maturity. Such a spiritual adult has learned the secret of getting "self" out of the way and allowing Christ (i.e., the Anointed One and His anointing) to live through him.[19] Not that every issue has been resolved, but this person is relying upon Yahweh and is sufficiently consecrated to His purposes such that he functions as a blessing to others as God intended.

Besides providing the model for harmony and integration of the endowment gifts, and supplying the unction for their operation within the body, Yeshua has given us His Spirit, which enables us to walk in the God-kind of love. This is the all-important ingredient for the church to fulfill its destiny, for only the God-kind of love gives the ability to overcome strife, division, and all manner of sin. The best way for the enemies of Yahweh to bring a congregation down is to reduce the believers' ability to walk in His love. The corporate anointing and spiritual atmosphere will wane. This will bring about an inverse of what occurred following the outpouring of the Holy Spirit on the day of Pentecost and during the early days of the church. It is for this reason that Jesus Christ delivered so stern a rebuke in His message to the church at Ephesus for having left its first love.[20] Clearly, it is more important to Yeshua to operate in His love than it is to accomplish great feats in His name without it. The results of what seem to be

The results of what seem to be real accomplishments for the kingdom will likely end up being fleeting if not based on the God-kind of love.

real accomplishments for the kingdom will likely end up being fleeting if not based on the God-kind of love.

THE GIFTED PASTOR AND LEADER

A basic requirement for successful ministry in God's eyes is that a pastor has a heart for his sheep. Once that condition has been met Scripture informs us that a pastor will be most effective when he is able to operate with integrity, discernment, and skillfulness.[21] The first quality, integrity, is related to the purity of his motives as well as his ability to carry through with what he knows is right. The second characteristic, discernment, is connected to his ability to understand the people he is leading as well as his sensitivity to the guidance of the Holy Spirit. The third quality, skillfulness, is associated with the pastor's ability to act with wisdom as he leads.

The integrity of any leader depends upon his wholeness as a person. Above all else, he must be "rooted and grounded in love." It is certain that he will be hindered in developing his gifting if there are strongholds in his mind or wounds in his heart. The personal integrity of a pastor, and the strength of character that it represents, is one of the most important attributes he can possess. This quality can be developed as he looks in the mirror of Scripture and is transformed as the Holy Spirit deals with his heart. As with everyone, the leader must "pick up his cross daily" and develop an intimacy with his Creator. As part of his calling he must have a genuine concern for the welfare of people as well. A true barometer of his success as a pastor has less to do with the number of his followers than it does with his relationship with both God and his fellow man. Unfortunately, many in the church have been more focused on "nickels and numbers" than on integrity—and the church has suffered for it.

> *A true barometer of success as a pastor has less to do with the number of his followers than it does with his relationship with God and his fellow man.*

The discernment of a pastor is highly dependent on his ability to understand and relate to people—both those close to him as well as the general flock for which God has made him responsible. To function competently in a leadership capacity, he must be able to deal with a wide variety of personality types and understand their underlying motivations and abilities. The pastor will be greatly helped in this regard as he learns to depend on the Holy Spirit.

Also, if his concern for people is genuine, he will know more about those in his care than what appears on the surface. While it is true that the gifts, talents, and interests of his people will become apparent as he gets to know them better, most people have a far greater potential inside of them that is hidden. Discerning the latent abilities in people is part of his responsibility as a pastor. He has been assigned with the task of equipping God's people to do the *"work of the ministry."*[22] In fulfilling that obligation the pastor must be familiar enough with those for whom he is responsible to be able to assess their spiritual DNA, understand their unrealized potential, and provide the training and opportunities necessary for them to grow in their gifting.

A leader's skillfulness will depend on many factors including his ability to keep a clear vision and purpose before the people and motivate them to become involved in that vision. Just as important is his capacity to understand people's needs, pinpoint their abilities, and place them so they can fulfill their function in the body of Christ. If a leader is unskilled in any of these areas the ministry will suffer. Also, if a leader has a faulty image of what leadership "looks like" he will be ineffective as well.

Jesus provided us with the truest image of leadership. He was the Good Shepherd who cared for His flock. He was the humble servant-leader who washed His disciples' feet. He was also one who dedicated most of His time and effort to training those whom He had chosen to carry the ministry forward. Yeshua understood not only His purpose and destiny, but He also appreciated the fact that He would need to leave a legacy to complete the vision Yahweh had given Him. Those closest to Him would be the ones carrying the message of God's kingdom to the farthest reaches of the world.

If the present-day body of Christ here on earth is to fulfill its destiny, those in leadership must focus on developing the endowment gifts of the people entrusted in their hands. Leaders must imitate Jesus as He led. A true leader will be as concerned about helping others reach their God-given destiny as he is with developing his own gifting. *"Equipping the saints to do the work of the ministry"* should be near or at the very top of his agenda.

The local church was designed to be a many-membered body and not a "one-man show"—with the spectators being the congregation—which it has become in too many cases. Such a condition, to the extent that it occurs in any local body of believers, is not only unscriptural it is also dysfunctional. For the church to move toward its potential, the people of God need to be trained by the equipping gifts: those who are called by Yahweh to serve as apostles, prophets, evangelists, pastors, and teachers. True New Testament Christianity will be restored when leadership develops a clear set of priorities in line with Jesus' example and the mandates of Scripture. As a church agenda that is crowded with non-essential activities comes into alignment with Yahweh's priorities, it will flourish in its calling and the body will fulfill its intended purpose.

For effective ministry, a leader must realize that it is just as important to understand the *weaknesses* of his gifting as it is to appreciate its *strengths*. For example, a mercy giver who is a pastor may be perceived by the flock as "weak" because he is consistently ruled by his heart rather than his head. This can cause great problems because if the people do not truly appreciate the mercy gift in him, they are not likely to respect his authority as they should. This can lead to turmoil as the people chafe, and perhaps even rebel, at his leadership. In order to avoid this type of difficulty, it is essential for such a pastor to cultivate a few close friendships and have a trusted inner circle of confidants who possess a complementary gifting, such as an endowment gift prophet or leader.[23] Having such friends who can serve as

> *It is just as important for a leader to understand the weaknesses of his gifting as it is to appreciate its strengths.*

sounding boards will help him in areas where he tends to be weak.[24]

For example, a gifted prophet will be able to see problems coming down the road even before they appear on the horizon to the mercy giver. So, rather than wondering what "hit him" after the fact, the pastor will be able to anticipate problems and take appropriate measures in advance with the counsel of this friend. Likewise, when a sticky situation arises, the trustworthy advice of someone with the gift of leadership will provide the insight and wisdom necessary for the pastor to swim through shark-infested waters and survive.

In addition to being able to share problems with trusted friends, the pastor should also have a diverse leadership team. To qualify for entrance into such a team a brother or sister must demonstrate commitment to the vision of the pastor, faithfulness in service, strength of character, and an exemplary lifestyle. Once these qualities have been proven the pastor should reflect upon the endowment gift mix of his leadership team. The goal is to develop a balanced team, one that reflects not only the needs of the church and the variety of gifts within it, but also one that addresses attributes that are lacking. For example, if the pastor's primary gift is teaching he may have a natural tendency to surround himself with others who teach. This will not produce as healthy a spiritual environment as when he consciously includes those with the gift of mercy or encouragement in the leadership team who will add passion as well as the warmth of "people skills." By so doing, the pastor will develop a healthier and more productive church environment.

Also, at some point as a local church grows in size, it will become important for the pastor to consider the gift mix in each area of ministry. The pastor would be wise to make inclusiveness a goal, with several gifts represented in each area of ministry to avoid potential pitfalls and maximize the effectiveness of each team. For example, in areas where the gift of compassion would most likely be attracted, such as prison outreach or hospital visitation, teams should not be comprised *exclusively* of mercy givers. Clearly there is a role for encouragers, servers, prophets, and teachers in such outreach efforts as well. In the long run it will strengthen the team's effort by having the perspective and abilities of a variety of gifts represented.

RELATIONSHIPS IN THE BODY

"And to each of us grace is given, according to the measure of the gift of the Messiah." Ephesians 4:7 (MNT)

The natural tendency for most people, including believers in Jesus Christ, is to assume that their point of view is also held by others, and when it is not, to assume that something is faulty on the other person's part. Perhaps the person doesn't really understand the situation. Or maybe they are just not sensitive enough to it.

Once a believer comes to at least a minimal understanding of the endowment gifts it should be clear that many differences in emphasis and opinion among God's people result from the unique grace package He has bestowed on each one of us. It is Yahweh who created diversity in the body of the Messiah. The gift mixture is what provides the body's overall strength. It also makes the church the attractive, bride-to-be that she is as well as the many-colored mosaic that she was meant to be. We as believers must be open to others' gifts and talents as well as appreciate their contribution to fulfilling Yahweh's purposes here on earth. The *"eyes of our understanding"* need to be enlightened among those of us to whom this has not yet been revealed.[25]

The secret to harmony is operating in the God-kind of love. The many differences among giftings should be seen as complementary aspects of a whole, each one meeting specific needs. If there is "sin in the camp," for example, that is not the time to gloss over the situation by dispatching a mercy giver. Perhaps a prophet should take the lead, but one whose motivation is to restore rather than merely expose the sin and denounce it. While a developing prophet may be irritated by the wishy-washy attitude of a mercy giver toward moral failures, the reality is that a judgmental attitude needs to be tempered by compassion.

A teacher is an excellent complement for an encourager in that he will be constantly steering an exhorter away from the dangerous shoals of deception and error. At the same time, the sunny disposition of the encourager will have a positive impact on a teacher, who may tend to become isolated from others. The teacher can have a positive impact on a leader who is heading off in the wrong direction if he uses his gift wisely. By presenting the truth in a non-confrontational way he may be able to persuade the leader to change course. A server's gift will combine in a complementary way with all of the other giftings. This is true across the board but is true to a lesser extent as the server relates to a mercy giver.

The generosity of the giver complements the spiritual DNA of all the other gifts in a positive way. However, the tendency of some givers toward being aloof means that they are likely to make a better combination with a "people-person," such as an encourager or a mercy giver. The warmth of either of these two gifts will balance the detachment of this type of sharer. The leader's easiest combination is with a server. Since the leader is endowed with a strong personality, unless he is well developed in his gifting, difficulties may arise with other combinations. On the other hand, if a leader manifests the fruit of the Spirit in his life, he can be an asset to any group and a complement to other giftings.

In reality, if a person with any of the gift packages is walking in love then compatibility will not be an insurmountable problem. An excellent vertical relationship with Yahweh will ensure a good horizontal relationship with others even if there is a tendency for some to "rub us the wrong way." The Holy Spirit will show us how to maneuver around difficulties and how to work with people and their quirks. A religious spirit on the other hand will tend to erect barriers and cause a person to take offense at differences that merely reflect God's  greatness. Such a person will have reduced Yahweh into the "box" of their own experience and limited understanding. God's grace is greater than we can imagine. As we abide in His love we will come together in the unity that He so zealously desires for His people!

Questions: Chapter Eight

1. Each member of the body of Christ has been gifted with a particular _____ DNA that enables him to perform a needed function in the body.

2. Most of God's children are grossly undeveloped in terms of their _____.

3. The endowment gift prophet brings the _____ of spiritual discernment to the body and is like a "canary in a coal mine" for God's people when it comes to spiritual hazards.

4. If the endowment gift of _____ is underappreciated or misunderstood the congregation is likely to become lax in regard to sin and self-examination.

5. The endowment gift minister serves as the _____ for the body.

6. The gift of service is the _____ of any local assembly.

7. The endowment gift of _____ serves as the brain for the body.

8. The positive impact of the teacher is maximized when he is able to both discern the heart of God and impart His _____ with integrity, wisdom, and understanding.

9. The encourager's role in the body is represented by the _____ because of the expressiveness connected with this gift.

10. The _____ orientation of the encourager is one of the key elements in fostering a warm, caring community.

11. The _____ serves as the arms of the body.

12. As the people of God seek for an ever-elusive "revival" perhaps we would be better served seeking for a _____ of gifts and qualities that have been lost—including a truer understanding of the gift of sharing.

13. The gift of leading in the body is symbolized by its _____.

14. While every believer has been given authority by the Messiah, a specific anointing for _____ is infused into every aspect of the leader's spiritual DNA.

15. The gift of _____ serves as the heart for the body.

16. A physical body is unable to function without a heart and it is the same with a _____.

17. Jesus not only supplies us with the model for all the gifts working in unity, He also supplies the _____ to get the job done.

18. The highest level of anointing and service will be found among those who have worked their way through most of the problems of their spiritual _____ and have come out on the winning side.

19. The long-term results of what seem to be real accomplishments for the kingdom will likely end up being fleeting if not based in the _____ of love.

20. A basic _____ for successful ministry in God's eyes is that a pastor has a heart for his sheep.

21. As a church agenda that is crowded with non-essential activities comes into alignment with Yahweh's _____, it will flourish in its calling and the body will fulfill its intended purpose.

22. In addition to being able to share problems with trusted friends, the pastor should also be mindful of the importance of having a _____ leadership team.

23. Even with a minimal understanding of the endowment gifts it should be clear that many _____ in emphasis and opinion among God's people result from the unique grace package He has bestowed on each one of us.

24. In reality, if a person with any of the gift packages is walking in love then _____ will not be an insurmountable problem.

Chapter Nine

THE TRULY ABUNDANT LIFE

Restoration and Walking in Wholeness

GETTING RID OF THE ENEMY'S FOOTHOLDS

"I beseech you therefore, brothers, by the mercies of God to present your bodies a living sacrifice, holy, pleasing to God, which is your reasonable service." Romans 12:1 (MKJV)

What is reasonable service for a Christian? At the very least, it involves presenting our bodies as *"a living sacrifice"* to God, just as the apostle Paul exhorted the saints in Rome to do. Since Yahweh has fashioned each of us, redeemed us from the curse of sin, and purchased us with His very own blood,[1] presenting ourselves back to Him as a living sacrifice would seem to be a reasonable expectation. Several other translations have rendered this well-known verse *"present all of [your] faculties"*[2] to God, not just your body. Considering the "first commandment" Jesus gave us—to love God with all our heart, soul, mind, and strength[3]—it appears that such a rendering is appropriate.

The sacrifice that pleases Yahweh involves more than just our bodies. We are to place everything we have been endowed with and *all* that we are—spirit, soul, and body—on the altar. Though this verse is familiar to most believers, it is apparent that Paul's exhortation has gone largely unheeded for most in the body of Christ. It is as if what the apostle calls a "reasonable" service is considered by many as going "above and beyond," something "unreasonable." Unfortunately for many in the body, what the Lord meant for our highest good has been viewed as a burdensome requirement—one that is optional. However, for any follower of the Messiah to look at the first commandment in this manner shows a rebellious nature, one that needs to be repented of speedily.

What Yeshua and Paul have put forth isn't complicated or difficult. We just have a natural tendency within us, which is called a "sin nature," to make what is clear and simple into something complicated so that we can avoid obeying the Lord's command. He told us that His "yoke is easy" and His "burden is light." He invited us to "taste and see that the Lord is good."[4] Will we take Him up on His offer?

When comparing the characteristics of each endowment gift in its "undeveloped" or "negative"[5] state with the perfection that Jesus Christ demonstrated, it is understatement to say that every one of us has a way to go to fulfill our potential and our destiny. The distortions in the soul realm of everyone's nature were symbolized in a vision I called the "twisted branches walking" vision at the start of Chapter Five. In the vision all types of people were going about their normal everyday routine, but the people appeared not as human beings but as twisted and gnarled tree branches, indicating they were damaged in some way on the inside—in their emotions, outlook, and other ways as well. The bottom line is that each one of us has wounds that have affected our heart and our mind, wounds that need healing. Every one of these represents a stronghold that must be brought down if we are to move toward God's best.[6] This is part of what it means to become a "living sacrifice."

Yeshua made a bold declaration that the enemy of our soul had no power over Him.[7] From this statement it is commonly understood that Satan had no authority over Jesus because He walked in sinless perfection. Such a conclusion is entirely warranted, but His testimony has further implications as well. While our Savior experienced rejection and humiliation and was sinned against in countless other ways, the evil perpetrated against Him did not produce wounds in His soul. In other words, He was never injured in His emotions, mind, or will by anything that came against Him. Because of this, the Master was in no way ruled by the hurts He endured. If what He suffered had caused a deformity in His nature in any way on the inside, then the enemy would have gained power over Him, which was definitely not the case. There were no footholds for Satan. Because Yeshua's Spirit man ruled over every hurt, He was able to walk in sinless perfection as well as the fullness of His gifting. Indeed, He was "the Branch who walked straight."

Jesus was able to accomplish mastery over potential wounds in His emotions, mind, and will as the Son of Man. Though He was tempted in all ways as we are—to become bitter and resentful, to harbor grudges, to become proud, to retaliate against His detractors—He was aware that by doing so He would be giving Satan a way to destroy God's purposes and His own destiny. Yeshua counted the cost and found that His Father's plan was infinitely more rewarding and fulfilling than giving in to any temptation, no matter how enticing.

Most Bible-believing Christians are fond of quoting the verse by the apostle John, *"Beloved, I wish above all things that thou mayest prosper and be in health, even as thy soul prospers."*[8] However, most of the interest in this verse is focused on the promised benefits of financial blessing and health, while scant attention is paid to the other major point, which is that both of these blessings depend on prospering in the soul. To be sure, a person who is crippled in his will, thought life, or emotions will be adversely affected in every area of his life—including his finances and physical health. Conversely, as the crippling effects of soul wounds are removed, these areas begin to improve as well. If a person neglects to do what is necessary to prosper in his soul then his finances will languish and his health will suffer.

An interesting comparison can be made between Israel's failure to focus on the God-given priority of rebuilding the Temple in the time of the prophet Haggai and Christians who focus on "prosperity" and "health" while ignoring the strongholds and wounds that hold them captive. In the case of the remnant of Israel, they left off from working together on God's house once the foundation was completed, and each one went his own way to focus on building his own personal "prosperity." The prophet told them that as long as they neglected the Temple their efforts would be fruitless.

> *Is it time for you yourselves to dwell in your paneled houses while this house [of the Lord] lies in ruins? Now therefore thus says the Lord of hosts: Consider your ways and set your mind on what has come to you. You have sown much, but you have reaped little; you eat, but you do not have enough; you drink, but you do not have your fill; you clothe yourselves, but no one is warm; and he who earns wages has earned them to put them in a bag with holes in it. Thus says the Lord of hosts: Consider your ways (your previous and present conduct) and how you have fared.*[9]

What God was saying is that His priority had to be that of His people or He would see to it that their efforts, no matter how hard they tried, amounted to nothing.[10] In the case of the church, the physical body of each believer is the temple of the Holy Spirit.[11] If the soul of that temple lies in ruins there is no way for God's child to enter into prosperity. A son (or daughter) of the Most High can devote himself to training for a career, make great sacrifices in service to the Lord, or work seventy hours a week for years, but in the end will find that it has all been for naught if his soul has not prospered first. Strongholds must come down and emotional wounds must be healed prior to experiencing true prosperity. As this process of restoration occurs the child of God will grow in his true purpose, which is to glorify Yahweh by fulfilling his personal destiny. By placing everything he is on the altar and offering it up as a "living sacrifice" the believer will move inexorably toward greater maturity of the gifts God has placed within him.

TRICKS OF THE ENEMY

The enemy of our soul is a trickster. He is a deceiver who plays with our mind and emotions to divert us from the will of God. His strategies are numerous and he is crafty. However, we as believers have the upper hand—if we rely on the Holy Spirit. The devil has been defeated and we are called to walk in that powerful truth. Jesus has given us all authority over this conniving enemy of our soul.

The primary arena of the enemy's deception is in the soul realm. He is the master of "virtual reality." The devil and his minions present us with a convincing view of reality that is removed from the truth. Whenever he and his cohorts are involved you can be sure that appearances *are* deceiving. While he is the

> *The primary arena of the enemy's deception is in the soul realm. He is the master of "virtual reality."*

"father of lies" and there is "no truth in him,"[12] under the right circumstances he is no match for us. We have the "greater One" living in us[13] and we are well equipped to uncover his schemes.

A stronghold is an area in which the enemy has convinced us of one of his deceptions. Some Christians have bought the lie that they are able to unmask the tricks of the adversary on their own. This is categorically false. Since he is a dark force only light can expose his lies—*supernatural* light. The Holy Spirit within us gives us the illumination we need. When we team up with Him we have the candlepower to shine the spotlight in every dark place where Satan has set his traps. Light always drives out darkness. As we rely on Him, the supernatural light of the Holy Spirit will reveal every device and plot of our wicked foe.

Dealing with a stronghold sometimes is like peeling an onion. You strip off the outer skin and find layer upon layer underneath. As you peel away you finally reach the center, the heart of the onion, and amazingly there is hardly anything there. Sometimes strongholds are like that—they are wrapped around a very small deception that was believed long ago. It's buried so deep within that perhaps you can't even remember how it all began. But it's there and it controls your thought life and your feelings up till this day. It all started with a lie—perhaps a little one at that.

Obvious strongholds are like the outer skin of an onion. Almost always they are merely a symptom of an underlying problem. For example, some Christians who profess to "love the Lord" spend a ridiculous amount of time in what they consider "harmless" pastimes—activities that are not necessarily sinful in and of themselves—that simply do not edify. Such a believer may be involved in a hobby such as video games, watching TV, talking on the phone, chatting online, or playing sports. Such diversions can consume many hours every week, and yet this type of adult Christian may claim to have difficulty finding time for fellowship or to attend Bible study. This person is exhibiting a stronghold that prevents him from experiencing the abundant life God has in store for him.

Wasting time on trivial pursuits instead of being engaged in activities that benefit himself, others, or the kingdom of God is evidence of a problem at a much deeper level. While such a person may not be totally adrift, he lacks direction and a sense of purpose. Such aimlessness results from not setting his affections on "things above." Being lukewarm about the things of God is unwise to be sure, but there is an underlying reason for it. One thing is certain: it began with a sin that turned into a deception.

Perhaps he was sinned against by someone else, or maybe it was his own sin. Whatever the case, at some point it resulted in a lie that he believed which in turn became a stronghold. Perhaps the person felt rejection or abandonment in his childhood and is trying to mask the pain with mindless activity. Maybe he feels trapped in a hopeless situation. Or it might be that the person is unwilling to face up to his responsibilities as a spouse or parent. The possibilities are nearly endless, but the root cause was a sin that caused a lie which was believed.

Many deceptions in our lives have been transmitted unwittingly by those we trusted the most—our parents, religious leaders, teachers, or friends. They *thought* they had our best interests at heart but were unaware that what they were teaching us amounted to "the wisdom of the world." It seemed believable enough, and so we swallowed their advice. To undo the damage takes divine intervention. We have these huge blind spots and by definition we don't see them. In fact, we don't even know what they are. We have false images, wrong ideas, even wrong feelings. What can be done?

BRINGING RESTORATION

A good place to begin the process of restoration is to ask the Lord to reveal our blind spots to us. He will show us as gently as He is able because He is our loving Father who cares for us and wants us to be free from deception. As this process unfolds Yahweh will deal with issues one by one in the order He knows is best. Even if trauma was involved at the root, He will use a method in which His love is present at all times to heal any wound exposed.[14]

Throughout Scripture we see God's desire to make His people whole. Jesus said at the very start of His ministry that He came to *"… heal the brokenhearted, to preach deliverance to the captives…to set at liberty them that are bruised."*[15] God yearns to take away every wound and injury we have suffered at the hands of the enemy. To show us how much our deliverance and healing means to Him, He chose to send His beloved Son to pay for it with His life. The least we can do is be thankful enough for what He has done to receive what cost Him so much.

Once blind spots that have created strongholds have come into the light of the Lord, issues of forgiveness will also come into play. If a sin was committed against a person, then the sinner will need to be forgiven. If the person has sinned against himself, he will need to ask the Lord for forgiveness and receive it. A huge amount of hurt may be involved that has gone on for decades following the original offense. Yeshua said that before a mountain is cast into the sea we must forgive anyone we hold anything against.[16] These deceptions we believed that created strongholds may have caused us immense pain and suffering and destroyed other people's lives in turn—all because of lies produced by sin that became strongholds.

The importance of forgiveness cannot be emphasized too much. If a person is unable to forgive he will effectively block the healing power Yeshua has made available and the enemy will continue to have an advantage by which he can harass a believer. Unforgiveness will poison the heart and create bitterness, making it impossible for him to receive God's healing grace. The light of the Holy Spirit is needed to reveal Satan's lies, but a failure to forgive will effectively extinguish that light.

> *Unforgiveness will allow the enemy a great advantage over the believer—allowing Satan to harass him.*

In his torment, Job exclaimed to his friends who brought accusations of wrongdoing against him, *"...I will speak out of the bitterness of my soul."*[17] Job had grown weary of life itself and was unable to see the light at the end of the tunnel after having lost everything. It was only when he chose to pray for his accusers that he was restored—the Lord returning double of everything he had lost.[18] Jesus taught, *"...if you do not freely forgive your brother from your heart his offenses"* you will be turned over to the tormenters.[19] Unforgiveness corrodes our relationship with the Lord, and if we cling to bitterness, as Job did, we will react to others around us from our pain and misery. Under such circumstances it is impossible for the Lord to bring about our restoration.

FIXING OUR EYES ON JESUS

Once a person has extended his mercy by forgiving those who sinned against him he must turn his attention toward seeking the Lord. During his time of communion in the "secret place" with his heavenly Father, those areas where the enemy has gained a foothold will be revealed. As they are exposed to the light, healing will start to flow.

The example of the Children of Israel in the wilderness demonstrates a truth about this process of healing. As they wandered through the desert they continued to complain about the Lord and Moses after having been warned many times about their grumbling.[20] Yahweh then sent poisonous snakes which bit many of them. Fearing for their lives, the people came to Moses and confessed their sin. Moses was given a divine method of healing that would deliver those who were bitten. He had a bronze serpent made and raised it up on a pole. Those who had been bitten were to focus all their attention on the bronze image and the Lord would heal them. Of course the temptation was to focus on the pain of the venomous bite and their fear of dying. But miraculously as they fixed their gaze on the bronze serpent they were healed.

What does this mean for us in terms of being healed of the wounds in our soul? First of all, our restoration will never come about by focusing on our wounds. As with any problem, focusing on the difficulty never brings about a solution. The healing that Yeshua purchased on Calvary's cross is for our soul as well as our physical body. The salvation He bought was for our *total* well-being. In fact, this is at the very heart of the gospel message. The completed work at Calvary provides for our every need.

We are to lay aside everything that distracts us or weighs us down and "fix our eyes on Jesus."[21] By so doing healing and restoration begin to flow. We don't need to comprehend how this happens any more than the Hebrews needed to understand Moses' instruction. But if we place our trust in the One who is the "author and completer"

Restoration never comes by focusing on our wounds. As we lay everything aside that would distract us or weigh us down and "fix our eyes on Jesus" healing and restoration begin to flow.

of our faith we will receive all that He has in store for us.

Jesus is not only the *"light of the world,"*[22] He is the light that we ourselves need for our own personal journey through life. The brilliance of His light was viewed by Peter, James, and John when He took them along to join Him at a mountain prayer meeting. It's significant that this happened a few days after He affirmed to Peter that He was indeed the Messiah, the "Anointed One."[23] Scripture tells us that after Yeshua began praying with them, His appearance was suddenly transformed. His face shone like the sun and His garments became as white as light itself. This astounding incident is not included in three of the Gospels just to pique our interest.[24] It is there for our edification. The image gives us a glimpse into His glorious presence and light. The last view of Jesus in His glory found in Scripture was revealed to the apostle John on the Isle of Patmos.[25] Again, He radiated light and glowed. What a glorious image!

Yahweh gave the prophet Malachi a word about the radiant presence of our Savior. The Amplified Bible describes the Lord's message this way:

> *But unto you who revere and worshipfully fear My name shall the Sun of Righteousness arise with healing in His wings and His beams, and you shall go forth and gambol like calves [released] from the stall and leap for joy.*[26]

The message Malachi delivered is that Yeshua will rise like the morning sun and in His radiance will shine beams of light that bring healing. These sunrays bring both physical and emotional healing. His brightness dispels all the works of darkness. Every distress, pain, grief, sorrow, affliction, burden, and suffering is chased away. The strongholds of the enemy are obliterated. And, as this happens, great joy springs forth. It is as if we are a calf released from a stall to frolic in a green meadow.

Having finally been set free the believer can then rest in the assurance that the work has been completed. He is free from the enemy's debilitating trickery, and the stronghold is vanquished. There is no anxiety or fear but instead a peace that *"passes all understanding."* The child of God experiences a genuine peace that will keep a vigilant watch over both his heart and mind, allowing him to enter unreservedly into God's presence.[27] The rest for our soul that Jesus offered becomes a living reality.[28]

In this process the believer has journeyed along the road toward his destiny. What once detained him is now in his past. As he fixes his eyes on Jesus and overcomes the strongholds that once held him back, he moves in the direction God always planned for him—to be more connected with Him. He now sees his situation more like God sees it. His feelings are more in tune with the way Yahweh feels. His spirit is "plugged in" to the Holy Spirit more than ever before. The believer has moved from "glory to glory" and is in a process of continuing transformation and growth.[29] His soul is being restored to what Yahweh had in His heart and mind at the very beginning. As each stronghold is removed his endowment gifts flourish and God's will is fulfilled in his life.

TRUE ABUNDANT LIVING

"For You have been my help, and in the shadow of Your wings I sing for joy." Psalm 63:7 (NASB)

As the strongholds come down one by one there is a sense of freedom and exhilaration. There's nothing quite like it. The believer can also take pleasure in knowing he is moving toward his God-ordained future. Knowing that you're on the right path brings optimism and produces confidence as well.

As barriers are broken that hindered our relationship with the Lord, our spiritual eyes become brighter. The glory of His presence lights our path and reveals the hidden things of God. It is His delight to show us those secret things that were once veiled.

The relationship we have with the Lover of our soul should be as the sweet fragrance of romance between the king and his beloved in the Song of Solomon. Our heavenly Father loves us fervently and desires for our eyes and our affection to be set on Him. He has sought us and brought us to a higher place. His passion for us was proved at the cost of His Son. We should be as eager to hear Him as the Shulamite woman waiting to hear the sound of her lover's voice. Since we were meant for each other, nothing should come between us. Our soul should cherish the words *"I am my beloved's and my beloved is mine...."*[30] Our heart's desire should be to bring Him joy and understand His needs.

You didn't know that God has needs? You did consider, of course, that He created us in His image and likeness for companionship. Have you been a faithful companion to Him? If not, then surely it is time to reconcile with the Lover of your soul.

For us to truly experience the abundant life He has in store for us we need to be preparing in this life to spend eternity with Him. The Great I AM is not an "add-on" to a selfish lifestyle. He is a jealous God who must be in first place.[31] Why would we even think that we will have the opportunity to spend eternity with Him in heaven if we haven't even gotten to know Him here on earth?[32]

Whatever has kept us from knowing Him must get out of the way. Our desire has to be for our heavenly Father and spending time in communion with Him. We need to get to know His Word better and obey His commands. As we learn to love what He loves we will be drawn nearer to Him than ever before. If we have

> *The Great I AM is not an "add-on" to a selfish lifestyle. He is a jealous God who must be in first place.*

held Him at arm's length because of our busyness we need to change our priorities. If we have said in our heart of hearts that we are not worthy of such a One as our loving Father, then we haven't appreciated the gift of righteousness He gave us.

The necessary change will only come about as we abide in Him and meditate on His Word. It starts on the inside as our heart and mind are transformed. As we enter in through the portal of worship we find that His transforming love is beyond what we have imagined. He actually loves us as much as He said in His Word. We knew about it with our head but now we've experienced it. This is the result of true worship. As we soak in His presence those unsightly things that have attached themselves to us become dislodged. It is a gentle process in which the longer we soak the easier the blemishes are removed.

It has been said of some that they are so heavenly minded they are of no earthly good. Our Master showed us how to be both heavenly minded and earthly good. Living the abundant life means walking toward our destiny and fulfilling the purpose for which we have been created. It is being led by the greater love that has been sent down from heaven. It manifests itself in extraordinary deeds of compassion. It reaches both upward and outward.

Never let things or busyness get in the way of true abundance. Why would a saint of God let "stuff" keep him from the true riches that his heavenly Father has in store? Pursue His plan for your life. Do not be so occupied with serving Him that you miss what is "the better part," being with Him. As we put His kingdom and righteousness first we will walk in the miraculous and talk with the Eternal.

He is the One who has your best interests at heart, and His plans include prospering you in every area of your life. King David said this about the goodness of Yahweh:

Your goodness is so great! You have stored up great blessings for those who honor you. You have done so much for those who come to you for protection, blessing them before the watching world.[33]

Those who revere the Lord, who trust in Him and His provision, will be greatly blessed. As we abide in Him our prosperity will not just be our own personal secret—it will become obvious to all, *"before the watching world."*

The world has its eyes upon us. As we dwell in the presence of the Lord the world will observe that a true facsimile of Jesus Christ is being developed in our lives. And as the world's prospects continue to dim, the promises of God manifested through us will shine ever more brightly. As we abide in Him our lives will increasingly become a reflection of His glory. A day will soon arrive in which Isaiah's prophecy becomes fully manifested in our lives:

Arise, shine; for your light has come, and the glory of the LORD has risen upon you. For behold, darkness will cover the earth and deep darkness the peoples; but the LORD will rise upon you and His glory will appear upon you. Nations will come to your light, and kings to the brightness of your rising.[34]

Have the unsaved and powerful been knocking on your door lately? They will, as we reflect His glory. As the world enters the time of spiritual darkness of which Isaiah spoke, we will shine with His light because of His abiding presence. The glorious reflection of His light in our lives will be there for all to see. The Spirit within us will exude abundance. What will intrigue the world is that we are seemingly ordinary people but with extraordinary powers. That is the essence of true abundant living—radiating His glory for all the world to see.

Questions: Chapter Nine

1. Since Yahweh has fashioned each of us, redeemed us from the curse of sin, and purchased us with His very own blood, presenting ourselves back to Him as a living sacrifice would seem to be a _____ expectation.

2. We are to place everything with which we have been endowed and _____ that we are—spirit, soul, and body—on the altar.

3. Our Savior experienced rejection and humiliation and was sinned against in countless other ways, but the evil perpetrated against Him did not produce wounds in His _____.

4. Because Yeshua's Spirit man ruled over every hurt, He was able to walk in sinless perfection as well as the _____ of His gifting.

5. To be sure, a person who is crippled in his will, thought life, or emotions will be adversely affected in every area of his life, including his _____ and his physical health.

6. Jesus was able to accomplish mastery over potential _____ in His emotions, mind, and will as the Son of Man.

7. As the process of restoration occurs the child of God will grow in his true purpose, which is to _____ Yahweh by fulfilling his personal destiny.

8. The enemy of our soul is a _____ who

plays with our mind and emotions in order to divert us
from the will of God

9. The _____ arena of the enemy's deception is
in the soul realm.

10. A stronghold is an area in which the enemy has
_____ us of one of his deceptions.

11. Many _____ in our lives have been
transmitted unwittingly by those we trusted the most—
our parents, religious leaders, teachers, or friends.

12. Since Satan is a dark force only _____ is able to
expose his lies—*supernatural* light.

13. As we rely on Jesus, the supernatural light of the _____
_____ will reveal every device and plot of our
wicked foe.

14. Obvious strongholds are like the outer skin of an onion.
Almost always they are merely a _____ of an
underlying problem.

15. Whether sinned against by someone else or a person's own
sin, at some point it resulted in a lie that was believed
which in turn became a _____.

16. A good place to begin the process of _____
is to ask the Lord to reveal any of our blind spots to us.

17. The healing that Yeshua purchased on Calvary's cross is for
our soul as well as our physical body. The salvation He
bought was for our _____ well-being.

18. We are to lay aside _____ that distracts us or weighs us down and "fix our eyes on Jesus."

19. As we purpose to fix our eyes on Jesus and overcome the strongholds that once held us back we move in the direction God always planned for us—to be more _____ with Him.

20. For us to truly experience the abundant life that He has in store for us we need to be preparing in this life to spend _____ with Him.

21. As we _____ in His presence those unsightly things that have attached themselves to us become dislodged.

22. Our Master showed us how to be both _____ minded and earthly good.

23. As we put His kingdom and righteousness first we will _____ in the miraculous and talk with the Eternal.

24. Never let _____ or busyness get in the way of true abundance.

Chapter Ten

EMBRACING YOUR DESTINY

Maturing in Your Gift

"Being confident of this very thing, that he which hath begun a good work in you will perform it until the day of Jesus Christ."
Philippians 1:6

SINKING YOUR ROOTS AND GROWING IN HIM

The first-century church in Ephesus had a lot going for it. Paul lived and taught there for three years, and his spiritual son, Timothy, pastored the flock for many years as well. Beyond that, the apostle John is said to have based his ministry in Ephesus for years during the latter part of his life before being exiled to Patmos. Certainly the Lord had poured a great deal into the saints living in Ephesus!

Paul felt a great burden for the church in Ephesus because of his long-term involvement with the people of God there. His letter to the Ephesians reveals his passionate desire for the saints to come to a greater realization of the immensity of the Father's love for them[1]. In his letter, in the midst of his magnificent prayer for the believers, Paul implored "...*that Christ may dwell in your hearts through faith; and that you,* **being rooted and grounded in love***...*" *would come... to know the love of Christ which surpasses knowledge....*"[2]

In other words, Paul's fervent desire was that the Messiah take up residence on the inside of them and that they be *"rooted and grounded in [His] love."* In this manner, the believers would develop an intimate relationship with Yeshua and draw their sustenance from His love. Paul's desire was that this love relationship would grow *far* beyond what the Ephesians could even conceive.

The apostle's burden for the saints in Ephesus in the first century is the same as Yahweh's concern for His people everywhere and at all times. We are to be "rooted and grounded in love." Our spiritual well-being depends upon it!

The growth of a tree is dependent on its root system. It's through the root structure that a tree is anchored to the ground and able to draw the nutrients and moisture from the soil that are necessary for its survival. As the prophet Isaiah said, we are to be *"...trees of righteousness, the planting of the LORD...."*[3] As we are *"rooted and grounded"* in the Father's love we come into a greater realization of our total dependency upon Him. It is He who has established us and it is by Him that we are sustained. Paul put it so clearly to the Athenians: *"For in Him we live and move and have our being...."*[4] Once a believer catches even a glimpse of this spiritual reality his whole way of being will be transformed and he'll be able to grow and even flourish.

There are three basic types of Christians, who develop in noticeably different ways after entering into the kingdom of God. The essential difference between these types depends on their spiritual "root structure." The spiritual reality of each type is aptly represented by the three basic types of root systems found among the varieties of trees throughout the world.

The first type of Christian is the one who has taken to heart Yeshua's instruction to "abide in Him."[5] This is the believer who has developed a close relationship with the Lord and has sent a "taproot" down

into the soil for his spiritual sustenance. Smaller roots branch off the primary one, but it is the taproot—his connection with Jesus Christ—that sustains him and everything he does. This main source of strength goes down to the deep, rich soil far beneath the surface and draws moisture and nutrients that are simply not available to the two other root structures. The primary root is able to sustain this believer even if a spiritual drought happens to spread across the land.

This "taproot" Christian is steady and sure and will develop in his gifting as God intended. As he draws his strength for every situation in life by being *"rooted and grounded in love"* he will be enabled to go far beyond the other two types of root systems in fulfilling his destiny. Also, when all is said and done, his works will be truly "of the Lord" and the fruit of this believer's life will endure.

The second type of Christian is far more common than the "taproot" believer. This person's walk with the Lord is not as profound as with the first type but is able to produce fruit for the kingdom. The root struc-ture that typifies this second kind of Christian is much more complicated than the simple taproot system. Tree scientists call it the "heart root" sys-tem. In this structure, many roots of various sizes are sent outward and downward in all directions.  This dispersed type of root pattern typifies the believer who has many commendable traits as a Christian. Typically, this person will do some or even many of the things a Christian ought to be doing and has developed at least a few godly pri-orities—perhaps he studies the Word regularly, has a good prayer life, and may even be an active member of the body. Though this Christian will fall short in some areas of his walk, at least his primary orientation is not toward the world: he wants to grow in the Lord and desires to put his gifts and talents to use for God's kingdom.

As this "heart root" Christian matures the fruit in his life may start to look similar to that of the "taproot" Christian. In fact, depending on his gifts, talents, and understanding of biblical principles, this believer may produce even more fruit than the first type of Christian. The main shortcoming of this believer, however, is that the fruit manifesting through his life will be more a product of self-effort than the fruitfulness of a joint venture with Yahweh. His skills may be honed and much may be accomplished, but the truth is that some or even most of what has been produced will in the end amount to *"wood, hay and stubble."*[6] His activities are religious in nature but they are not born from relationship. Since he has been self-reliant and never truly depended on the Lord for guidance, what he has done was based on what "seemed good" and may or may not have had much to do with God's priorities. This believer's main problem stems from not being *"rooted and grounded in love."* Only by having a close relationship with the Lord will this happen. What he needs are "close encounters of the first kind"—by drawing near to God and experiencing His love.

The third kind of Christian is represented by a shallow root structure. The roots of this "flat root" system are sent out in every direction, but all are near the surface. The Christian represented by this superficial pattern has a more worldly orientation than the "heart root" believer and has never submitted more than a small portion of his life to the Lord. He basically has "one foot in the world and one foot in the church" and typically has never developed consistent, godly disciplines in his life—such as regular prayer or meditating on the Word.

The "flat root" Christian may experience a "touch" from the Lord now and again, but because his relationship with Yahweh is so shallow he knows very little of the dimensions of God's great love. Typically he will have little fruit to show in terms of a changed life or building God's kingdom. The gifts and talents of this third type of believer may or may not be developed, but it is sure that if they have been developed they will be used more for self-advancement than kingdom purposes. As a general rule the "flat root" Christian knows very little of self-denial and usually is unwilling to apply the Word in his life if it "costs" him something. He will be able to survive as a Christian, and not fall by the wayside, as long as he stays sufficiently close to a Christian-friendly environment. In short, this "flat root" believer lacks a passion for the things of God, has experienced little or nothing of the presence of God, and lacks both the power and the vision to live an overcoming Christian life.

The "taproot" model for Christian living is the one that Jesus demonstrated through His life and also the one He taught His disciples to follow.[7] He developed His gifting and fulfilled His destiny by being *"rooted and grounded in love."* Why is it that so much of present-day "churchianity" operates according to the "heart root" model? It is all too typical for "successful" evangelical churches to suffer from an overcrowded schedule filled with events and programs, which is a reflection of the majority of the believers' lives as well. It is clear from the fruit being produced in this spiritual environment that the church's agenda, as well as our own personal agenda, is being set according to something other than what is on the Lord's heart.

> *The "taproot" model of Christian living is the one that Jesus demonstrated and the one He taught His disciples to follow.*

The difference between the "taproot" and "heart root" approach to Christian living is as clear as the contrast between Mary sitting at the Master's feet, hanging on His every word, and Martha scurrying around trying her best to serve Him. Unfortunately, there has been a continuing battle of wills between the head of the church—the Lord Jesus Christ—and many members in His body, the church. His clear instruction is to abide in Him. From that condition of abiding we can then "do ministry." Have we become so "filled with ourselves" that we have found a better way than following His instructions?

It is startling to realize that despite Paul's fervent desire for the church in Ephesus to come to a greater understanding of the immensity of God's love, in the end they settled for "good works" instead. Many years after Paul's letter to them, the Lord Himself addressed the church at Ephesus as recorded in Revelation.[8] Yeshua commended the church for its many good works and even its spiritual discernment. However, He sternly rebuked the saints there for having left the most important thing—their "first love." In other words, they had great programs and events. They were mature believers with the ability to discern and judge many things properly. But even with so much that was worthy of commendation, their failure to heed the call to do things His way was about to jeopardize their very witness. This is what the Lord had to say about their failure to return to be "rooted and grounded in love":

> *Be mindful, therefore, of the height from which you have fallen. Repent at once, and act as you did at first, or else I will surely come and remove your lampstand out of its place—unless you repent.*[9]

Jesus was referring to more than having lost the passion they once felt. Actually, the text indicates He was referring to their having left what was of primary importance. Their "doing" wasn't grounded in their "being"—they were no longer rooted and grounded in Him.

What characterized the church at Ephesus is also true of many believers today. The potential of our spiritual DNA cannot be realized without the love of God present in our lives. That's the way we were made. The grace package of our endowment gifting cannot mature without the God-kind of love.

In the case of both the "taproot" Christian and the "heart root" believer there is potential for growth. The long-term potential of the first type is much greater, however, since it is as God instructed, being *"rooted and grounded in love."* Its fruit will endure and will be of the *"gold, silver and precious stones"* variety.[10]

The biggest problem with the "heart root" Christian is that God is not *really* the focus, even if the believer has convinced himself otherwise. The tendency is to justify himself defensively with the attitude, "I'm doing this [whatever it may be] for the Lord, what do you mean that it's not about Him?" The reality, however, is that the motives of the "heart root" believer are primarily centered on self—the need to feel worthy, a sense of guilt and obligation, seeking recognition, and the like. A basic difference between the two approaches is that the first acts out of obedience to the revealed will of God and the other represents a mixture of motives. Ministry should be done this way: from Him, through us, to others. If the flow hasn't begun with the true Source, its origin is self. The only way to reach the highest potential of our gifting over the long run and reach our destiny is to do things His way.

For a Christian who is more accustomed to leaning on his own understanding than relying upon Yahweh, the only way to improve is to repent, submit his will to the Lord's, and do things His way. Growing in His great love should be our motive. There is a marvelous reward for those who do so:

> *The righteous man will flourish like the palm tree; he will grow like a cedar in Lebanon. Planted in the house of the LORD, they will flourish in the courts of our God. They will still yield fruit in old age; they shall be full of sap and very green....*[11]

Palm trees and the cedars of Lebanon are both known for their ability to grow very tall. The Lord has promised that we will flourish as we are "planted" in His presence. He will increase us in stature and bring us to new heights. Furthermore, while most fruit trees tend to decrease in production as they grow older, that is not the case with the palm tree. Most palms do not bear fruit until they are mature, which can take many years. However, once a palm starts producing, the fruit grows sweeter as the tree ages! The righteous "will flourish like the palm tree...like a cedar in Lebanon...in the courts of our God." We will grow to new heights, and our latter years will be more productive and even sweeter than the former years. That's God's way!

DRAWN AWAY

"Temptation comes from our own desires, which entice us and drag us away." James 1:14 NLT

We have given the enemy an opening to harass us when we suffer from soul wounds and our thinking is off-base. However, there is a third problem that is just as serious. It occurs when we allow ourselves to be enticed by anything that draws us away from the true and living God.

There is an adage that goes: "Don't climb the ladder of success only to find it's leaning on the wrong wall." Most people live their lives in such a way that proves they are blind to the truth of this statement. They do not first consider what God has in store for them; they only know what *they* want. "*My* will be done" could be their motto. Their lives reflect a self-seeking pursuit of what seems at the time to be potentially rewarding. It is a quest that King Solomon discovered, after searching for meaning in his life for decades, ends up with the inevitable conclusion that *"all is vanity."*[12]

Solomon was a "believer" who was successful by any worldly standard. Yahweh had given him great wisdom in his earlier years. He knew more godly principles than anyone else in his day. After all, he wrote most of the book of Proverbs. But even godly precepts will only get a person so far. Clearly there is more to finding true fulfillment.

So what is it that can get even a "wise" king, said to be one of the richest human beings to ever walk the earth, to pursue things that proved in the end to be vexing to his spirit and void of meaning?[13] His basic problem was that while Solomon knew much about God, he was drawn away from the Source of all his blessings. His relationship with the Lord fell by the wayside as he increased in wealth, wives, and renown.

Truly, *"Godliness with contentment is great gain."*[14] The Apostle of Love, John, wrote: *"For the world offers only a craving for physical pleasure, a craving for everything we see, and pride in our achievements and possessions. These are not from the Father, but are from this world."*[15] There is an enemy lurking within us. It manifests itself with a desire for "more"—more of the world. It seeks meaning and significance in worldly ambition. It is enticed by that which pleases the senses or excites the mind. It is an enemy born in selfishness and disobedience. Its birth-place was the Garden of Eden and it was born of the "father of lies."

To overcome this treacherous foe we need to submit to Yahweh, for His way is best. He is not a grumpy kill-joy, as some would imag-ine, but the Lover of our soul. He wants wholeness and true fulfill-ment not only as our destination but also as something we experi-ence on our journey. He wants the trip to be joyful, blessed, and bountiful—with eternal rewards in the end. If you're driving a car and see that the road you're on isn't what you expected and won't get you where you want to be, why not hit the brakes and turn the car around? There is a better way.

In our search for significance and our pursuit of happiness, why not consult with our Maker? He knows how you're "wired." He knows the way to get to where you're going. He has the roadmap and He wants to guide you along the journey so that you avoid going down any more dead-ends.

He is the God who knows *"the end from the beginning,"*[16] and since He has your best interest in His heart, you should find out from Him how to be a success. First, you will need to put aside your own notions, if you haven't done so already, as to what success actually means. Fulfill-ing the destiny that Yahweh has planned for you is the only real success there is on this side of eternity. He has everything *"...all planned out— plans to take care of you, not abandon you, plans to give you the future you hope for."*[17]

Your success is both a heart and a head issue. Renew your mind with the Word until you are convinced in your "heart of hearts" that seeking after anything that stands between you and God will only drag you down. The lie that began in the Garden of Eden was that man could find fulfillment outside of Yahweh. However, when you view life from the perspective that your relationship with the Lord is of para-mount importance, you will be able to agree with the apostle Paul that *"...everything else is worthless when compared with the infinite value of knowing Christ Jesus my Lord. For His sake I have discarded everything else, counting it all as garbage, so that I could gain Christ."*[18]

CALLED TO BE YOU

"Don't let the world around you squeeze you into its own mould, but let God re-mould your minds from within, so that you may prove in practice that the plan of God for you is good, meets all his demands and moves towards the goal of true maturity." (Romans 12:2, PNT)

Imitation Is Limitation

Some of the most frustrated people in the world are those who are trying to be someone other than themselves or do something they were never called to do. If a person truly appreciates the value of his uniqueness he will avoid much disappointment and frustration in life. He realizes the best thing for any person to be is what Yahweh has made him to be. To fulfill the potential within him is his highest calling.

A believer will avoid much disappointment when he realizes the best thing to be is what Yahweh made him to be.

An analogy was made in the first chapter of how we can discern our purpose by observing our God-ordained design just as the purpose of a vehicle, such as a boat or a car, may be determined by looking at its characteristics. A car has wheels, which show that it was made for travel on the land. A boat has a water-tight hull, and therefore we can deduce that it was made to travel on the water.

Let's take the analogy a bit further to make a point about the uniqueness of our calling. As we all are aware, there are many kinds of boats. For example, there are canoes, cabin cruisers, sailboats, oil tankers, submarines, tugboats, and aircraft carriers. It wouldn't make any sense for one type of boat to try to fulfill the purpose of another type.

A canoe simply cannot fulfill the function of an aircraft carrier!

A problem with many human beings is the tendency to emulate others who are similarly gifted but who have a completely different calling. For example, you may be an evangelist just like Reinhard Bonnke is an evangelist; but then again, you're probably not just like Reinhard Bonnke! He is one of the "aircraft carriers" of evangelists. That is his purpose and calling and he was designed accordingly. However, perhaps your calling is to be a "cabin cruiser" type of evangelist. You don't travel on the high seas; you usually stick close to your home port. You minister in your local area but occasionally go to a nearby state. You're effective at what you do and the fruit of your ministry will last for eternity. Your calling is not a "lesser" calling than evangelist Bonnke's, it is just a different one—the one for which you were designed.

There is a place in God's kingdom for both types of callings and many others as well. There are "submarine" evangelists who have been called to work with the underground church in the Muslim world. There are "tugboat" evangelists who work alongside other evangelists in a supportive role. There are "canoe" evangelists who are called specifically to evangelize one-on-one or be paired with another in street witnessing. A "cabin cruiser" evangelist can reach people that Reinhard Bonnke will never meet. If you are an evangelist of any type, you are not insignificant even if you never have the opportunity to preach to millions of Nigerians. What God had in mind when he made you was no less special than what he had in mind for Reinhard Bonnke.

There is nothing wrong with having role models who have set high standards toward which you aspire. Emulation of others who have proved to be worthy is commendable. No matter what field of endeavor, there will be those who have gone before us who set a good precedent that can be followed. The mistake that is often made is to feel that in order to succeed we must attain their same level of achievement. However, the only personal ambition a Christian should have is to be faithful in the area to which he has been called, keeping in mind that his accountability is to his loving Father, who is by no means a harsh taskmaster.[19] While wanting to strive for excellence is a God-given desire, the basic motive behind such efforts should be to advance God's kingdom and bring glory to our Maker. Self-aggrandizement is a form of pride which, in the end, will bring a person down.[20]

Alignment with Your Assignment

The only expectations a mature person should try to live up to are those which have been developed in consultation with Yahweh. Some Christians have the mistaken notion that the only worthy calling in life is one that involves full-time service within the church. However, since Jesus' preaching and teaching focused on the Good News of God's kingdom, and His instruction to His followers is to bring that same message to the world,[21] it is a limited and faulty view to regard ministry in the marketplace as a lesser calling.

We are to be salt and light to the world. In order to engage those who have not yet entered God's kingdom we must bring the gospel to them, wherever they might be—at school or work, the store, sporting events, and whatever places their needs and interests take them.

Joseph served the Lord's purposes as an overseer for the Pharaoh and prime minister of Egypt.[22] The mighty prophet Daniel was second in command under the king of Babylon and later under the king of the Persian Empire. Paul worked with his hands making tents during certain periods of his ministry. He also proved to be very effective in advancing the kingdom of God from a jail cell in Macedonia as well as when he was under house arrest in Rome.[23] In other words, with a proper mindset that is in line with God's thinking, wherever a person finds himself he can be used mightily by God to fulfill His purposes.

You will find provision and flourish as you please the Lord through your obedience in doing what you've been called to do.

If your gifts and calling are to be an auto mechanic or a plumber, then serve the Lord with all your heart in your trade. If you work most of your life as a farmer or raising livestock, do it unto the glory of God.

Aspire only to that which Yahweh has purposed for you. Outside of His will produces only sparse results.

You will find provision and flourish as you please the Lord through your obedience in doing what you have been called to do. Limiting His reign to certain areas is more a reflection of insecurity or immaturity in a believer. It is also more in line with a pagan worldview which seeks to limit Christian influence. Since *the earth is the Lord's and the fullness thereof,*[24] do not preclude any field of endeavor from coming under the jurisdiction of His kingdom. Bringing light to the world is what we are called to do!

LIVING FROM WITHIN

The simple truth is that far too many Christians who profess to "know" the Lord have only a nodding acquaintance with Him. "Hello, Jesus" they say as they nod and pass along, going about their own business. But I am not referring only to "flat root" Christians, who are content to live in the "shallows" of their faith and are unwilling to take upon themselves a meaningful role in the body of Christ. Rather, it is those who shoulder many of the burdens of ministry who have yet to come into close fellowship with the One who has called us *"friend."*[25] Surely, they are His servants and are active in ministry—usually too busy to take the time to consult with "headquarters."

For most of these, it takes a process of maturing to eventually graduate to a deeper level of faith. But it doesn't need to take a matter of years. What is required is a willingness to accept the centrality of our own need to take up the cross of self-denial. "Ouch!" says the flesh. And your ego wants to tell you it's a "no-go." But if there is to be real spiritual progress there needs to be a process of peeling off the many layers of contamination that have caused our eyes to be blurry and our hearts to be dull.

Introspection. Reflection. Listening. Heeding. Doing. Each is a necessary part of the process. So is renewing our mind with the Word. It's so simple. But it must be done in faith to yield any results.

As we pass through the stages of life the basic questions we ask ourselves tend to change. Most youngsters will ask themselves, "What do I want to be when I grow up?" Then, as they pass through their teen years, questions like "Where do I fit in?" and "Who am I really?" figure more prominently. In adulthood, questions like "What do I really want to accomplish in life?" and "How can I make a difference?" come to the fore. Then, in later years, some of the major questions include, "Have I made a difference?" and "Will there be a legacy when I am gone?" Certainly most of us do not consciously ask ourselves these questions, but an inner dialogue goes on within each of us whether or not we are aware of it.

Before personal questions regarding purpose and significance can be answered, we have to know something about the spiritual DNA the Lord programmed within us. Your destiny is within you, but it is up to you to discover it and then get there. It should be obvious that there is no way you can arrive at your destination on your own. In fact, you will need all the help you can get. In the meantime, while you are still trying to make sense of it all, the enemy will make countless attempts to sow confusion into your life and get you off track so that you end up in a ditch. Since he operates in the supernatural realm as well as the natural, you need to be "plugged in" to the Most High to have any chance at all.

For this reason Yeshua said, *"For the gate is small and the way is narrow that leads to life, and there are few who find it."*[26] Most Christians will breeze over that familiar passage, thinking, "Of course, I'm counted among that small number." That likely is the case, but there are some who will be in for a surprise in the end. Just a few moments after telling the assembled crowd that not many will make it, Jesus said some will come saying "Lord, Lord" as they try to enter God's kingdom, but they will be rejected because He doesn't know them.

An individual can be involved in all kinds of religious activities in the name of the Lord and still not know Him in a personal way. Unless a believer is developing his relationship with the Lord day-by-day, and following His instructions, he may not end up in eternity with Yeshua as he thinks. You may wish to disagree, but that is what Jesus Christ told His listeners at the Sermon on the Mount.[27] Even if such a person does make it, his rewards in eternity will be slim to none.[28] Isn't it much simpler to learn to "abide in Him" as He instructed? Then there is no guesswork involved.

He has called us out of darkness into the light so that we may partake of His divine nature.[29] Developing a deeper life in Him is the way to do that. Whether you are a student, banker, prophet, waitress, or pastor your highest calling in life is to be in fellowship with your Maker.

THE TIME OF RESTORATION

Each one of us has a need to feel significant: "I am somebody." How much more significant could it be than that the Lord of the universe made you the way you are so that you can take part in His plan for the ages? It doesn't get any better than that!

These are exciting times in which to be alive as a Christian. Ancient prophecies concerning God's kingdom and the nation of Israel are being fulfilled right before our very eyes.[30] As the prophet Isaiah foresaw, it would be a time in which the world would be plunging into a deep darkness while the glory of the Lord's presence would shine on His people.[31]

In short, you couldn't have been born at a better time to take part in the plan of God. Revelation knowledge is flowing as never before, and we are living in the *"times of refreshing,"* spoken of by the apostle Peter, which will *"...come from the presence of the Lord."*[32] This same period, which the apostle spoke of, is also *"...the period of restoration of all things about which God spoke by the mouth of His holy prophets from ancient time."*[33]

This is the grand finale in which everything is being brought back to its original state. Even our spiritual DNA is being restored in this process. We have the divine pattern before us—Jesus Christ. As we gaze upon His glory we are being transformed. That which is lacking in us is able to reach its fulfillment. Because of this, we can reflect His glory to the world. This is our "time of refreshing" in which all things are being restored because we have "...come from the presence of the Lord."

We are special and we are living in an extraordinary time. If we can only grasp the immense significance of this simple truth it will make all the difference in our attitude. We will be energized to do the works to which He has called us. We will have the passion necessary to tear through the apathy and alienation that surround us. We will have the perseverance to overcome the obstacles the enemy throws our way. We will seek to please the Lord like never before. We will reach our destiny!

Questions: Chapter Ten

1. The apostle Paul's fervent desire was that the Messiah take up residence on the inside of the believers in Ephesus and that they would be "_____ *and grounded in [His] love.*"

2. The Christian who has taken to _____ Yeshua's instruction to "abide in Him" is the one who has sent a "taproot" down into the soil for his spiritual sustenance.

3. The "taproot" Christian is steady and sure and will develop in his _____ as God intended.

4. As a "taproot" Christian draws his _____ by being *"rooted and grounded in love"* he will go far beyond the other two types of root systems in fulfilling his destiny.

5. The main shortcoming of a "heart root" type of believer is that the fruit manifesting through his life will be more a product of _____ than the fruitfulness of a joint venture with Yahweh.

6. What the "heart root" Christian needs are "close _____ of the first kind"—by drawing near to God and experiencing His love.

7. The "flat root" Christian may experience a "touch" from the Lord now and again, but because his relationship with Yahweh is so _____ he knows very little of the dimensions of God's great love.

8. As a general rule the "flat root" Christian knows very little of self-denial and usually is unwilling to apply the Word

in his life if it "_____" him something.

9. The "flat root" believer lacks a passion for the things of God and has experienced little of the presence of God. He lacks both the power and the vision to live an _____ Christian life.

10. The "taproot" model for Christian _____ is the one that Jesus demonstrated through His life and also the one He taught His disciples to follow.

11. Ministry should be done this way: _____ Him, through us, _____ others. If the flow hasn't begun with the true Source, its origin is self.

12. The only way to reach the highest potential of our gifting over the long run and reach our destiny is to do things _____ way.

13. We have given the enemy an _____ to harass us when we suffer from soul wounds and our thinking is off-base.

14. In our search for significance and our pursuit of happiness why not _____ with our Maker?

15. Fulfilling the _____ that Yahweh has planned for you is the only real success there is on this side of eternity.

16. Some of the most _____ people in the world are those who are trying to be someone other than themselves.

17. A problem with many human beings is the tendency to want to emulate others who are _____

gifted but who have a completely different calling.

18. The only _____ that a mature person should try to live up to are those which have been developed in consultation with Yahweh.

19. In order to engage those who have not yet entered God's kingdom we must _____ the gospel to them, wherever they might be.

20. With a proper _____ that is in line with God's thinking, wherever a person finds himself he can be used mightily by God to fulfill His purposes.

21. You will find provision and flourish as you please the Lord through your _____ in doing what you have been called to do.

22. The simple truth is that far too many Christians who profess to "_____" the Lord have only a nodding acquaintance with Him.

23. A believer can be involved in all types of activities in the name of the Lord and still not know Him in a _____ way.

24. Which type of believer best describes you? (check one)
"Taproot" Christian _____ "Heart Root" Christian _____ "Flat Root" Christian _____

APPENDIX A

Two Kinds of Prophets, Two Kinds of Teachers

W hen reading the Scriptures it is important to keep in mind the simple fact that a word can have two (or more) very different meanings when used in various contexts. While we run across examples of this all the time in everyday life, normally we don't give it much thought. Here are a few examples.

If I were to tell you:

◈ "In our ministry we **train** pastors and church leaders," I'd be letting you know that we *teach and equip* those individuals.
◈ However, if I said, "I just saw an old lady get on the **train**," I'd be telling you that an elderly woman entered *a railroad car*.

Now if I were to inform you:

◈ "That's a **lean** piece of steak," I'd be communicating that the piece of meat *doesn't have much fat* on it.
◈ On the other hand, if I said, "I saw the boy **lean** against the streetlamp," I'd be telling you that a youngster was *standing there, resting against* a light pole.

To give a third and final example, if I told you that:

◈ "We are to **bear** the burdens of those who are weak," I'd be meaning that we're supposed to *carry* the load for others who are less able.

◈ However, if I said, "The papa **bear** hibernated all winter long," I'd be informing you that a rather *large, furry mammal* slept during the cold months of the year.

In each pair of sentences the same word is used—but with totally different meanings.

Dozens of words we use all the time have two or more meanings. It's not unique to the English language either; it's the same in every language, including the Greek in which the New Testament was written.

This is critical when considering the various spiritual gifts mentioned in the Bible because there are two instances in the New Testament in which the same word is used to describe two different gifts: the gift of "prophecy" and the gift of "teacher." There is the endowment gift of "prophecy"[1] as well as the manifestation gift of "prophecy,"[2] and there is also the endowment gift "teacher"[3] as well as the equipping gift "teacher."[4]

As we've seen from the examples above, though the same word is used it doesn't necessarily mean the same thing or that they are the same gift. The endowment gift called "prophecy," in fact, is very different from the manifestation gift "prophecy"[5] and, in a similar manner, the endowment gift "teacher" is not the same thing as an equipping gift "teacher."

This becomes clearer as we consider the fundamental difference between the three sets of gifts. The endowment gifts are really about "who we are," or more precisely, "who God created us to be." They are about our "spiritual DNA," which includes our personality traits and characteristics, motivations, abilities and talents. On the other hand, each of the manifestation gifts represents one of the various operations of the Holy Spirit—or "what He does through you, as He wills"—at a given time and place. In addition to these two sets of gifts, a believer may also have been called by God to be an equipping gift, which is still quite another matter. As an equipping gift a person is called by Yeshua to minister to his body with the purpose of training the saints for service and bringing each one to maturity in the faith.

So "prophecy" as an endowment gift is a "way of being" while prophecy as a manifestation gift is an act of "speaking forth" or "prophesying" as an oracle of God. Likewise with the teacher; the endowment gift teacher has been fashioned by God with the spiritual DNA that is characteristic of that gift. The equipping gift teacher, however, is someone Jesus Christ has called and prepared to teach His body, and he functions in that manner. While an equipping gift teacher may have the gift of teaching as his primary endowment gifting, it is not a prerequisite. Also, since a primary endowment gift has been given to every person that has been born, many with the endowment gift of teaching—those who have not been born again—do not qualify to be called by Yeshua to serve as an equipping gift teacher. A prerequisite for someone to be called as any of the equipping gifts is to have become part of God's family—being born again.

APPENDIX B

Answers to the Questions for Each Chapter

Chapter One

1. treasure
2. knew
3. mind
4. spirit

5. before
6. spirit, soul
7. designed
8. characteristics

9. design
10. spiritual
11. DNA
12. creation

Chapter Two

1. searching
2. within
3. secret
4. purpose
5. counsel
6. spiritual

7. signficance
8. experiment
9. manifestation
10. spiritual
11. every
12. motivational

13. endowment
14. humilty
15. endowed
16. find

Chapter Three

1. glorify
2. look, motivated
3. vital
4. intended
5. grace
6. glasses
7. heart
8. characteristics
9. harmony
10. fulfills
11. important
12. train
13. right
14. comfort
15. gifts
16. blessing
17. teamwork

Chapter Four

1. seven, spiritual
2. truth
3. God
4. practical
5. long
6. honest
7. truth
8. Scripture, change
9. experience
10. sound
11. encourage
12. heart
13. confidence
14. conduit
15. provider
16. generational
17. resources
18. born
19. Loyalty
20. Authority
21. feelings
22. heart
23. emotional

Chapter Five

2. natural
3. arrived
4. strongholds
5. true
6. solving
7. sensitivity
8. pessimistic
9. forgiveness
10. resentment
11. negligent
12. identity
13. pride
14. insecurities
15. confidence
16. application
17. priorities
18. manipulating
19. trusting
20. fear, doubt
21. compassion
22. difficult
23. sensitive
24. evade
25. identified
26. sin
27. vulnerable
28. God-kind

Chapter Six

1. interaction
2. weaknesses
3. purpose
4. obedience
5. loyalty
6. receiving
7. true
8. weakness
9. relationship
10. truth
11. teacher
12. generations
13. encouraged
14. development
15. advancing
16. generosity
17. lack
18. prophecy
19. plan
20. motivational
21. organizing
22. stranger
23. cost
24. necessary

Chapter Seven

1. grace
2. proof
3. perfection
4. hearts
5. truth
6. prophecy
7. minister
8. humility
9. obedience
10. growing
11. searched
12. judging
13. kindness
14. development
15. spiritual
16. model
17. gift
18. generosity
19. done
20. organization
21. authority
22. care
23. compassion
24. recognize

Chapter Eight

1. spiritual
2. potential
3. eyes
4. prophecy
5. hands
6. lifeblood
7. teacher
8. counsel
9. mouth
10. people
11. giver
12. restoration
13. shoulders
14. governance
15. mercy
16. congregation
17. anointing
18. adolescence
19. God-kind
20. requirement
21. priorities
22. diverse
23. differences
24. compatibility

Chapter Nine

1. reasonable
2. all
3. soul
4. fullness
5. finances
6. wounds
7. glorify
8. deceiver
9. primary
10. convinced
11. deceptions
12. light
13. Holy Spirit
14. symptom
15. stronghold
16. restoration
17. total
18. everything
19. connected
20. eternity
21. soak
22. heavenly
23. walk
24. things

Chapter Ten

1. rooted
2. heart
3. gifting
4. strength
5. self-effort
6. encounters
7. shallow
8. costs
9. overcoming
10. living
11. from, to
12. His
13. opening
14. consult
15. destiny
16. frustrated
17. similarly
18. expectations
19. bring
20. mindset
21. obedience
22. know
23. personal

RECOMMENDED RESOURCES

Brennfleck, Kevin and Kay Marie. *Live Your Calling: A Practical Guide to Finding and Fulfilling Your Mission in Life*. San Francisco, CA: Jossey-Bass, 2005.

Fortune, Don and Katie. *Discover Your God-Given Gifts*. Grand Rapids, MI: Chosen Books, 1987.

Johnson, Regina. *What's Your Spiritual DNA?: The Seven Foundational Gifts*. DVD series available through www.global-transformationnetwork.org.

Leider, Richard. *The Power of Purpose: Creating Meaning in Your Life and Work*. San Francisco, CA: Berrett-Koehler, 2004.

Munroe, Myles. *The Principles and Power of Vision*. New Kensington, PA: Whitaker House, 2003.

Varner, Kelley. *Corporate Anointing: Christ Manifest in the Fullness of His Body*. Shippensburg, PA: Destiny Image, 1998.

Walston, Rick. *Unraveling the Mystery of the Motivational Gifts*. Fairfax, VA: Xulon Press, 2002.

NOTES

Preface

1 One of the most eminent books on the subject is *Discover Your God-Given Gifts* by Don and Katie Fortune (Grand Rapids, MI: Chosen Books, 1987).

Chapter 1: The Mystery of the Treasure Within

1 Jeremiah 1:5.
2 See Acts 10:34.
3 Psalm 139: 13,14,16 (GWT).
4 See John 4:24.
5 Such phrases as "outward man" and "inner man" refer to humankind—both male and female.
6 Alternatively referred to as "mind and heart" in the *New English Translation*.
7 I am refraining from use and repetition of awkward phrases that refer to both genders, such as "his or her" and "he and she," though every observation, unless noted otherwise, applies equally to both men and women.

Chapter 2: Appreciating Our Endowment

1 See Matthew 6:33.
2 1 Corinthians 12:7-11. Each of the three sets of gifts in the Bible is "spiritual" in that they are given by God who is Spirit, and so it is improper to elevate the gift set of 1 Corinthians 12 to the place of being the "spiritual gifts," which implies that the other two groups of gifts are somehow less spiritual, which is far from true.
3 Ephesians 4:11-12. Though each of the labels used to describe these two sets of

gifts is somewhat imprecise, using the term "manifestation gifts" for the gifts in 1 Corinthians 12 is perhaps best—at least it provides the sense that these nine gifts involve an operation or manifestation of the Holy Spirit. The term "equipping gifts" best portrays the purpose for which these five gifts in Ephesians 4 were given to the church: to equip the saints.

4 The term "endowment gifts" emphasizes the fact that they have been bestowed—to both the individual believer and also corporately to the body of Christ. It also carries with it a sense of their intrinsic or essential nature. The more common term "motivational gifts" is inadequate because it is limited to only one aspect of the profound nature of these gifts.

5 Romans 12:6-8 (MKJV).

6 The endowment gift names in parentheses are the corresponding gift names used in various translations other than the Modern King James Version (MKJV).

7 See Appendix A, which clarifies the difference between "prophecy" as an endowment gift and "prophecy" as a manifestation gift, as well as the difference between an endowment gift of "teaching" and an equipping gift "teacher."

Chapter 3: Adding Greater Dimension

1 When the apostle Paul pointed out that "…we have gifts that differ according to the grace given to us …" the word translated there as "gifts" was the Greek word charisma in the original text.

2 Romans 12:3.

3 See Romans 12:4-5 and 1 Corinthians 12:12.

4 Ephesians 4:11-12.

5 Hosea 4:6.

Chapter 4: Good Things Come in Sevens

1 This environment includes the spiritual environment as well as such things as family and socio-economic and cultural influences.

2 1 Corinthians 13:1.

3 See Acts 17:11.

4 See 2 Timothy 4:3.

5 Obviously other factors have been involved such as his humility, following the leading of the Holy Spirit, and obeying God's instructions.

6 This gift has four other names by which it is known as well: the gift of administration, organizing, ruling, and facilitating.

7 What is referred to here as the "God-kind of love" is agape in the Greek. It is a type of love that is far beyond human love, or even human understanding.

8 Paul told the believers in Rome that "… God's love has been poured into our hearts by the Holy Spirit, who has been given to us" (Romans 5:5).

Chapter 5: Growing in Grace

1 Jeremiah 17:9.

2 Matthew 15:19 (NASB).

3 1 Samuel 16:7.

4 "Therefore if any man be in Christ, he is a new creature: old things are passed away; behold, all things are become new" (2 Corinthians 5:17).

5 "For those whom He foreknew, He also predestined to become conformed to the image of His Son, so that He would be the firstborn among many brethren" (Romans 8:29, NASB).

6 The Lord desires that each one of His children will develop to become "…mature in the Lord, measuring up to the full and complete standard of Christ" (Ephesians 4:13, NLT).

7 Jesus Christ warned that, "*Many* will say to me…Lord, Lord, have we not prophesied in thy name? and in thy name have cast out devils? and in thy name done many wonderful works? And then will I profess unto them, I never knew you: depart from me, ye that work iniquity" (Matthew 7:22-23, emphasis added).

8 Jesus told His disciples to "abide in me, and I in you. As the branch cannot bear fruit of itself, except it abide in the vine; no more can ye, except ye abide in me" (John 15:4). Judging by the high percentage of "casual Christians" today, many are trying to walk the Christian walk in their own power, which is "fruitless."

9 The apostle Paul instructs us that "…the gifts and calling of God are without repentance" (Romans 11:29) which means that God has chosen not to take back any of the gifts He's given—and that applies even if a person is not walking closely with Him. However, Jesus warned of the dire consequences for many deluded "Christians" who fail to abide in Him; they will be told by the Lord to "depart" because "I never knew you" even though they had done many "marvelous works" (Matthew 7:22-23).

10 The proper approach in such a situation is provided by the apostle Paul: "Even if a man should be detected in some sin, my brothers, the spiritual ones among you should quietly set him back on the right path, not with any feeling of superiority but being yourselves on guard against temptation" (Galatians 6:1, PNT).

11 Make the fact that "God's love has been poured out in our hearts through the Holy Spirit Who has been given to us…" a living reality in your everyday walk (Romans 5:5b).

12 Romans 12:3.

13 The apostle Paul wrote in 1 Corinthians 8:1b that "…knowledge puffs up, but love edifies," by which he was referring to the tendency for knowledge to produce an inflated ego.

14 John 15:5.

15 Ecclesiastes 3:1.

16 Genesis 13:13; Genesis 19:5,24.

17 1 Samuel 2:22.

18 1 Samuel 2:34, 1 Samuel 4:11.

19 See James 3:1.

20 See Acts 17:10-11.

21 As when God used a donkey to speak to the prophet Balaam in Numbers 22:1-35.

22 See 2 Timothy 4:3,4.

23 You can find a major part of the sad tale of King Saul in 1 Samuel 15.

24 Proverbs 29:25 (NLT). The secret to a trap is that it's concealed, because if a bird or animal knew what was waiting for him he'd go around it.

25 1 Samuel 30:6b "….David encouraged and strengthened himself in the Lord his God." It was King David himself who encouraged himself in the Lord. Don't look to others—you take the initiative, for you're promised that if you "come close to God…He will come close to you" (James 4:8, MKJV).

26 Psalm 138:2b says, "…for thou hast magnified thy word above all thy name."

27 1 Corinthians 13:4. "Love is patient…."

28 1 Thessalonians 5:14b. "…be patient toward all men."

29 Romans 15:4-5 (NLT). "Such things were written in the Scriptures long ago to teach us. And the Scriptures give us hope and encouragement as we wait patiently for God's promises to be fulfilled. May God, who gives this patience and encouragement, help you live in complete harmony with each other, as is fitting for followers of Christ Jesus."

30 Luke 12:16-21.

31 Proverbs 11:24-25 (NKJV).

32 See Joshua 1:8.

33 See John 15:16.

34 See Matthew 28:19-20.

35 See Matthew 25:31-46. Jesus, speaking of acts of mercy done for those He calls brothers, said this: "Inasmuch as ye have done it unto the least of these my brethren, ye have done it unto me" (Matthew 25:40b).

36 Matthew 6:3.

37 Jesus warns every believer, "Do not lay up treasures on earth for yourselves, where moth and rust corrupt, and where thieves break through and steal. But lay up treasures in Heaven for yourselves, where neither moth nor rust corrupt, and where thieves do not break through nor steal" (Matthew 6:19-20).

38 The apostle Paul encouraged the Philippians to give "…[not] because I want a gift from you. Rather, I want you to receive a reward for your kindness" (Philippians 4:17, NLT). From God's perspective (and that's the only one that really counts) giving is for our own benefit.

39 In His message to the church in Laodicea, Jesus sternly rebuked them for their self-sufficient attitude. "Because you say, I am rich and increased with goods and have need of nothing, and you do not know that you are wretched and miserable and poor and blind and naked" (Revelation 3:17). Christians must realize that they are not their own, for they have been "…bought with a price…" (1 Corinthians 6:20).

40 Luke 6:38 (MSG)."Give away your life; you'll find life given back…given back with bonus and blessing. Giving, not getting, is the way…."

41 Jesus put it this way: "For where your treasure is, there will your heart be also" (Matthew 6:21).

42 The apostle Paul's wise counsel to Timothy concerning riches was the following: "But godliness with contentment is great gain. For we brought nothing into this world, and it is certain we can carry nothing out. And having food and raiment let us be therewith content. But they that will be rich fall into temptation and a snare, and into many foolish and hurtful lusts, which drown men in destruction and

perdition. For the love of money is the root of all evil: which while some coveted after, they have erred from the faith, and pierced themselves through with many sorrows" (1 Timothy 6: 6-10).

43 This ability is much like that of the encourager.

44 See John 15:5.

45 Jesus expressed His views on leadership to His disciples when He gathered them together and said, "You know that the rulers in this world lord it over their people, and officials flaunt their authority over those under them. But among you it will be different. Whoever wants to be a leader among you must be your servant…" (Matthew 20:25-26, NLT).

46 Matthew 7:12 (NASB).

47 Jesus counseled the multitude gathered at the Sermon on the Mount to "give, and it shall be given unto you; good measure, pressed down, and shaken together, and running over, shall men give into your bosom. For with the same measure that ye mete withal it shall be measured to you again" (Luke 6:38). This timeless spiritual law applies in every realm.

48 Matthew 10:16. "Behold, I send you out as sheep in the midst of wolves. Therefore be as wise as serpents and as harmless as doves."

49 Luke 6:37. "Judge not, and ye shall not be judged: condemn not, and ye shall not be condemned: forgive, and ye shall be forgiven."

50 2 Peter 1:4.

51 See Romans 5:5.

52 1 Corinthians 13:8(a).

53 Paul's letter to the church at Colossae unveils the magnificent truth that the "… mystery which has been hidden from ages and generations…now has been revealed to His saints…which is Christ in you, the hope of glory" (Colossians 1:26-27). The *cristos* (the Greek word translated as Christ) to which Paul is referring is both the anointing (of Christ) in us and the person of Christ, by the indwelling Holy Spirit, who tabernacles (takes up residence) within. In fact, it's by reason of this anointing that we're called "Christians" (literally, "little anointed ones").

Chapter 6: Seven Endowment Portrait Gifts

1 See Genesis 3:8.

2 James 5:17 (NLT).

3 Obviously the Good Samaritan in Jesus' parable, illustrating the gift of mercy, may not have been a real-life person.

4 See Acts 2:14, 2:23, 3:12, 4:8, 5:3-10, 5:29-42, 11:4; Matthew 14:28, 15:15, 16:16, 16:33, 17:4, 18:21, 19:27; Luke 5:8; and John 6:38, 6:67-69; 13:6.

5 This statement is made in Matthew 16:16. In John 6:69, which occurred earlier, Peter proclaimed that Jesus was "the Holy One of God," a phrase which held the same significance for first-century Hebrews (NLT).

6 Matthew 16:17 (NLT).

7 Great conviction was brought to thousands on the day of Pentecost when Peter pointed out, "…Ye have taken [Jesus], and by wicked hands have crucified and slain [Him]" (Acts 2:23).

8 This story of Jesus and Peter walking on the water is recorded in Matthew 14:24-33.

9 This incident is described in John 6:60-69.

10 Matthew 16:21-23.

11 See John 13:4-9.

12 See Luke 5:4-9. After Peter hadn't caught so much as a minnow working all night, he went out at Jesus' advice and caught so many fish that his and the other fishermen's nets were filled to the point of breaking. After this, Peter "...fell down at Jesus' knees, saying, Depart from me; for I am a sinful man, O Lord.'"

13 See Luke 10:38-42; John 11:1-45, 12:1-11.

14 This story is recounted in the last five verses of Luke chapter 10 (Luke 10:38-42).

15 See Luke 10:25-37.

16 See John 11:1-45 and John 12:1-11.

17 Luke 10:40 (NASB).

18 Luke 10:41 (AMP). Several translations use an alternative phrase here, "worried and bothered."

19 Luke 10:42 (NLT).

20 From the little information we have in Scripture about Mary, it appears that her endowment gift was mercy. Many times people with this gift are worshippers. Though Mary's adoring attitude toward the Lord is only hinted at during this incident, it became the centerpiece of a later occasion when she poured precious ointment on Jesus' feet and wiped them with her hair (John 12:3).

21 See Ezra 7:1-10:44; Nehemiah 8:1-10:39.

22 The name Ezra means "Help" or "Helper" in Hebrew.

23 All but a few copies of the Torah had been destroyed after the fall of Jerusalem. Ezra labored arduously for many years, piecing together a complete version of the Scriptures from extant manuscripts.

24 Ezra 7:12 (MSG).

25 Ezra 8:26.

26 This same observation about the hand of the Lord being upon him was made six times in the book of Ezra and twice in Nehemiah.

27 "For Ezra had prepared his heart to seek the Law of the Lord, and to do it, and to teach statutes and ordinances in Israel" (Ezra 7:9).

28 See Deuteronomy 32:10 and Lamentations 2:18.

29 The last three prophets to address Judah—Haggai, Zechariah, and Malachi—were contemporaries of Ezra. From that time forward, the nation of Israel would enter a period known by Christians as the "four hundred years of silence," until the time of John the Baptist, the forerunner of Jesus Christ.

30 It was also a time in which synagogues started to be organized throughout the diaspora. The role of the synagogue in Jewish life, and the teaching which occurred there, became increasingly significant while Temple worship waned in importance.

31 This dramatic scene is recorded in detail in Ezra 9:1-10:44.

32 Nehemiah 8:6-9.

33 See Deuteronomy 7:3.

34 Ezra 9:11 (MSG).

35 The essence of his words of encouragement to Ezra were, "…there is still hope for Israel…Take charge—we're behind you. Don't back down" (Ezra 10:2,4).

36 This action was necessary solely because of the spiritual pollution that the pagan and idolatrous foreign wives had caused. It has no bearing on inter-marriage between different ethnic groups when both parties are believers. However, God still maintains the same strict boundaries as He did then in the case of marriage between a believer and a non-believer. A believing Christian is never to enter into such a relationship because the result will be that he or she is "unequally yoked" (see 2 Corinthians 6:14).

37 There is a striking contrast between the example of Ezra, who taught by his actions as well as his words, and Solomon, who, though he had great insight, brought corruption to Israel by marrying idolatrous pagans for the sake of building alliances for the kingdom.

38 See Acts 3:21.

39 It was also a time of great miracles and persecution. A man who had been crippled from birth had just been healed at the Beautiful Gate by the Temple, and the apostles Peter and John were released by the ruling Sanhedrin after having been jailed for their preaching. According to Acts 4:4 the number of men who had become believers at that point was about five thousand.

40 See Acts 4:34-35.

41 Acts 4:36 (NLT). Though most translations do not refer to Barnabas as an apostle in this verse, he is referred to as an apostle in Acts 14:14 and 1 Corinthians 9:5-6 in nearly all translations.

42 Other translations refer to him as "Son of Comfort," "Son of Exhortation," "one who encourages others," or "Son of Consolation."

43 Colossians 4:10 informs us that John Mark was Barnabas' relative, with some translations referring to him as a cousin. He is recognized by most Bible scholars as the author of the Gospel of Mark.

44 See Acts 11:24.

45 At the time, Antioch was the third largest city in the Roman Empire.

46 See Acts 9:26-28.

47 See Acts 13:1-3.

48 See Acts 13:13.

49 Luke, the author of the book of Acts, begins referring to Saul as Paul during the first missionary journey. See Acts 13:9.

50 The strongest component of Saul's grace package was that of an endowment gift prophet.

51 Later on Paul implicitly acknowledged that Barnabas had been right in not giving up on John Mark when he wrote that he had become "useful" to Paul in ministry (2 Timothy 4:11).

52 Though the Gospel of Mark was composed by an anonymous author, it was attributed to the evangelist John Mark as early as the start of the second century. It is said to have been the first of the Gospels written and was based on the firsthand account of the apostle Peter.

53 See Acts 14:12. Barnabas' presence and power so impressed the heathens as he ministered on his missionary journey in Asia Minor that some said he was Zeus (Jupiter), the most powerful of their deities. They also postulated that Paul was the messenger of the gods, Mercury, because he was the principal speaker.

54 The name Abraham was given at birth was "Abram," which means "exalted father" in Hebrew. However, Yahweh changed his name to "Abraham," which means "father of many nations," as part of the covenant He made with him when Abram was ninety-nine years old (see Genesis 17:5).

55 See Genesis 12:1-3.

56 See Acts 7:2, Romans 4:1, 12, 16, and James 2:21.

57 Abram's wife was named "Sarai," which means "my princess" in Hebrew. Her name was changed to "Sarah" by the Lord twenty-four years after their arrival in Canaan from Mesopotamia. This name change occurred at the time of the covenant agreement made between the Lord and Abram, when his name was changed to Abraham (see Genesis 17:15). The new name "Sarah" means "princess," and the significance of the name change was that from this time forward she would no longer just be a princess to a certain few (her family) but a princess to many (humanity).

58 Genesis 13:2.

59 See Genesis 13:10.

60 See Genesis 13:14-17.

61 Genesis 14:22-24.

62 From Genesis 17:1 we see that Abraham was ninety-nine years old.

63 See Genesis 18:1-2.

64 See Genesis 18:10 and Romans 9:9.

65 Abraham referred to himself as a stranger and a sojourner when he met with the sons of Heth to purchase a cave to bury Sarah's body (Genesis 23:4). The writer of Hebrews says the same of Abraham in Hebrews 11:9.

66 Hebrews 11:9. "By faith he sojourned in the land of promise, as in a strange country, dwelling in tabernacles with Isaac and Jacob, the heirs with him of the same promise."

67 See Hebrews 11:10.

68 "And the scripture was fulfilled which saith, Abraham believed God, and it was imputed unto him for righteousness: and he was called the Friend of God" (James 2:23).

69 The inspiring story of Nehemiah and the rebuilding of the walls of Jerusalem is found in Nehemiah chapters 1-6.

70 Nehemiah means "Yahweh comforts" in Hebrew.

71 Nehemiah 2:7-8. Artaxerxes provided letters of authorization for Nehemiah's travel to Judah as well as an order to the keeper of the king's forest for a supply of timber sufficient for the beams of the Temple fortress, to build Jerusalem's walls and for Nehemiah's own house.

72 Nehemiah 2:17-18.

73 Nehemiah 3:5. It was only the nobles from among the Tekoites who refused to "pitch in" and get their hands dirty by getting involved in the construction.

74 Nehemiah 3:12. Shallum, one of the mayors of Jerusalem, had the help of his daughters in working on the wall section allotted to him.

75 Nehemiah 2:10.

76 Nehemiah 4:9,16,17.

77 Nehemiah 6:3 (NLT).

78 Just prior to Jesus telling the Parable of the Good Samaritan the scribe had said, "You must love the Lord your God with all your heart and with all your soul and with all your strength and with all your mind; and your neighbor as yourself" (Luke 10:27). This was his own response to Jesus' question, "How do you read the Law?"

Chapter 7: A Portrait of Perfection

1 See John 14:6.

2 1 Peter 1:20 (AMP). "It is true that He was chosen and foreordained (destined and foreknown for it) before the foundation of the world...."

3 "...He gave up His divine privileges; He took the humble position of a slave and was born as a human being. When He appeared in human for ..." (Philippians 2:7, NLT). The Revised Version puts this verse another way: "[He]...emptied himself, taking the form of a servant, being made in the likeness of men...."

4 John 5:19 (NASB).

5 For example, concerning His disciples, the Scripture says, "But Jesus, as He perceived the thoughts of their hearts..." (Luke 9:47, AMP), and, regarding the Pharisees, "And Jesus knew their thoughts..." (Matthew 12:25).

6 Luke 8:46 (MKJV). "And Jesus said...Someone has touched Me, for I know that power has gone out of Me."

7 See Matthew 12:34 and Matthew 23:27.

8 Matthew 21:13.

9 See John 8:52 and Mark 3:22.

10 See John 1:14.

11 See 1 Corinthians 15:55 and Revelation 1:18.

12 See Matthew 14:23, Mark 6:46, and Luke 6:12.

13 An endowment gift prophet's primary orientation is vertical toward God. As such, a prophet will normally have only a few close friendships.

14 See Isaiah 53:3, 11.

15 Luke 2:7.

16 See Matthew 5:3-8.

17 See Matthew 7:24-27 (NLT).

18 Matthew 11:29 (MKJV).

19 See John 6:38.

20 Philippians 2:7-8 (NET). "But emptied himself by taking on the form of a slave, by looking like other men, and by sharing in human nature. He humbled himself, by becoming obedient to the point of death—even death on a cross!"

21 See John 5:1-9.

22 See Matthew 13:58, Mark 6:3-6, and Mark 9:23-27.

23 See Matthew 20:26-28, Mark 9:35, and Mark 10:43.

24 For example the incident described John 5:12-13.

25 See John 13:1-17. Consider also that Judas was among the Twelve, so Yeshua washed the feet of the disciple who would soon betray Him unto death.

26 Mark 10:45 (NASB). "For even the Son of Man did not come to be served, but to serve, and to give His life as a ransom for many...."

27 See Luke 2:40-49. There is only one observation in the Gospels concerning the Messiah's years growing up: "And the Child grew and became strong in spirit, filled with wisdom; and the grace (favor and spiritual blessing) of God was upon Him" (Luke 2:40, AMP).

28 See Luke 2:46-47 (AMP). Responding to a question with a question was a teaching technique commonly practiced in Israel at Jesus' time. The Scripture does not specifically indicate whether that was so in this instance, but it is likely the Messiah was engaging the leadership with this teaching technique rather than seeking their views on the Torah.

29 Luke 4:18-19 (NASB).

30 Mark 6:2 (NLT).

31 See Matthew 4:23-24 and 12:9; Mark 1:22,27,29,39; Luke 4:15,16,44, 13:10.

32 John 7:1.

33 John 7:15 (NASB).

34 See John 3:2 (MSG).

35 Some have the mistaken idea that Yeshua mainly taught at large gatherings such as the Sermon on the Mount. His normal public venue, however, was teaching at the local synagogue in whatever town He was in at the time. See Matthew 4:23, 24; Mark 1:39; Luke 4:15.

36 While Jesus did not openly preach about immorality He certainly counseled against it. For example, when He spoke privately with a woman caught in the act of adultery, after He had forgiven her, Yeshua told her, "Go and sin no more." Another example: after healing a man at the pool of Bethesda He told him to "... not sin anymore, so that nothing worse happens to you" (John 5:14, NASB).

37 John 7:16.

38 Rabbi is the Hebrew word for "my teacher," not just "teacher." The word in Hebrew for disciple is talmid.

39 While perhaps most believers think of Jesus as the "carpenter from Nazareth," He was referred to in Scripture forty-one times as a teacher, thirteen times as rabbi, and only once as a carpenter.

40 This can be surmised because each was already engaged in a trade or occupation when Jesus called them. It was customary in Israel that by the age of fifteen a young man either had been chosen to study under a local rabbi or was earning a living.

41 See Luke 10:1,17. Beside the "twelve" there was also a group of "seventy." These were other followers whom Jesus also trained and sent out. These seventy are mentioned in Luke's Gospel only. Some Bible versions refer to the "seventy-two" instead of the "seventy" because while some ancient Greek manuscripts show their number to have been seventy, others have the number of "other disciples" as seventy-two.

42 Rabbi Yeshua used five principal Hebrew teaching methods to train His disciples: modeling, instruction, direction, rebuke, and skill-sharpening.

43 See John 7:46-47 (MSG).

44 See John 9:16,24.

45 The story of the Samaritan woman at the well is found in John 4:4-30.

46 John 4:27 (MSG).

47 See John 19:39. Nicodemus helped in the burial of the Messiah's body after He was crucified.

48 Matthew 26:36 (NASB).

49 See Matthew 26:75 and Luke 22:62.

50 See Matthew 6:9-13 and Luke 11:2-4. This model prayer is oftentimes called the "Lord's Prayer" but its more apt label is the "Disciple's Prayer" because it provided a pattern for them to use.

51 See Matthew 6:33.

52 See Mark 11:22-25.

53 Luke 6:27-37.

54 See Matthew 8:20 and Luke 9:58 (NASB).

55 John 5:19.

56 John 3:16.

57 2 Corinthians 8:9 (NASB).

58 Matthew 6:32 (NASB). "For the Gentiles eagerly seek all these things; for your heavenly Father knows that you need all these things."

59 Matthew 6:19,20 (NASB).

60 Matthew 6:24 (NLT). In fact, the harsh reality is that if a person is a friend of this world and its system he has made himself an enemy of God (see James 4:4).

61 Matthew 13:22.

62 Matthew 6:1-4.

63 Matthew 18:23-35. The Parable of the Wicked Servant.

64 Luke 6:30 (AMP).

65 Luke 6:38 (MKJV).

66 The story of the feeding of the five thousand is found in Mark 6:31-44.

67 2 Corinthians 1:20.

68 Galatians 3:29 (NLT).

69 The number of attendees enumerated at the various events did not include women and children.

70 Luke 9:23 (NLT).

71 See Acts 1:4-5; Ephesians 3:19; John 3:15-16; John 15:4; John 17:3; Romans 5:21; Romans 6:23; 2 Corinthians 5:1; 1 John 2:25; 1 John 5:11,13; and 1 Corinthians 2:9.

72 Luke 10:1-17.

73 See Mark 3:13-14.

74 See Matthew 26:37; Mark 9:2-9, 14:33.

75 Yeshua throwing the moneychangers out of the Temple is depicted in Matthew 21:12-13; Mark 11:15-17; Luke 19:45, 46; and John 2:14-16. The synoptic Gospels portray the incident as being near the end of the Messiah's ministry while John evidently described another similar incident at the Temple that occurred near the start of Jesus' ministry.

76 The episode of the ferocious storm on the Sea of Galilee is found in Matthew 8:23-27, Mark 4:35-42, and Luke 8:22-25.

77 When Jesus rebuked the wind He was actually rebuking the force behind the storm, the "prince of the power of the air" (see Ephesians 2:2).

78 This incident in Gadara is described in Matthew 8:28-34, Mark 5:1-20, and Luke 8:26-39.

79 Mark 5:8 (NASB).

80 Mark 5:7 (NASB).

81 Isaiah 61:1-2 (NASB). When Yeshua read this prophecy He purposely omitted the last portion which spoke of "…the day of vengeance of our God…." This will be fulfilled at the time of His second coming.

82 Luke 7:11-17. The woman was a widow. Since she had lost both her husband and son she was left in a desperate situation, likely without means of support.

83 Mark 10:14-15 (MKJV).

84 Luke 13:10-17. This is just one of many incidents in which the Promised One showed Himself sensitive to the plight of a woman in need.

85 Luke 13:12 (NLT).

86 This incident is recorded in Matthew 8:2-4 and Mark 1:40-44.

87 John 11:33,35.

88 Matthew 23:37.

89 Luke 19:41.

90 Luke 23:34.

Chapter 8: The Gifted Church

1 This true story of the hidden "golden buddha" is from various Internet sources.

2 See Ephesians 4:11-12 (ISV).

3 Ephesians 5:25 (NASB).

4 See Revelation 19:7-9.

5 See Acts 6:1-4.

6 1 Corinthians 8:1 (NET). "Knowledge puffs up, but love builds up."

7 Acts 2:44-47 (NLT).

8 See Isaiah 9:6. Modern-day idioms reflect a similar concept as well, such as "to shoulder a burden" and having "the weight of the world on our shoulders."

9 John 1:12a (AMP). "But to as many as did receive and welcome Him, He gave the authority (power, privilege, right) to become the children of God…." The church's authority was also symbolized by the keys that Yeshua promised to give to Simon Peter when He said, "And I will give you the keys of the Kingdom of Heaven. Whatever you forbid on earth will be forbidden in heaven, and whatever you permit on earth will be permitted in heaven" (Matthew 16:18, NLT).

10 Ephesians 3:17.

11 See Revelation 2:4.

12 2 Timothy 3:1. "This know also, that in the last days perilous times shall come."

13 Genesis 1:4.

14 Genesis 1:31 (MKJV).

15 Dr. Kelley Varner, Corporate Anointing (Shippensburg, PA: Destiny Image,

2002). Dr. Varner's book was the source of several insights concerning fullness and the corporate anointing.

16 See 2 Corinthians 5:17.

17 Psalm 133:1-2 (NASB).

18 Acts 2:43-47 (NASB).

19 In other words, this believer is living the type of life that the apostle Paul wrote about in Galatians 2:20: "I have been crucified with Christ, and I live; yet no longer I, but Christ lives in me. And that life I now live in the flesh, I live by faith toward the Son of God, who loved me and gave Himself on my behalf. "

20 See Revelation 2:1-7.

21 Psalm 78:72 (AMP). "So [David] was their shepherd with an upright heart; he guided them by the discernment and skillfulness [which controlled] his hands." This subject was also touched upon in chapter three in the section "Leading Requires 'Skillful Hands.'"

22 See Ephesians 4:11-12.

23 The worth of counsel from those who have a different perspective is acknowledged in the proverb, "As iron sharpens iron, so a friend sharpens a friend" (Proverbs 27:17, NLT).

24 It needs to be acknowledged that close friendships are not common among those in leadership positions such as pastors. The advice here is to have a few trusted friends who will be able to offer sage counsel when requested.

25 See Ephesians 1:18.

Chapter 9: The Truly Abundant Life

1 See Acts 20:28.

2 The WNT translates the Greek "...present all your faculties to Him..." which of course includes all of our being—our mind, heart, will, gifts, talents, and abilities. Several translations render this verse as such, including the Amplified Bible, which says, "I APPEAL to you therefore, brethren, and beg of you in view of [all] the mercies of God, to make a decisive dedication of your bodies [presenting all your members and faculties] as a living sacrifice, holy (devoted, consecrated) and well pleasing to God, which is your reasonable (rational, intelligent) service and spiritual worship" (Romans 12:1, AMP).

3 "And thou shalt love the Lord thy God with all thy heart, and with all thy soul, and with all thy mind, and with all thy strength: this is the first commandment" (Mark 12:30).

4 Psalm 34:8.

5 This analysis was the theme of chapter five.

6 2 Corinthians 10:4-5.

7 See John 14:30. Various versions render this verse as he has "no power over me," "nothing in me," and "no claim over me." The Amplified Bible brings out all various shades of meaning: "...for the prince (evil genius, ruler) of the world is coming. And he has no claim on Me. [He has nothing in common with Me; there is nothing in Me that belongs to him, and he has no power over Me.]"

8 3 John 1:2.

9 Haggai 1:4-7 (AMP).

10 This is also reminiscent of what the Lord said in Psalm 127:1 (NASB)."Unless the LORD builds the house, they labor in vain who build it; unless the LORD guards the city, the watchman keeps awake in vain."

11 1 Corinthians 6:19 (NLT). "Don't you realize that your body is the temple of the Holy Spirit, who lives in you and was given to you by God? You do not belong to yourself...."

12 See John 8:44.

13 1 John 4:4 (NASB). "You are from God, little children, and have overcome them; because greater is He who is in you than he who is in the world."

14 In some cases, the Lord will use a competent Christian counselor to help heal soul wounds. His healing ministry is not limited to physical ailments but includes anything from which one of His children is suffering.

15 See Luke 4:18 (KJV).

16 See Mark 11:23-25.

17 Job 10:1.

18 Job 42:10.

19 See Matthew 18:34-35.

20 See Numbers 21:4-9.

21 Hebrews 12:2 (NASB). "Fixing our eyes on Jesus, the author and perfecter of faith, who for the joy set before Him endured the cross, despising the shame, and has sat down at the right hand of the throne of God."

22 John 8:12 (NLT). "Jesus spoke to the people once more and said, 'I am the light of the world. If you follow Me, you won't have to walk in darkness, because you will have the light that leads to life.'"

23 See Matthew 16:15-17.

24 See Matthew 17:1-9, Mark 9:2-10, and Luke 9:28-36.

25 Revelation 1:14-15. "His head and His hair were white like white wool, like snow; and His eyes were like a flame of fire. His feet were like burnished bronze, when it has been made to glow in a furnace, and His voice was like the sound of many waters."

26 Malachi 4:2 (AMP).

27 Philippians 4:7(NLT). "Then you will experience God's peace, which exceeds anything we can understand. His peace will guard your hearts and minds as you live in Christ Jesus."

28 Matthew 11:28-30 (NLT). "Then Jesus said, 'Come to Me, all of you who are weary and carry heavy burdens, and I will give you rest. Take My yoke upon you. Let Me teach you, because I am humble and gentle at heart, and you will find rest for your souls. For My yoke is easy to bear, and the burden I give you is light.'"

29 The apostle Paul commented on this process: "But we all, with unveiled face, beholding as in a mirror the glory of the Lord, are being transformed into the same image from glory to glory, just as from the Lord, the Spirit" (2 Corinthians 3:18, NASB). Because it is we who reflect His glory, the Weymouth Translation of this verse comes closer to the original meaning of the Greek text: "And all of us, with unveiled faces, reflecting like bright mirrors the glory of the Lord, are being trans-

formed into the same likeness, from one degree of radiant holiness to another, even as derived from the Lord the Spirit" (2 Cor 3:18, WNT, emphasis added).

30 Song of Solomon 6:3 (NASB).

31 The Lord said that He is jealous at least seven times in the Scriptures. See Exodus 20:5, 34:14; Deuteronomy 4:24, 5:9, 6:15; Joshua 24:19; and Nahum 1:2. The Lord being in first place is the Great Commandment. See Deuteronomy 6:4-5; Matthew 22:36-38; Mark 12:29-30; and Luke 10:27.

32 See Matthew 7:22-23.

33 Psalm 31:19 (NLT).

34 Isaiah 60:1-3 (NASB).

Chapter 10: Embracing Your Destiny

1 See Ephesians 3:14-19.

2 Ephesians 3:16,17,19 (NASB).

3 Isaiah 61:3b.

4 Acts 17:28.

5 See John 15:4,5.

6 See 1 Corinthians 3:12.

7 See John 5:19-20 and John 15:4-5.

8 See Revelation 2:1-7.

9 Revelation 2:5 (WNT).

10 See 1 Corinthians 3:12.

11 Psalm 92:12-14 (NASB).

12 Ecclesiastes 1:2 and 12:8 (NASB). "'Vanity of vanities,' says the Preacher, 'all is vanity!'"

13 See Ecclesiastes 1:14, 2:11, 2:17, 2:26, 4:4, 4:16 and 6:9. Solomon, the man who "had it all," indicated how frustrated he was with many of his various pursuits by saying that he found in them "vanity and vexation of spirit."

14 1 Timothy 6:6.

15 1 John 2:16 (NLT).

16 See Isaiah 46:10.

17 Jeremiah 29:11 (MSG).

18 Philippians 3:8 NLT.

19 See Matthew 11:30. His "yoke is easy" and His "burden is light."

20 Proverbs 16:18 (MKJV). "Pride goes before destruction, and a haughty spirit before a fall."

21 See Mark 16:15 and Matthew 24:14.

22 See Genesis chapters 39-47.

23 See Acts 16:23-34 and Acts 28:30-31.

24 1 Corinthians 10:26.

25 John 15:14-15 (PNT). Jesus, speaking to His disciples in the Upper Room, said, "You are my friends if you do what I tell you to do. I shall not call you servants any longer, for a servant does not share his master's confidence. No, I call you friends, now, because I have told you everything that I have heard from the Father."

26 Matthew 7:14 (NASB).

27 See Matthew 7:21-27.

28 See 1 Corinthians 3:15.

29 See 2 Peter 1:4.

30 Just to name a few: the outpouring of the Holy Spirit on all nations and peoples (Joel 2:28-29 and Acts 2:17-18), the knowledge of His glory covering the entire earth (Habakkuk 2:14), the enemies of Israel forming an alliance against her to "wipe her off the face of the earth" (Psalm 83:4), and the gospel of the kingdom going to the ends of the earth (Matthew 24:14).

31 See Isaiah 60:1-3.

32 Acts 3:19 (NASB). The apostle Peter enlightened his Hebrews listeners outside the Temple in Jerusalem with the message: "Therefore repent and return, so that your sins may be wiped away, in order that times of refreshing may come from the presence of the Lord...."

33 Acts 3:21 (NASB).

Appendix A

1 In Romans 12:6.

2 In 1 Corinthians 12:10.

3 In Romans 12:7.

4 In Ephesians 4:11.

5 To complicate things even further, among the equipping gifts we find there is the gift of "prophet," which is yet another gift—different from the equipping and the manifestation gifts of "prophecy."

amazon.com

Item Price	Total
$14.49	$14.49

$14.49
$3.99
$18.48
$18.48
$0.00

B

amazon.com

Your order of December 23, 2012 (Order ID 102-2504198-8743855

Qty.	Item
1	**Called to Be, Called to Do: Finding Your Purpose and Destiny in Your Unique** Wollensack, Peter --- Paperback **(** ** P-1-Q33C147 ** **) 1936443015**

Subtotal
Shipping & H
Order Total
Paid via cred
Balance due

This shipment completes your order.

Have feedback on how we packaged your order? Tell us at www.amazon.com/pa

Made in the USA
Lexington, KY
23 December 2012